Social Capital

A Theory of Social Structure and Action

In *Social Capital*, Nan Lin explains the importance of using social connections and social relations in achieving goals. Social capital, or resources accessed through such connections and relations, is critical (along with human capital, or what a person or an organization actually possesses) to individuals, social groups, organizations, and communities in achieving objectives.

This book places social capital in the family of capital theories (the classical and neoclassical theories), articulates its elements and propositions, presents research programs, findings, and agendas, and theorizes its significance in various moments of interactions between individual actions and social structure (for example, the primordial groups, social exchanges, organizations, institutional transformations, and cybernetworks). Nan Lin eloquently introduces a groundbreaking theory that forcefully argues and shows why "it is who you know" as well as "what you know" that make a difference in life and society.

Nan Lin is Professor of Sociology and Director of the Asian/Pacific Studies Institutes at Duke University. He is author of *The Struggle for Tiananmen* (1992); *Social Support, Life Events and Depression* (with Alfred Dean and Walter Ensel, 1986); *Foundation of Social Research* (1976); and *The Study of Human Communication* (1973). He is coeditor (with Peter Marsden) of *Social Structure and Network Analysis* (1982). His work has appeared in *American Sociological Review*, *American Journal of Sociology*, *Journal of Health and Social Behavior*, and *Social Forces*, among other journals.

Professor Lin is former Vice President of the American Sociological Association (1999–2000) and Academician at Academia Sinica, Taiwan. He is also honorary or advisory professor at numerous international universities in China, including People's University, Huazhong University, Nankai University, Fudan University, and Zhongshan University, among others.

D1292575

Structural Analysis in the Social Sciences

Mark Granovetter, editor

The series, *Structural Analysis in the Social Sciences*, presents approaches that explain social behavior and institutions by reference to *relations* among such concrete entities as persons and organizations. This contrasts with at least four other popular strategies: a) reductionist attempts to explain by a focus on individuals alone; b) explanations stressing the causal primacy of ideas, values and cognitions; c) technological and material determinism; d) explanation using "variables" as the main analytic concepts, as in "structural equation" models, where the structure connects variables rather than actual social entities.

One important example of structural analysis is the "social network" approach. The series also features social science theory and research that is not framed explicitly in network terms but stresses the importance of relations rather than the atomization of reductionism or the determinism of ideas, technology, or material conditions. Such efforts typically grapple with the complex balance between structure and agency, increasingly a key issue in the human sciences. Examples of the structural approach are scattered across many disciplines, and the *Structural Analysis* series hopes, by pulling them together under a single rubric, to expose this very fruitful style of analysis to a wider public.

Structural Analysis in the Social Sciences | 19

Social Capital

A Theory of Social Structure and Action

NAN LIN

Duke University

CAMBRIDGE
UNIVERSITY PRESS

PUBLISHED BY THE PRESS SYNDICATE OF THE UNIVERSITY OF CAMBRIDGE
The Pitt Building, Trumpington Street, Cambridge, United Kingdom

CAMBRIDGE UNIVERSITY PRESS
The Edinburgh Building, Cambridge CB2 2RU, UK
40 West 20th Street, New York, NY 10011-4211, USA
477 Williamstown Road, Port Melbourne, VIC 3207, Australia
Ruiz de Alarcón 13, 28014 Madrid, Spain
Dock House, The Waterfront, Cape Town 8001, South Africa

http://www.cambridge.org

First published 2001
First paperback edition 2002
Reprinted 2003

Printed in the United States of America

Typeface Sabon 10/12 pt.   *System* QuarkXPress [BTS]

A catalog record for this book is available from the British Library.

Library of Congress Cataloging in Publication Data

Lin, Nan, 1938–
Social capital: a theory of social structure and action / Nan Lin.
p.   cm. – (Structural analysis in the social sciences)
Includes bibliographical references and index.
ISBN 0-521-47431-0
1. Social networks. 2. Social action. I. Title. II. Series.
HM741.L56 2000
302.4 – dc21

                                        00-036289

ISBN   0 521 47431 0   hardback
ISBN   0 521 52167 X   paperback

To Alice, Ho, and Ping

Contents

Preface

Sociology, to me, is the study of choices in social relations. It explores the motivations for taking actions, examines what choices are available (perceived or real) in relations, and studies the consequences of such choices. Therefore, central to sociology is the analysis of both action and structure: choice behaviors in the context of structural opportunities and constraints. Choices are made within such opportunities and constraints, and choices interacting with structural opportunities and constraints can also alter or create structural opportunities and constraints. These processes necessarily shift between the macrostructure and the microstructure. How to capture and demonstrate these dynamics is what occupies sociologists' time and efforts.

This monograph is about a theory that suggests that actors (whether individual or corporate) are motivated by instrumental or expressive needs to engage other actors in order to access these other actors' resources for the purpose of gaining better outcomes. The core proposition is that such accessed resources embedded in social relations, or social capital, bring about better outcomes. Thus, social capital is social and useful. It is ingrained in social relations and facilitated or constrained by them. But within such structural opportunities and constraints, action makes a difference; given the same extent and array of relations for two actors, the outcomes may differ, depending on their choice behaviors. In this formulation, I accept the prevailing effects of structure and relations. Nevertheless, I want to stress the theoretical significance of choices.

To do this, I divide the monograph into two parts. In Part I, I begin with a historical account of capital theories (Chapter 1) and the ideas of social capital (Chapter 2). The next three chapters describe the theory from the structural perspective "down" to relational and action dynamics. Chapter 3 describes how resources are embedded in structures, including networks, and Chapter 4 describes how motivations and interactions propel actors to make choices. Chapter 5 summarizes the elements of the theory and introduces the propositions systematically. Two more chapters demonstrate the research utilities of the theory. Chapter 6 summarizes the research tradition linking social capital to status attainment, and Chapter 7 highlights the important research agenda of inequality in social capital.

In Part II, in extending the theory to several arenas of research, I turn the dynamics around, from choice actions to institutional and structural contexts. I begin with the micro- and mesodynamics to give more emphasis to choice actions. Chapter 8 explores the theoretical possibility that choice actions lead to social structure, and Chapter 9 extends this argument by showing how social exchange, in contrast to economic exchange, carries its own rationality. I continue the discussion of choices in the more constrained context of hierarchical organizations in Chapter 10. Chapter 11 turns to the topic of social change – how the theory of social capital, as formulated in this monograph, may help explain societal transformations, both within the context of existing institutions and in the creation of capital through social networking and alternative institutions. Chapter 12 explores the explosion of cybernetworks – social relations in cyberspace – and their significance for reevaluating the premature proclamation that social capital may be declining or dying, again highlighting how actions and choices in relations and networks retain and even gain vitality and power in a globalized and technologically advanced society.

Given the limited space of this monograph, certain choices had to be made regarding the coverage. I have decided to focus on the instrumental aspect of social capital and thus shortchange the expressive aspect of social capital, not that my own research efforts have ignored the latter (Lin 1979; Lin, Dean, and Ensel 1986; Lin and Ensel 1989; Lin and Lai 1995; Lin and Peek 1999; Lin, Ye, and Ensel 2000). The significance of expressive action in a theory of social capital is made clear in the discussion of the formulation of the theory in Chapters 4 and 5. I also mention how expressive action operates in several extensions of the theory (Chapters 8 to 11). However, to fully cover the expressive aspect of social capital would require perhaps another monograph of comparable size. Instead, I chose to focus on social capital for instrumental action in order to parallel discussions of two other similar topics: human capital and cultural capital. In human capital, as espoused by economists, the focus is on the returns in the labor market, especially economic returns. In cultural capital, à la Bourdieu, the concern is with the reproduction of the dominant class. In both cases, the instrumental use of capital is salient. Only in the Epilogue do I reintegrate expressive action, somewhat abbreviated still, in a full model of analysis for social capital.

I have also abbreviated the coverage of social capital as a collective asset, as my evaluation has convinced me that its theoretical and research viability can be extended from the formulations as outlined in this monograph, rather than being treated as a separate and independent entity (see Chapters 2, 8, and 12).

The work represented in this monograph can be traced back to the late 1960s and early 1970s, when I began research on social networks in the United States, Central America, and Haiti. And I have continued to benefit from such comparative research experiences, which are now extended to East Asia as well. Along the way, I have benefited a great deal from many collaborators, including Ron Burt, John Vaughn, Clifford Melick, Walter Ensel, Ron Simeone, Mark Tausig, Mary Dumin, Mary Woelfel, Gina Lai, Yanjie Bian, Kristen Peek, Yushu Chen, Chih-jou Chen, Ray-May Hsung, Yang-Chih Fu, Xiaolan Ye, and Marc Magee. My intellectual network has extended to and included, among many others, Mark Granovetter, James Coleman, Henk Flap, Bonnie Erickson, Ron Breiger, Judith Blau, Robert Merton, Peter Marsden, Peter Blau, Jeanne Hurlbert, Harrison White, Barry Wellman, Edward Tiryakian, John Wilson, and Lulin Cheng. I have also benefited from interactions and friendships with colleagues at the Department of Sociology, SUNY–Albany, and the Department of Sociology, Duke University. They have been my vital social capital.

My research work, extending to several continents and stretching over three decades, has received important support from the National Science Foundation (the Sociology program and the International Program), the National Institute of Mental Health, the U.S. Department of Labor, the New York Department of Health, the Luce Foundation, the Chiang Ching-Kuo Foundation, the American Council of Learned Societies, the Research Foundation of SUNY, and the Research Council of Duke University. Without their funding, it would not have been possible to conceive and examine many aspects of the theory presented in this monograph.

I also wish to thank three publishing houses for permission to reprint portions of the following pieces in this monograph:

Cambridge University Press: 1990. Lin, Nan. "Social Resources and Social Mobility: A Structural Theory of Status Attainment." In Ronald Breiger (ed.), *Social Mobility and Social Structure*, Cambridge University Press, pp. 247–271 (Chapter 10).

JAI Press: 1994. Lin, Nan, "Action, Social Resources and the Emergence of Social Structure," in *Advances in Group Processes*, Volume 11, edited by Barry Markovsky, Jodi O"Brien, and Karen Heimer (Chapter 8).

Annual Reviews: 1999. Lin, Nan. "Social Networks and Status Attainment," *Annual Review of Sociology* 25:467–488 (Chapter 6).

Part I

Theory and Research

1

Theories of Capital

The Historical Foundation

One of the far-reaching explanatory schemes in contemporary sociology and economics focuses on the concept of capital. What is *capital*? I define it as *investment of resources with expected returns in the marketplace*. Capital is resources when these resources are invested and mobilized in pursuit of a profit – as a goal in action. Thus, capital is resources twice processed. In the first process, resources are being produced or altered as investment; in the second, the produced or altered resources are being offered in the marketplace for a profit. In one instance, capital is the outcome of a production process (producing or adding value to a resource); in the other, it is the causal factor in a production (the resource is exchanged to generate a profit). These are processes because both investment and mobilization involve time and effort. In the past two decades, social capital in its various forms and contexts has emerged as one of the most salient forms of capital. While much excitement has been generated, divergent views, perspectives, and expectations have also raised a serious question: is this a fad, or does it have enduring qualities that will herald a new intellectual enterprise?

The purpose of this volume is to present a theory of social capital, a theory eliciting the central theme that capital is captured in social relations and that its capture evokes structural constraints and opportunities as well as actions and choices on the part of the actors. Firmly anchored in the general theory of capital, this theory will, it is hoped, contribute to an understanding of capitalization processes explicitly engaging hierarchical structures, social networks, and actors. This theory, and its research enterprise, argue that social capital is best understood by examining the mechanisms and processes by which embedded resources in social networks are captured as investment. It is these mechanisms and processes that help bridge the conceptual gap in the understanding of the macro–micro linkage between structure and individuals.

3

This chapter will explore the nature of capital and various theories of capital, a context essential in leading up to the presentation and analysis of social capital, which begins in the next chapter.

The Classic Theory: The Marxian View of Capital

To understand social capital, we must first clarify the notion of capital. The notion of capital can be traced to Marx (1849, 1865/1933/1935, 1867/1995; Brewer 1984) in his analysis of how capital emerges from social relations between the bourgeoisie (capitalists) and laborers in the processes of commodity production and consumption. Marx saw capital as part of the surplus value (created through the processes of commodities production and exchange) that creates further profit (Marx 1867/1995, Vol. 1, Chap. 4, and Vol. 2, Chap. 1). The production of commodities engages labor, land, rents, and materials (including facilities, technology, and transportation). Each of these elements incurs a use (or production) value for the producer. However, while a laborer is paid a fixed weekly or monthly wage, the laborer puts out more than the necessary number of hours in producing the commodity (socially necessary labor), and the produced commodity thus carries a lower cost of labor for the producer. That is, the generated use value surpasses the exchange value in payment to support the laborer's subsistence. Thus, a surplus value (or profit) results. Further, the producer (or rather the capitalist) then engages in an exchange process in which the produced commodity is exchanged for another commodity (in the modern world, usually a medium of commodities, i.e., money). The field of exchanges may engage the producer and the consumer either directly or through intermediaries such as traders and merchants. The commodity generates a market value in these exchanges. If the market value exceeds the use (production) value or cost, then further surplus value, or capital, results from the exchange. Figure 1.1 depicts my rendition of Marx's notions of how capital emerges from social relations between capitalists and laborers in the processes of commodity production and consumption.

The processes begin with the capitalist, who is bestowed with resources (capital) to begin with (e.g., land ownership, aristocracy inheritance) and who engage in commodity production by establishing an exchange relation with laborers, who contribute their labor in the production process. In return, the capitalist assesses the value of the commodity produced and pays the laborers in accordance with this value (known as the *exchange value*), usually in money. As presented in Figure 1.1, this relationship is represented by the production exchange between a capitalist and a laborer in the production of Commodity 1.

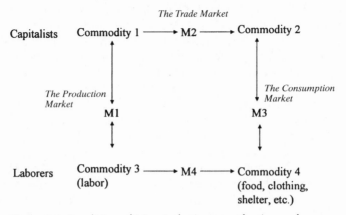

Figure 1.1 Rendition of Marx's thesis on production and consumption relations.

Commodity 1 is the outcome of the production, and Commodity 3 is the labor contributed by the laborer. M1 represents the payment of the capitalist to the laborer for the work performed (Commodity 3) on the production of Commodity 1. The exchange value represents the "socially necessary value" for the production, or what is deemed necessary to pay the laborer for the labor performed (Commodity 3).

The produced commodity (Commodity 1) is then moved through a trade market (from Commodity 1 to Commodity 2) and to the consumption market (from Commodity 2 to Commodity 3). Thus, in the simplest process, Commodity 1 is directly offered as Commodity 2 by the producers to the consumers. The consumers, to a large extent, are the laborers who use the money earned in the production process (M1) to purchase the essential commodities (Commodity 4) for survival. They pay a price (M3) to get these commodities. Marx presents the following arguments:

1. M1 is essentially the same as M4 in value. That is, the payment for labor received by the laborer is the same value that the laborer uses to purchase essential commodities for survival. It is the exchange value, representing no gain or loss of value.
2. M2 is greater than M1 and/or M3 is greater than M1. That is, the selling value of the commodity in the trade and consumption markets is greater than its production value.

Thus, these two processes, the production process and the trade/consumption process, result in two important and separate consequences for laborers and capitalists. Laborers earn the value for their labor

(Commodity 3), which is in turn exchanged to get the essential goods (Commodity 4) for survival, and they earn no surplus value in the process (M1 = M4). Capitalists gain a surplus value (M3 − M1), part of which becomes capital.[1] Thus, the circulation of commodities sustains laborers' subsistence so that they can continuously provide the commodity (labor) necessary in the production process, but no more. On the other hand, the capitalists gain surplus value from the circulation of commodities, of which a significant portion can become capital. The processes are usually more complex, of course. For example, the capitalists can trade the produced commodities among themselves or to other capitalists, from Commodity 1 to Commodity 2, and gain a surplus value (M2 > M1). These other capitalists (traders, merchants) create their own surplus values by circulating the commodities to the consumption market (M3 > M2). Thus, there are capitalists other than those directly engaged in production within the circulation system (the nodes along the circulation of commodities or the chains in the forms of C-M-C and M-C-M, such as traders, merchants, etc.). Capitalists are the ones who get to keep the capital, usually in the form of money.

This system of commodity circulations and social relations between capitalists and laborers sustains itself so long as (1) M1 is kept at a minimum (socially necessary value) and is always nearly equal to M4 and (2) M3 is always greater than M1 (or M2 > M1 and M3 > M2), so that the surplus value (and capital) is generated. When this system is sustained, there is assumed to be no mobility from laborers to capitalists, since, first of all, the capitalists control the means of production (assembling materials, instruments, and labor) and, second, the laborers will never accumulate capital and the capitalists will continue to accumulate capital. Thus, capital is a return (of surplus value) on an investment in the production of useful commodities in the marketplace. Capital can appear in the forms of money, the capacity to control the means of production, and/or further investment to produce more useful commodities. When the focus is on the process of producing surplus value, *capital may be defined as an investment with expected returns in the marketplace*.

In summary, then, in Marx's analysis, capital is part of the surplus value captured by capitalists or the bourgeoisie, who control production means in the circulation of commodities and monies between the production and consumption processes. In this scheme of a capitalist society, capital represents two related but distinct elements. On the one hand, it

---

[1] Surplus value has two components: revenue (part of which will be used for the repeated production processes and part of which will be used to sustain luxury-leisure or lifestyle expenditures) and capital (an increment of the valued resources).

is part of the *surplus value* generated and pocketed by the capitalists (and their "misers," presumably the traders and sellers). On the other hand, it represents an *investment* (in the production and circulation of commodities) on the part of the capitalists, with expected returns in the marketplace. Capital, as part of the surplus value, is a product of a process; capital is also an investment process in which the surplus value is produced and captured. It is also understood that the investment and its produced surplus value refer to a return/reproduction of the process of investment and of more surplus values. It is the dominant class that makes investments and captures the surplus value. Thus, Marx's theory is a theory based on the exploitive social relations between two classes.

Central to this theory are several important notions concerning capital. First, capital is intimately associated with the production and exchange of commodities. Commodities, in the theory of Marx, are mainly material goods that carry price tags in both the production and exchange processes. Labor, labor power, and labor value are part of the price tag and are seen as "socially necessary" in the production of a commodity. But it is commodities, through their production and exchange, that generate capital. Labor is a necessary factor in the process of producing a commodity, but it is subservient to the commodity itself.

Second, capital involves processes rather than simply a commodity or value, even though it may be the final result. Capital represents an investment process on the part of the capitalist, as production requires assembling and organizing labor, land/rents, equipment, facilities, and so on. These entail investment of initial capital, effort, and social activities of coordination and persuasion. When the processed commodity is exchanged for a profit, it also entails a process in the marketplace.

Third, as a result of these processes, any resultant capital is an added value (surplus value or profit). The existence of capital means that the market value of a commodity exceeds its production value or cost to produce. If the market value is the same as or less than the cost, there will be no capital from the commodity, and in fact there may be a deficit or debt.

Fourth, capital is intrinsically a social notion. Capital entails processes of social activity. The production process, as mentioned, involves social activities. For example, Marx explicitly describes use value as dependent on "socially necessary labor," since there is no objective value or worth that can be used to calculate the value or cost of labor. The exchange process, by definition, is also social.

Fifth, capital is captured by the capitalist or producer from the circulation of commodities through the cycle of commodity production and exchange and capital accumulation. Capital is a process and an end result that lies by definition in the hands of those who control the means of production. The means of production create and accumulate in the form of capital. Capital, in turn, consolidates control over production means (e.g., circulation of commodities and circulation of capital; see Marx 1867/1995, Vol. 1, Chaps. 3–5). In Marx's formulation, laborers are paid wages to meet their subsistence needs, and no more. In other words, capital is the surplus value generated from the capitalist's investment in the production and is captured by the capitalist.

I will call the notion of capital and its features as described by Marx the *classic theory* of *capital*. The basic idea that capital is the investment of resources for the production of profit has been maintained in all subsequent capital theories. However, in the Marxian scheme, both investment and profit are vested in the capitalists. The labor involved in the process of production does not generate or accumulate capital for the laborers. The classic theory of capital is based on the explanatory argument that class differentiation is fundamental in capitalist society, where the exploiting class controls the means of production and collects all the surplus value generated from the labor provided by the exploited class. The evolution of capital theory in the last four decades into what can be called *neo-capital theory* essentially modifies or eliminates the class explanation as a necessary and required theoretical orientation. These alternative renditions of capital notably include human capital, cultural capital, and social capital.

Neo-Capital Theory: Human Capital

Human capital, which assumes that capital can rest with the individual laborer, can be traced to Adam Smith, who included all the acquired and useful abilities of the population in a country as part of capital (1937). In the late nineteenth and early twentieth centuries, this notion occasionally surfaced in the economic literature (von Thunen 1875; Fisher 1906). Contemporary understanding of human capital can be attributed to the works of Johnson, Schultz, and Becker (Johnson 1960; Schultz 1961; Becker 1964/1993). Johnson (1960) argued that laborers have become capitalists, not from a diffusion of the ownership of corporation stocks, as capitalist public relations would have it, but from the acquisition of knowledge and skills that have economic value. That is, with knowledge and skill, the laborers can demand from the capitalists payment beyond the exchange value for their labor. Presumably, their knowledge and skills enable the hourly worth of their labor to exceed that of others who do not have such knowledge and skills.

However, the first systematic presentation of the human capital argument was made by Theodore W. Schultz in his presidential address at the 1960 meeting of the American Economic Association (1961). In this seminal piece, "Investment in Human Capital," he forcefully condemned "the failure to treat human resources explicitly as a form of capital, as a produced means of production, [and] as the product of investment, [which] has fostered the retention of the classical notion of labor as [only] a capacity to do manual work requiring little knowledge and skill, a capacity with which, according to this notion, [all] laborers are endowed about equally" (p. 3). In addition, Becker (1964) explicated human capital most forcefully in terms of education, but later also in terms of a host of other factors.[2]

Schultz's challenge and proposal formed the basis of the human capital theory, elaborated by other economists, Becker (1964) being the principal one among them. Human capital, unlike physical capital, is the value added to a laborer when the laborer acquires knowledge, skills, and other assets useful to the employer or firm in the production and exchange processes. The important distinction between physical and human capital is that human capital is the added value embedded in the laborers themselves. Typically, human capital is operationalized and measured by education, training, and experience. Investment in human capital on the part of laborers is good not only for the firm/producer, but also for the laborers themselves. Human capital adds the value of the labor, and part of the value can be negotiated and retained by the laborers as wages and benefits, beyond the minimal amount required for subsistence needs.

Thus conceived, human capital may be seen as any investment on the part of the laborers that will result in increased worth (M1) in commodity production process. This value affords three types of expenditures, according to Schultz: expenditures for (1) consumption, (2) investment (human capital), and (3) both consumption and investment. Because of the difficulty of disentangling the third type of expenditure from the first two (i.e., decomposition of M4 in terms of these three expenditures), Schultz proposed that the effects of human capital should be estimated by its yield rather than its cost; "the resulting increase in earnings is the yield on the investment" (p. 8). In essence, for human capital, there is no substantial change in the definition of capital relative to the Marxian notion. It remains an investment with an expected return in the marketplace. From the Marxian point of view, this added value

---

[2] For example, Schultz also proposed that not only skill and knowledge acquisition but also health and migration would yield additional economic value. Becker added a host of other factors. There is a danger, however, of including all things that sustain or improve life itself as human capital. I choose to focus on the original intent.

(knowledge, skills) enables the capitalist (the employer or firm) to increase the capacity of labor (e.g., labor power; Marx 1867/95, Vol. 1, Chap. 6). As a result, the market value of the commodity or production is increased (either in quality, quantity, or both). So long as the increased wage for such added capacity grows at a lower rate than the use value from the capacity generated, profit will increase, adding to the capital of the capitalist. Thus, human capital can be seen as consistent with the theoretical scope of Marxian analysis: capital is viewed from the capitalist's, producer's, employer's, or firm's perspective in the production and exchange of commodities.

However, the classical capital theory received a major challenge: that the immobility of class distinctions between the capitalists and the laborers no longer holds. If laborers can acquire skill, knowledge, and other capital to increase the value of their hourly labor, two things can happen:

1. M1 may no longer be mere exchange value for the laborers. Payment for skilled labor may exceed the socially necessary value of the labor without required skill. Rather than acting as replaceable commodities on the assembly line, certain laborers can now claim and charge higher value for their labor because, for the same labor unit (hour), more production may be accomplished. Thus, M1 contains use value for the laborers and capitalists alike.

2. M1 is no longer equal to M4 – the earnings necessary to sustain lives. Instead, M1 is greater than M4. There is a surplus value of labor for laborers with capital. That is, after expenditures for essential commodities for survival (Commodity 4), there is a residual value that can be used as (1) revenue, which can be used to invest in capital-generating activities or to support leisure and lifestyle needs, and (2) capital (e.g., accumulation of money and other valued resources).

Thus, while the human capital theory does not deviate substantively from the classical (Marxian) theory in the definition of capital, it challenges the classical theory regarding who can or cannot acquire capital. The vision of the social structure is altered. Everyone can invest and acquire capital. Far from being a homogeneous society, there are different opportunities or motivations in the acquisition or nonacquisition of human capital, so that the worth of labor as a commodity varies across individuals. Nevertheless, the social structure is now envisioned as a hierarchy of many grades of capitalists, with extensive cross-grade mobility possible, rather than a rigid two-class system.

This alternative view challenges the classic theory of capital in its fundamental stance: that in the capitalist state the capitalist, as controller of resources for production, extracts capital from low-skilled and interchangeable laborers. By arguing that laborers themselves can accumulate capital by investing in skills and knowledge that are economically productive, Schultz and Johnson turn laborers into potential capitalists and subvert the Marxian premise of class differentiation and conflict. This challenge, however, does not violate the principal notion of capital as an investment of resources in the production of surplus value. Rather, it incorporates skills and knowledge as resources, and thereby claims that skilled, knowledgeable laborers themselves hold such capital.

In summary, human capital theory deviates substantially from classical Marxian theory in several ways. First, while Marxian theory focuses on the production and exchange of commodities, human capital focuses on a process associated with the *laborer*. This change of focus is enormously significant. In the classic theory, value is assessed relative to labor costs rather than to the laborer, since laborers are considered interchangeable members in a large, available, competitive pool of workers who simply provide the socially necessary minimal and similarly skilled labor in production. Capital results from a successful calculus between the relative costs of production and prices in the exchange of commodities. In human capital theory, however, it is the laborers themselves, rather than the labor they perform, who figure centrally in the calculus of capital. In this view, capital is seen and calculated as the added value to the laborer, not to labor or the commodity. In other words, the major theoretical orientation has been changed. Labor, rather than being treated as a contributing factor in the exploitive relationship between the capitalist and the laborer, is seen as generative of capital for the laborers themselves. The social relations between capitalists and laborers are modified. Laborers can no longer be treated as replaceable commodities; differential values and payments are due to different laborers, depending on the capital they bring to bear on production – the human capital. Where do laborers acquire human capital? By gaining education, on-the-job training, or work experiences; by remaining physically healthy and able; by migrating to places where demands are higher; and so forth. This stance completely subverts the core orientation of the classic theory, which ties capital to the control of production means resting solely in the hands of the capitalist.

Secondly, and related to the first point, the laborer can now be seen as the *investor*, or at least as a party in the investment scheme. In the original Marxian analysis, laborers offer their labor in exchange for a wage to sustain their subsistence needs. Human capital clearly assumes that laborers may be in a position to gain profit if profit is defined as a surplus value to what it costs merely to sustain their lives. The temptations of luxury and lifestyle, as well as the possibilities for reinvestment, seen by Marx as exclusively in the capitalist's possession, are now presumably within the effort and grasp of the laborer as well. In other words, capital, as it is being produced and exchanged, is meaningful and possible for both the capitalist and the laborer engaged in the production process.

A third departure of the concept of human capital from the Marxian notion of capital is that because there is a potential reward in increased wages and other forms of profit, the laborer is now *motivated* to acquire skills and knowledge. Marx recognized that labor is a purposive act (1867/1995, Vol. 1, Chap. 7). However, he argued that in the capitalist system, the purpose is "provided" or imposed by the capitalist. Thus, the purposive acts of the laborers are appropriated for the purposes of production. Action on the part of the laborers no longer represents or expresses their free will. From the perspective of human capital theory, however, investment in the acquisition of skills and knowledge is motivated by a cost–benefit calculus on the part of laborers themselves. This calculus drives their investment in acquiring skills and knowledge. It reflects a rational choice, and the action taken is a purposive act consistent with the laborer's self-interest.

Finally, capital in its classic theory is tied to the processes of production and exchange. In the final instance, capital develops as surplus value or profit relative to investment or cost – the outcome of the production and exchange processes. In this formulation, investment in labor is part of the cost calculation. But in the human capital theory, nothing is explicitly delineated concerning the production and exchange processes. Nor is labor calculated as merely cost (expenditure). Rather, it is considered as effort or investment. In fact, an explicit decision is made in the formulation of human capital theory that human capital should be assessed as a function of *return or yield* to the laborer. Thus, "the resulting increase in earnings is the yield on the investment" (Schultz 1961, p. 8). Human capital development in the acquisition of skills and knowledge generates economic value, allowing laborers to become capitalists (Johnson 1960; Schultz 1961, p. 3).

The shift of analytic attention to the microstructure of production of skills and knowledge as investment in laborers does not necessarily negate the macrostructure process of production of surplus value for capitalists in the classic theory. Laborers with better human capital make themselves available in the labor market so that capitalists and managers can capture this human capital by hiring these laborers. However, the labor obtained is no longer an easily interchangeable element in the production process, as Marx assumed. Differential distribution of human capital among laborers makes it necessary for producers and capitalists to calculate the added value of human capital embedded in each of their hired laborers relative to their relative cost (wages and benefits). Presumably, if the added human capital makes it worthwhile for capitalists to pay hired laborers wages and benefits beyond what are required for the workers' subsistence and survival, that is what they will pay when there are no cheaper alternatives. Attractive wages and benefits keep the laborers with better human capital and entice them to contribute quantitatively and qualitatively to the market value of the commodities produced. Better benefits also allow these laborers to enjoy leisure or to invest in further production of their own capital (more education and training).

The enormous significance of this subversion of the classic theory can be seen in two epistemological implications of human capital research. First, laborers can become capitalists, as they enjoy the surplus value of their labor. Thus, there is a blurring of the two classes. Since laborers become capitalists by acquiring human capital or, at the minimum, since capital is conceived of as being shared (however unequally) by the capitalist and the laborer in production and exchange, the worker's acquisition of human capital is now in the interest of both the capitalist and the laborer. The confrontation and struggle between classes becomes a cooperative enterprise – "What's good for the company is good for the worker, and vice versa."

Research can now focus on the laborer's acquisition of and investment in human capital. The production process and its utility for (and manipulation by) capitalists recedes into the background. Rather, since human capital entails purposive action in the laborers' self-interest, the simple investment–return calculus is now applied to the laborers themselves, independent of the context of commodity production and exchange. Thus, the only meaningful context for laborer–capitalist relations is the labor market, where the exchange is between the supply of human capital as embedded in laborers and the demand for such human capital. Instead of focusing on the appropriation of labor for the capitalists' profit, analysis examines the fit between human capital supply and demand. It is the laborer, instead of the manager or capitalist, who is rewarded for or deprived of the price and value of labor power. If labor's value is low, for example, this is due to a lack of human capital rather than the expropriation of surplus value or capital by the capitalist.

Second, research on the link between education and wages constitutes a core area of human capital analysis. Since educational attainment is seen as a major indicator of investment in skills and knowledge, this becomes individuals' major asset in the labor market, resulting in their entering better firms and receiving higher wages. Note that nothing in the appropriation of other kinds of capital enters into this equation. The critical analytic tool used by Marx in his theory of exploitation and appropriation of labor – capitalists' control of the means of production – now becomes the means for analyzing production due to the free will and self-interest of laborers themselves.

I call the human capital theory a neo-capital theory because its rendition of *social relations* in the production and consumption markets radically differs from the fundamental structure assumed in the classical capital theory.

Cultural Capital: A Contention

Not all neo-capital theorists agree with the interpretation of human capital as the product of workers' free will or self-interest. A distinctive alternative theoretical explanation of human capital is the theory of cultural capital. Bourdieu (1990; Bourdieu and Passeron 1977) defines culture as a system of symbolism and meaning (Jenkins 1992, p. 104). He argues that a society's dominant class imposes its culture by engaging in pedagogic action (e.g., education), which internalizes the dominant symbols and meanings in the next generation, thus reproducing the salience of the dominant culture. Thus, cultural capital, as conceptualized by Bourdieu (1972/1977, 1983/1986), derives its analytic contribution from the notions of social practice and social reproduction of symbols and meanings. For the purpose of the present discussion, I will focus on his work on social reproduction, which is intrinsically related to the idea and processes of practice.

To Bourdieu (Bourdieu and Passeron 1977), social reproduction is the imposition of "symbolic violence" by the dominant class on the dominated class. Symbolic violence occurs in that pedagogic action through which the culture and values of the dominant class are legitimated as the "objective" culture and values of the society, so that they are not seen or noticed at all as culture and values that support and sustain the dominant class. In other words, through pedagogic action, the culture and values of the dominant class are "misrecognized" as the culture and values of the entire society. Such pedagogic action occurs in the family, in informal groups and on informal occasions, and, most important, through education, especially schooling (institutionalized education). In the education system, not only do the agents (teachers and administrators) acquire and misrecognize the dominant culture and values as universal and objective, but they transmit "knowledge" by rewarding students who carry out the reproduction of the dominant culture and values in the next generation.[3]

The result is an internalized and durable training, *habitus*, in the reproduction of the culture. Symbolic violence through misrecognition and the process of social reproduction carries over to the labor market (the social "field"), which serves to reinforce the pedagogic rewards (Bourdieu 1990). Students who have acquired and misrecognized the culture and values as their own are rewarded in the labor market by being employed by the organizations controlled by the dominant class. Thus, misrecognition is reinforced in the education system so that other students continue the misrecognition of the need and the merit of acquiring the culture and values being transmitted.

The most important feature of symbolic violence is, then, the pedagogic processes by which the dominant culture and values are accepted and taken in as one's own without any resistance or even conscious awareness on one's part. The acquisition and misrecognition of the dominant culture and its values (legitimized knowledge) is called cultural capital. Such is the sorcery in social reproduction – the reproduction of dominant class values.

It is clear to Bourdieu that education, or indeed any training that can be taken as human capital by some, can in fact be seen as cultural capital by others. The different viewpoints are more than different perceptions of the same empirical phenomenon (e.g., education); they represent a fundamental divide in theoretical explanations. Bourdieu's symbolic violence and social reproduction are consistent with Marx's theoretical stance. They reflect the imposition by one class (the capitalists or a dominant group) of its values on another (the laborers or the dominated group); the appropriation of the latter's labor to the benefit of the former is justified by this value system. Further, Bourdieu also sees profit (capital) as what is at stake in the perpetual struggle in society or the social field (Wacquant 1989). In fact, he identifies a wide range of capital as being at stake, such as economic capital, social capital (relationships with significant others), cultural capital, and symbolic capital (prestige and honor) (Bourdieu 1980, 1983/1986). It is clear that Bourdieu considers these forms of capital as largely in the hands of the dominant class, since it occupies the top positions in society.

We may trace the lineage of this rendition of capital to Marx. The

---

[3] Bourdieu himself has time and again argued that he is not a structuralist or a Marxist. Whether the interpretations here are consistent with his work can be judged by reading what he has written. It seems more accurate to rely on what a scholar practices (writes) than on what he claims, as Bourdieu himself has advised.

social relations described by Marx are also assumed; there is a class, capitalists, that controls the means of production – the process of pedagogic action or the educational institutions (in homes, in schools, etc.). In the production (schooling) process, laborers (students or children) invest in the educational process and internalize the culture of the dominant class. Acquisition of this culture permits or licenses the laborers to enter into the labor market, earn payments, and sustain expenditures for their lives. The capitalists, or the dominant class, gain cultural capital that supplements their economic capital and accumulate capital of both types in the circulation of commodities (educated mass) and domination of production means (the educational institutions).

Yet, at the same time, Bourdieu's work on cultural capital shares features with Schultz's and Becker's work on human capital. Unlike Marx, Bourdieu focuses on the laborer and on relations between acquired capital and the market. He clearly argues for the significance of external social structure (i.e., the dominance of one class and its culture and values) for the process of symbolic violence and social reproduction, and of the pedagogic actions it uses to create and impose misrecognition on its agents and laborers. Yet, for Bourdieu, the dominant group always remains only as the latent force implied in the background rather than in the forefront of the analysis. That is, the analysis of cultural capital engages the micro- and mesostructures rather than the macrostructures.

Bourdieu (1972/1977) does not seem to rule out purposive action or choices of behavior either. In his analysis of social behavior and interactions (practice), he clearly sees a calculation (strategizing) between opportunities and constraints, and between what is desirable (subjective expectation) and what is probable (objective probability) (1990). Bourdieu is also less rigid than Marx in the demarcation between the exploiting and exploited classes, since he sees society (field or fields) as a network of positions, the better ones of which are struggled over (Wacquant 1989). In fact, some members of the dominated group may contest for and occupy positions holding such capital, as they have misrecognized and acquired the dominant values. These features reflect the neo-capital theoretical stance of the cultural capital theory, as distinguished from Marx's classic theory of capital.

Another break from Marx can be seen in the fact that Bourdieu does not assume perfect correspondence between the accumulation of economic capital and cultural capital. Some economic capitalists do not possess cultural capital, and some cultural capitalists are not economically endowed. This less than perfect correspondence would seem to open a possible path for some laborers, allowing them to use their cultural habitus to gain a foothold in the dominant class. It is conceivable that they can become part of the educational institutions and gain returns in the labor market due to their cultural capital. Bourdieu does not carry his analysis this far, but he seems to leave open the process of social mobility and the possibility of agency.

As a rendition relative to the one depicted in Figure 1.1, one can describe Bourdieu's work as misrecognized or reproduced symbols and meanings constituting the necessary labor, or Commodity 3, that is exchanged for employment and compensation in the production market dominated by the cultural elites or capitalists, who can use the labor in the reproduction of the culture and their dominance, which constitute their surplus value and capital. However, at the same time, the laborers, by offering their culturally reproduced labor to the elites, can in turn acquire compensations, presumably generating a surplus value and capital as well, so that they themselves can reinvest in the accumulation of cultural symbols and meanings to advance further in their relations with the elites and therefore improve their relative standing in the society. In this rendition, I conceive Bourdieu's cultural capital as a neoclassical capital theory with elements from the classical theory.

Neo-Capital Theoretical Explanation: Structurally Constrained Actions

We may now briefly summarize the two critical elements that these neo-capital theories share. For one, there has been a clear shift of explanation from the macroanalytic level employed by the classic Marxian theory to the microanalytic level used in the neo-capital theories. Rather than seeing capital as part of the process of class exploitation in society, the neo-capital theories favor a microlevel explanation of how individual laborers as actors make the necessary investments in order to gain surplus value of their labor in the marketplace.

This shift to a microlevel explanation does not rule out the effects of the larger macrolevel or structural influences in the process of capitalization. Cultural capital theory clearly stresses the "invisible hand" of the dominant class behind the capitalization process. Yet, it is the individual actor, a laborer or potential laborer, I argue, who is the focus of analytic attention.

Second, action or choice has emerged as an important element in neo-capital theories. In the classic theory, action resides solely with the capitalists, while laborers are helpless interchangeable components in the scheme of production to generate surplus value for the capitalists. As such, the laborers have no choice but to provide cheap labor to the production process in exchange for a subsistence livelihood. In the neo-capital theories, laborers are now capable of gaining and keeping some surplus value of their own labor. To an extent, it is up to the individual laborers to decide whether and how much of an effort or investment they wish to make to acquire useful skills and knowledge, which they can "sell" to the producers for a larger share of the surplus value of the labor in the production process. This choice action is the primary and sometimes the only explanatory force employed in the human capital theory.

To be sure, there are constraints to the availability and range of choices for different individuals. Physical health and mental health, whatever their origins, vary among individuals and account for choice differentiations of capitalization. Human capital theorists even take into account family and other individual characteristics (gender, race, etc.). Cultural capital theory, in fact, emphasizes the role of the class structure in society and what it does to individual actions. Not only do structural or class positions define the types of capital having differential values in the market place, but, more important, they dictate what actions the under-privileged must take to acquire such valued skills and knowledge.

In short, neo-capital theories stress the interplay of individual actions and structural positions in the capitalization process. While each particular theory places emphasis either on the former or the latter element, it is recognized that it is this interplay, or choice actions within structural constraints, that accounts for the capitalization process.

However, this interplay remains largely in the background of both human capital and cultural capital theories. Human capital theory clearly chooses to focus on choice behavior in capitalization. Cultural capital theory strongly argues for the dominant class's vested interest in the types of capital and the imposition of their acquisitions in an indoctrination process. Yet, this explanation is largely assumed rather than demonstrated. Dominant values or culture, observable in every society (e.g., there is no society without culture), are assumed to be dictated by a dominant class, and pedagogic indoctrination and misrecognition of these values and culture are assumed to be the process of schooling.

A more explicit explication of the interplay between structure and action is afforded by still another neoclassic capital theory – the social capital theory. It is this theory that will be this volume's primary focus of analysis. The next chapter considers its development.

2

Social Capital

Capital Captured through Social Relations

The premise behind the notion of social capital is rather simple and straightforward: *investment in social relations with expected returns in the marketplace*. This general definition is consistent with various renditions by all scholars who have contributed to the discussion (Bourdieu 1980, 1983/1986; Lin 1982, 1995a; Coleman 1988, 1990; Flap 1991, 1994; Burt 1992; Putnam 1993, 1995a; Erickson 1995, 1996; Portes 1998). The market chosen for analysis may be economic, political, labor, or community. Individuals engage in interactions and networking in order to produce profits. This represents a major extension of the capital theory in general and a significant expansion of the neo-capital theory. Both neo-capital theories discussed so far – human capital and cultural capital – see capital as an investment of personal resources for the production of profit; while they differ in terms of the nature of production (skills and knowledge versus values and norms) and profit (economic return for individuals versus reproduction of the dominant culture), they both address capital as resources invested and vested in individual actors. Capital is seen as the investment or production of individual actors, whether seen as independent, atomized elements randomly located in society, as in the case of human capital theory, or as individuals indoctrinated into adopting the dominant values, as in the case of cultural capital.

But this individual perspective has been expanded with a major advance in neo-capital theory, the notion of social capital – capital captured through social relations. In this approach, capital is seen as a social asset by virtue of actors' connections and access to resources in the network or group of which they are members.

Why Does Social Capital Work?

Generally, four explanations can be offered as to why embedded resources in social networks enhance the outcomes of actions. For one,

19

the flow of *information* is facilitated. In the usual imperfect market situations, social ties located in certain strategic locations and/or hierarchical positions (and thus better informed on market needs and demands) can provide an individual with useful information about opportunities and choices otherwise not available. Likewise, these ties (or their ties) may alert an organization (be it in the production or consumption market) and its agents, or even a community, about the availability and interest of an otherwise unrecognized individual. Such information would reduce the transaction cost for the organization to recruit better (be it in skill, or technical or cultural knowledge) individuals, and for individuals to find better organizations that can use their capital and provide appropriate rewards. Second, these social ties may exert *influence* on the agents (e.g., recruiters or supervisors of the organizations) who play a critical role in decisions (e.g., hiring or promotion) involving the actor. Some social ties, due to their strategic locations (e.g., structural holes) and positions (e.g., authority or supervisory capacities), also carry more valued resources and exercise greater power (e.g., greater asymmetry in dependence by these agents) on organizational agents' decision making. Thus, "putting in a word" carries a certain weight in the decision-making process regarding an individual. Third, social ties, and their acknowledged relationships to the individual, may be conceived by the organization or its agents as certifications of the individual's *social credentials*, some of which reflect the individual's accessibility to resources through social networks and relations – his or her social capital. "Standing behind" the individual by these ties reassures the organization (and its agents) that the individual can provide added resources beyond the individual's personal capital, some of which may be useful to the organization. Finally, social relations are expected to reinforce identity and recognition. Being assured of and recognized for one's worthiness as an individual and a member of a social group sharing similar interests and resources not only provides emotional support but also public acknowledgment of one's claim to certain resources. These *reinforcements* are essential for the maintenance of mental health and the entitlement to resources. These four elements – *information, influence, social credentials,* and *reinforcement* – may explain why social capital works in instrumental and expressive actions not accounted for by forms of personal capital such as economic or human capital.[1]

---

[1] Another element, control, has also been mentioned for the usefulness of social capital. I consider control, reflecting both the network's location and the hierarchical position, as central to the definition of social capital itself. Thus, information, influence, social credentials, and reinforcement are all reasons why social capital works or controls.

Differing Perspectives and
Converging Conceptualizations

Social capital has been a relatively recent development in theory and research. While earlier scholars (Loury 1977, 1987; Ben-Porath 1980) pointed to the phenomenon of resources or capital through social relations or even employed the term *social capital*, only in the 1980s, when several sociologists, including Bourdieu, Coleman, and Lin, independently explored the concept in some detail, did it catch the attention of the research community.

Two perspectives can be identified relative to the level at which return or profit is conceived – whether the profit is accrued for the group or for the individual. In one perspective, the focus is on the use of social capital by individuals – how individuals access and use resources embedded in social networks to gain returns in instrumental actions (e.g., finding better jobs) or to preserve gains in expressive actions. Thus, at this relational level, social capital can be seen as similar to human capital in that it is assumed that such investments can be made by the individual with an expected return (some benefit or profit) to the individual. Aggregation of individual returns also benefits the collective. Nonetheless, the focal points for analysis in this perspective are (1) how individuals invest in social relations and (2) how individuals capture the embedded resources in the relations to generate a return.

Lin (1982), for example, argued that there are two types of resources an individual can gain access to and use: personal resources and social resources. Personal resources are resources possessed by an individual and may include ownership of material as well as symbolic goods (e.g., diplomas and degrees). Social resources are resources accessed through an individual's social connections. Depending on the extensity and diversity of their social connections, individuals have differential social resources.

Further, these resources can be "borrowed" for the purpose of making a gain. A car borrowed from a friend to move household goods and a good word put in by an old classmate of one's father for a job possibility are examples of the use of social resources. As will be made clear later in this volume, in both quantity and quality, social resources far outweigh personal resources in their potential usefulness to individuals.

For Flap (1988, 1991, 1994), social capital also includes mobilized social resources. Flap specifies three elements of social capital: (1) the number of persons within one's social network who "are prepared or obliged to help you when called upon to do so," (2) the strength of the relationship indicating readiness to help, and (3) the resources of these persons. Social capital, for Flap, is resources provided by alters who have strong relationships with ego. Thus, it is the product of availability of social resources and the propensity by alters to offer such resources for help.

Burt's work (1992) also reflects this perspective. Network locations represent and create competitive advantages. Locations that link nodes and their occupants to information and other resources unlikely to be accessible otherwise constitute valuable capital for the occupants at these "structural hole" positions, and at other locations and for other occupants accessing them.

Another perspective focuses on social capital at the group level, with discussions dwelling on (1) how certain groups develop and more or less maintain social capital as a collective asset and (2) how such a collective asset enhances group members' life chances. Bourdieu (1980, 1983/1986) and Coleman (1988, 1990) have discussed this perspective extensively, and Putnam's empirical work (1993, 1995a) is exemplary. While acknowledging the essentiality of individuals interacting and networking in developing payoffs of social capital, the central interest of this perspective is to explore the elements and processes in the production and maintenance of the collective asset.

Bourdieu (1983/1986) sees capital in three guises: as economic capital, as cultural capital, and as social capital. For him, social capital is "made up of social obligations or connections." It is the aggregation of "actual or potential resources which are linked to possession of a durable network of institutionalized relationships of mutual acquaintance and recognition – or in other words, to membership in a group" (p. 248). The group provides its members with the collectivity-owned capital, which allows them credit. Capital, in this form, is represented by the size of the network and the volume of the capital (economic, cultural, or symbolic) possessed by those to whom a person is connected. In other words, for Bourdieu, social capital depends on the size of one's connections and on the volume or amount of capital in these connections' possession. Nevertheless, social capital is a collective asset shared by members of a defined group, with clear boundaries, obligations of exchange, and mutual recognition.

Further, Bourdieu sees social capital as a production of the group's members. It takes repeated exchanges that reinforce mutual recognition and boundaries to affirm and reaffirm the collectivity of the capital and each member's claim to that capital. Finally, for Bourdieu, social capital is a mere disguise for economic capital. In the final analysis, "economic capital is at the root of all the other types of capital," including social capital and "every type of capital is reducible in the last analysis to economic capital" (pp. 252–253). In summary, then, Bourdieu sees social capital as a form of capital possessed by members of a social network or group. Through connections among the members, the capital can be used by members as credits. In this sense, social capital is a collective asset endowing members with credits, and it is maintained and reinforced for its utility when members continue to invest in the relationships.

For Coleman, social capital consists of two elements: it is an aspect of a social structure, and it facilitates certain actions of individuals within the structure (1990, p. 302). Whether any structural aspect is a capital depends on whether it serves a function for certain individuals engaged in particular activities. For this reason, social capital is not fungible across individuals or activities. Social capital is the resources, real or potential, gained from relationships. In his scheme of social action, Coleman (1990) delineates how actors exercise control over resources in which they have an interest, and how they are also interested in events (or the outcome of events) that are at least partially controlled by other actors. Thus, in order for their interests to gain from the outcome of an event, actors engage in exchanges and transfers of resources. These social relationships serve important functions in facilitating the actions of individual actors; they form the basis of social capital.

Coleman (1990) illustrates this point by using the examples of how clandestine groups among South Korean students (p. 302) or workers' cells in the prerevolutionary communist movement in Russia (p. 304) not only provided social capital for individual participants, but also constituted social capital for the revolutionary movements themselves. Parent–teacher associations (PTAs) and other social organizations allow individual parents and students to achieve personal goals, but they also offer resources to the school and to all administrators, teachers, students, and parents affiliated with the school. Coleman uses the example of a mother who moved from Detroit to Jerusalem because her children would be safer when going to the park and school by themselves as another illustration of how individual actors adapt to the social capital available in a collecitivity – the community. Thus, for Coleman and Bourdieu, dense or closed networks are seen as the means by which collective capital can be maintained and reproduction of the group can be achieved.

Putnam's work on participation in voluntary organizations in democratic societies such as the United States strongly reflects the use of this perspective. He argues that such social associations and the degree of participation indicate the extent of social capital in a society. These associations and participation promote and enhance collective norms and trust, which are central to the production and maintenance of the collective well-being (Putnam 1993, 1995a).

While the two perspectives describe social capital differentially in terms of the level at which the utility or outcome can be assessed, all scholars remain committed to the view that it is the interacting members who make the maintenance and reproduction of this social asset possible. This consensual view puts social capital firmly in the neo-capital theory camp.[2] Thus, Bourdieu, Coleman, Lin, Flap, Burt, Erickson, Portes, and others all share the understanding that social capital consists of resources embedded in social relations and social structure, which can be mobilized when an actor wishes to increase the likelihood of success in a purposive action. Like human capital, it is an investment on the part of the actor to increase the likelihood of success in purposive actions. Unlike human capital, which represents investment in training and other programs of activities to acquire skills, knowledge, and certifications, social capital is an investment in social relationships through which resources of other actors can be accessed and borrowed. While the concept has been applied to a wide range of actions (e.g., moving to a different community that is safer for one's children, mobilizing participants in a social movement; see Coleman 1990), and to both macro- (e.g., number of participants and scope of participation in voluntary and community organizations and social groupings; see Putnam 1993, 1995a) and microlevels (e.g., job searches and promotions; see Lin, Ensel, and Vaughn 1981; Burt 1997) of research, there is a converging consensus (Portes, Burt, Lin) that social capital, as a theory-generating concept, should be conceived in the social network context: as resources accessible through social ties that occupy strategic network locations (Burt) and/or significant organizational positions (Lin). This is the conceptualization I will use in this volume.

In this conceptualization, social capital may be defined operationally

---

[2] Two major and different theoretical positions distinguish scholars in the collective asset camp. For Bourdieu, social capital represents a process by which individuals in the dominant class, by mutual recognition and acknowledgment, reinforce and reproduce a privileged group that holds various forms of capital (economic, cultural, and symbolic). Nobility and titles characterize such groups and their members. Thus, social capital is another way of maintaining and reproducing the dominant class. I would characterize this theoretical position as one that views social capital as class (privilege) goods. The other position on social capital as a collective asset is represented by the works of Coleman and Putnam. Coleman, while defining social capital as consisting of any social-structural features or resources that are useful to individuals for specific actions, stresses social capital as a public good. These collective assets and features are available to all members of the group, be it a social group or a community, and regardless of which members actually promote, sustain, or contribute to such resources. Because social capital is a public good, it depends on the good will of the individual members to make such efforts and not to be free riders. Thus, norms, trust, sanctions, authority, and other structural features become important in sustaining social capital. If one were forced to trace the theoretical lineage of these two explanatory schemes, one could argue that the privileged-good view is principally an extension and elaboration of the social relations in Marx's capital theory and that the public-good view is primarily an extension and elaboration of the integrative or Durkheimian view of social relations.

as the *resources embedded in social networks accessed and used by actors for actions*. Thus, the concept has two important components: (1) it represents resources embedded in social relations rather than individuals, and (2) access and use of such resources reside with actors. The first characterization, socially embedded resources, allows a parallel analysis between social capital and other forms of capital. For example, human capital, as envisioned by economists (Schultz, Becker) represents investment on the part of individuals to acquire certain skills and certifications that are useful in certain markets (e.g., the labor market). Social capital can also be envisioned as investment by individuals in interpersonal relationships useful in the markets. The second component of social capital, therefore, must reflect that ego is cognitively aware of the presence of such resources in her or his relations and networks and makes a choice in evoking the particular resources. There may be ties and relationships that do not appear in ego's cognitive map and thus not in her or his awareness of their existence. Only when the individual is aware of their presence, and of what resources they possess or can access (these ties have their networks as well), can the individual capitalize such ties and resources. A systematic presentation of this conceptualization will begin in the next chapter.

Issues and Clarifications

Before I embark on the conceptual presentation, certain issues need to be discussed and clarified. Specifically, the divergence in perspectives has created some theoretical and measurement confusions. Further confusion arises from the fact that some discussions have flowed freely between levels. For example, Bourdieu provides a structural view in pointing to the dominant class and nobility groups' reproduction as the principal explanation of social capital, which is represented by aggregating (1) the size of the group or network and (2) the volume of capital possessed by members (Bourdieu 1983/1986, p. 248). This representation makes sense only when it is assumed that all members maintain strong and reciprocal relations (a completely dense or institutionalized network), so that the strength of relations does not enter into the calculus. Yet, Bourdieu also describes how individuals interact and reinforce mutual recognition and acknowledgment as members of a network or group. Coleman (1990, Chap. 12), while emphasizing how individuals can use sociostructural resources in obtaining better outcomes in their (individual) actions, devotes much discussion to the collective nature of social capital in stressing trust, norms, sanctions, authority, and closure as parts or forms of the concept. It is important to identify and sort through these views and

Table 2.1. *Controversies in Social Capital*

Issue	Contention	Problem
Collective or individual asset (Coleman, Putnam)	Social capital as a collective asset	Confounding with norms, trust
Closure or open networks (Bourdieu, Coleman, Putnam)	Group should be closed or dense	Vision of class society and absence of mobility
Functional (Coleman)	Social capital is indicated by its effect on particular actions	Tautology (the cause is determined by the effect)
Measurement (Coleman)	Not quantifiable	Heuristic, not falsifiable

reach some understandings before we proceed to build a coherent theory of social capital. I identify some of these issues in Table 2.1.

One major controversy generated from macro- versus relational-level perspectives is whether social capital is collective goods or individual goods (see Portes's 1998 critique). Most scholars agree that it is both collective and individual goods; that is, institutionalized social relations with embedded resources are expected to benefit both the collective and the individuals in the collective. At the group level, social capital represents some aggregation of valued resources (e.g., economic, political, cultural, or social, as in social connections) of members interacting as a network or networks. The difficulty arises when social capital is discussed as collective or even public goods, along with trust, norms, and other collective or public goods. What has occurred in the literature is that some terms have become alternative or substitutable terms or measurements. Divorced from its roots in individual interactions and networking, social capital becomes merely another trendy term to employ or deploy in the broad context of improving or building social integration and solidarity. In the following, I will argue that social capital, as a relational asset, must be distinguished from collective assets and goods such as culture, norms, trust, and so on. Causal propositions may be formulated (e.g., that collective assets, such as trust, promote relations and networks and enhance the utility of embedded resources, or vice versa; see Chapter 13), but it should not be assumed that they are all alternative forms of social capital or are defined by one another (e.g., trust is capital; Paxton 1999).

Another controversy related to the focus on social capital's collective aspect is the assumed or expected requirement that there is closure or density in social relations and social networks (Bourdieu 1983/1986; Coleman 1990; Putnam 1993, 1995a). Bourdieu, from his class perspective, sees social capital as the investment of the members in the dominant class (as a group or network) engaging in mutual recognition and acknowledgment so as to maintain and reproduce group solidarity and preserve the group's dominant position. Membership in the group is based on a clear demarcation (e.g., nobility, title, family) excluding outsiders. Closure of the group and density within the group are required. Coleman, of course, does not assume such a class vision of society. Yet, he also sees network closure as a distinctive advantage of social capital, because it is closure that maintains and enhances trust, norms, authority, sanctions, and so on. These solidifying forces may ensure that network resources can be mobilized.

I believe that the requirement for network density or closure for the utility of social capital is not necessary or realistic. Research in social networks has stressed the importance of bridges in networks (Granovetter 1973; Burt 1992) in facilitating information and influence flows. To argue that closure or density is a requirement for social capital is to deny the significance of bridges, structural holes, or weaker ties. The root of preferring a dense or closed network lies rather in certain outcomes of interest (Lin 1986, 1990, 1992a). For *preserving or maintaining resources* (i.e., expressive actions), denser networks may have a relative advantage. Thus, for the privileged class, it would be better to have a closed network so that resources can be preserved and reproduced (e.g., Bourdieu 1983/1986) or for a mother to move to a cohesive community so that her children's security and safety can be assured (Coleman 1990). On the other hand, for *searching for and obtaining resources* not presently possessed (i.e., instrumental actions), such as looking for a job or a better job (e.g., Lin, Marsden, Flap, Burt), accessing and extending bridges in the network should be more useful. Rather than making the assertion that closed or open networks are required, it would be theoretically more viable to (1) conceptualize for what outcomes and under what conditions a denser or sparser network might generate a better return and (2) postulate deduced hypotheses (e.g., a denser network would be more likely to promote the sharing of resources, which in turn would maintain group or individual resources; or an open network would be more likely to access advantaged positions and resources, which in turn would enhance the opportunity to obtain additional resources) for empirical examination.

A third controversy that requires clarification is Coleman's statement that social capital is any "social-structural resource" that generates returns for an individual in a specific action. He remarks that "social capital is defined by its function" and that "it is not a single entity, but a variety of different entities having two characteristics: They all consist of some aspect of a social structure, and they facilitate certain actions of individuals who are within the structure" (1990, p. 302). This *functional* view may implicate a tautology: social capital is identified when and if it works; the potential causal explanation of social capital can be captured only by its effect; or whether it is an investment depends on the return for a specific individual in a specific action. Thus, the causal factor is defined by the effectual factor. Clearly, it would be impossible to build a theory in which causal and effectual factors are folded into a singular function. This is not to deny that a functional relationship may be hypothesized (e.g., resources embedded in social networks make it easier to obtain better jobs). But the two concepts must be treated as separate entities with independent measurements (e.g., social capital is the investment in social relations, and better jobs are represented by occupational status or supervisory position). It would be incorrect to allow the outcome variables to dictate the specification of the causal variable (e.g., for actor X, kin ties are social capital because they channel X to get a better job, and for actor Y, kin ties are not social capital because they do not channel Y to get a better job). The hypothesized causal relationship may be conditioned by other factors (e.g., family characteristics may affect differential opportunities for building human and social capital) that need be specified in a more elaborate theory. A theory would lose parsimony quickly if the conditional factors become part of the definitions of the primary concepts. In fact, one would question whether it remains a theory if it is required to make a good prediction for every case and every situation.

Perhaps related to this indistinguishable view of social capital from its outcome – and perhaps given his view that social capital, as a collective good, can also be seen in many different forms, such as trust, norms, sanctions, authority, and so on – Coleman questions "whether social capital will come to be as useful a quantitative concept in social science as are the concepts of financial capital, physical capital, and human capital remains to be seen; its current value lies primarily in its usefulness for qualitative analyses of social systems and for those quantitative analyses that employ qualitative indicators" (1990, pp. 304–305). Again, the confusion can be seen as resulting from extending the notion of social capital beyond its theoretical roots in social relations and social networks, and the unattainable theoretical position that prediction holds for every individual case. Once these issues are resolved, social capital should and must be measurable.

3

Resources, Hierarchy, Networks, and Homophily

The Structural Foundation

It has been proposed that social capital, as an investment in social relations with an expected return in the marketplace, should be defined as *resources embedded in a social structure that are accessed and/or mobilized in purposive actions*. In this definition, three critical components present themselves for analysis: (1) the resources, (2) being embedded in a social structure, and (3) action. I contend that resources are at the core of all capital theories, especially social capital. A theory of social capital should accomplish three tasks: First, it should explain how resources take on values and how the valued resources are distributed in society – the structural embeddedness of resources. Second, it should show how individual actors, through interactions and social networks, become differentially accessible to such structurally embedded resources – the opportunity structure. Third, it should explain how access to such social resources can be mobilized for gains – the process of activation. This chapter will focus on the first two of these tasks: embeddedness of valued resources in society and the opportunity structure relative to such resources. Chapter 4 will conclude the explication of the theory by discussing the action component.

Resources and Their Social Allocation

A fundamental concept of the theory presented here is resources, defined *as material or symbolic goods* (Lin 1982).[1] Beyond the basic physical resources needed to sustain and enhance human life, individuals and groups ascribe meanings and significance to other resources as well.

[1] Sewell (1992, p. 9) identified two types of resources in structure: nonhuman and human resources. While nonhuman resources are consistent with physical resources, human resources include both physical (physical strength, dexterity) and symbolic (knowledge, emotional commitment) resources.

29

Here, three principles are proposed as assumptions about how meanings and significance are assigned to resources.

First, in any human group or community, *differential values are assigned by consensus or influence to resources* to signal their relative significance (Lin 1982). Value assignment of a resource is dictated in part by its scarcity relative to the demand or expectations for it (e.g., gold in one society or seashells in another). But it is also determined by the unique historical, geographical, and collective experiences of each group.

The assignment of values to resources may be achieved through one of three processes of influence: persuasion, petition, or coercion (Lin 1973; and see related discussions in Kelman 1961 and Parsons 1963). *Persuasion* is a process by which fellow actors are convinced, through communication and interaction, of the merit of a resource, resulting in the internalization of the value of a resource among the actors. Members supposedly see the intrinsic value of a resource. Persuasion results in assigning value to a resource without the threat or imposition of external sanction or punishment. *Petition* indicates the appeal or lobbying of a group of individual actors and represents normative pressure. Individual actors accept the value of a resource because they wish to remain members of a group or identify with the group, and they are willing to accept what the group's values even if they do not understand or accept the resource's intrinsic merit. *Coercion* is the process by which fellow actors are forced to recognize the merit of a resource or face certain sanction or punishment. Individual actors do not see the intrinsic value of a resource or voluntarily accept its value because they wish to identify with the group. Rather, they are confronted with either recognizing the authoritative assignment of value or suffering undesirable consequences (physical or mental harm, for example).

The assigned value of a resource may change due to internal (civil war, revolution, upheaval, disaster, authoritative revision, discoveries, changes in fashion or taste, etc.) and external (trade, war, invasion, conquest, exchange of ideas, etc.) forces. For example, the status of females, while universally distinct, is expressed differently in different communities and epochs. For women in the Qing dynasty of imperial China, bound feet signaled high status; the smaller the foot, the more highly the lady was regarded. For women in mid-twentieth-century Europe and North America, high heels similarly signaled high status. Both resources are valuable in their respective contexts and time, perhaps for women to attract mates who have other valued resources. While the value of each resource is time-bound, some resources are more enduring or universal (e.g., money, ethnic or racial ranking, pierced body parts) than others (e.g., bound feet, kilts for men, and wigs for judges or high priests).

Second, we assume that *all actors will take actions to promote their self-interests by maintaining and gaining valued resources if such opportunities are available.* An *actor* here is either an individual or a collective group. The collectivity, or the community, promotes its self-interest by conferring relatively higher statuses on individual actors who possess more valued resources. There is a good reason why the collectivity would confer such status on or "empower" (Sewell 1992) individual actors. It reinforces the social consensus of the collectivity on the values of the resources – a sense of community. It is a reward to an individual actor for his or her demonstrated adherence to the social consensus on the assigned values. The status conferral serves to promote the unity, and thus the survival and persistence, of the collectivity. Conferred status further reinforces the loyalty to the collectivity of the individual actors in possession of the valued resource, because it confirms and protects the values of the resources. Thus, status conferral for possession of valued resources promotes the mutual interests of the community and the participating individual actors.

The reciprocal relationship between the persistence of a community and its conferral of status on individual actors possessing valuable resources has important consequences for collective action. Individual actors holding more valued resources, and therefore higher standings, tend to be given the opportunity to make decisions on behalf of or in the name of the collectivity, including ways to allocate and distribute the valued resources. Such an opportunity is offered by assigning to these individual actors decision-making positions in the collectivity. This structural opportunity will be discussed further in the next section on the macrostructure of resources. In any case, the consequence is that individual actors in possession of valued resources are more likely to be involved in decisions regarding the rights (use, transfer, disposition) of these resources (e.g., valued properties).[2] Actors in decision-making positions are expected to reinforce the community consensus, because there is an incentive for them to sustain and promote their standing in the community. Self-interest is thus served because it is consistent with collective interest. These powerful individual actors can further advance their standing by either gaining more valued resources, or manipulating value consensus to promote the value of resources that they possess or can access. Higher positions in the collectivity offer more opportunities to promote self-interest.

On the other hand, individual actors with less valued resources and

---

[2] For a discussion of property rights, see Alchian (1965), Alchian and Demsetz (1973), Gilham (1981), and Willer (1985). For the relationships between property rights and class structures, see Dahrendorf (1959), Bourdieu (1986), and Kornai (1992).

thus lower standings in the community experience greater structural constraints and less opportunities to innovate. There are two types of actions
these individuals can take: either appropriate more valued resources or
change the values assigned to various resources. Appropriation of valued
resources can employ means legitimated and sanctioned by the community, that is, institutionalized channels such as going through the educational system. Or it can employ means not sanctioned or considered
legitimate by the community, that is, deviant actions. Merton (1940), in
his work on social structure and anomie, has theorized how individual
actors can violate group norms to achieve individual goals.

To change the values of resources requires more than individual
actions; it needs the mobilization of other actors who make similar
demands. Such mobilization can range from the formation of social networks promoting alternative value assignments to resources to revolutions that aim to replace the community's decision makers (for further
discussion, see Chapter 11).

These deviant actions, of course, risk sanctions from the community.
Sanctions may range from demotion in community standing (incarcera-
tion or deprivation of valued resources and higher status) to expulsion.
Such is the force of structure on individual actors to act responsibly. Yet,
the fact remains that structural constraints and opportunities go hand in
hand (Merton 1995). The focal point, for both individuals and the community, remains contention for valued resources, and actions are taken
to promote self-interest by gaining and preserving such resources.

In ordinary times, when actions and interactions are carried out
routinely, the significance of the constraint–opportunity synergy is not
clear to the actors themselves, since the decisions seem to be made by the
collectivity's invisible hand for the well-being of every member. It becomes
more explicit when the community's survival is challenged. In time of
external crisis, a unified community follows a strategy that protects those
with the most valued resources and sacrifices those with the least valued
resources. In facing an external threat, for example, a collectivity would
tend to let go the non–decision makers first or in higher proportions,
while the managers who authorize or control such layoffs tend to survive
unless the collectivity is on the verge of collapse. During the waning phase
of World War II, Japan sent its low-ranking and younger pilots on
kamikaze missions while holding back the higher-ranked and more experienced pilots in preparation for the final battle to defend the motherland.
Preservation of the community and preservation of individual actors in
possession of valued resources are mutually serving and sustaining.

The third principle regarding valued resources assumes that *maintaining and gaining valued resources are the two primary motives for
action, with the former outweighing the latter* (Lin 1994a). Both the

community and its individual actors strive, first, to maintain the valued resources they possess or to which they can gain access. Only when the existing valued resources are secured do actors seek to gain additional valued resources. There are secondary and peripheral motives for actions; however, we assume that these two motives are primary and dictate the overwhelming proportion of actions. A further deliberation on the significance of this principle and its consequences for action will appear in Chapter 4.

The Macrostructure of Resources: Hierarchies and Social Positions

Once resources are defined and their values and significance assumed, we next consider how resources are embedded in the collectivity. The following description below focuses on several topics: (1) the nature of a social structure, (2) the hierarchy in a social structure, (3) the pyramidal shape of the hierarchical structure, and (4) complex social structures and resource transactions.

Social Structure

A *social structure* is here defined as consisting of (1) a set of social units (*positions*) that possess differential amounts of one or more types of valued resources and that (2) are hierarchically related relative to *authority* (control of and access to resources), (3) share certain *rules* and procedures in the use of the resources, and (4) are entrusted to *occupants* (*agents*) who *act on* these rules and procedures (for related discussion, see Sewell 1992).

The first element links the embeddedness of resources to social positions (for a discussion of the positional view of structure, see Burt 1992). The occupant of a position may change, but the resources are attached to the position. Therefore, resources embedded in a structure are distinguished from resources possessed by individual actors. A structure remains stable as long as the positions with their embedded resources persist (Weber 1947).

The second element describes relations among the positions. *Authority* is one form of power, defined as the relative control over and access to the valued resources (see discussion of this definition in Emerson 1962; Cook and Emerson 1978; Bourdieu 1983/1986; Coleman 1990, pp. 780–782), identifying the relative ranking between any pair of positions. Authority implies coercion, with explicit legalistic sanctions. A structure is more hierarchical the more the relative authority among its positions differs.

The third element describes the shared procedures and rules guiding how positions (and the agents) ought to act and interact relative to the use and manipulation of valued resources (for a discussion of rules in structure, see Sewell 1992).[3] The rules and procedures lead to uniform actions and interactions among social positions, so that the value of the resources is upheld and maintaining and expanding such resources remain the purposes of collective actions.

The final element is the occupants of these positions, which highlights the fact that they are expected to behave in accordance with these rules and procedures. Thus, social structure, with its rules and procedures, represents the principle, and the individual actors who occupy positions and are empowered to act out the rules and procedures are the agents. This is a very important principle and a paradox as well. On the one hand, enactment of the rules and procedures is critical to the persistence of the structure, so that selection of occupants favors those who are socialized and trained to carry out these rules and procedures. On the other hand, because occupants must carry out these rules and procedures, individual actors in these positions gain opportunities to act according to their own interpretations. The paradox is that while these occupants are favored because of their skills and knowledge, and the expectation that they will carry out the rules and procedures that sustain the community, these agents are also given opportunities to act according to their whims – a reliance on their ability and willingness to interpret "properly" and act effectively and creatively. This agency principle (for a discussion of agency and agents in structure, see Sewell 1992) runs the risk that occupants may consider interests other than those of the collectivity in their interpretations or err in applying the rules and procedures to actual situations.

These four elements – *positions, authority, rules,* and *agents* – collectively define the social macrostructure as a system of coordination for the maintenance and/or acquisition of one or more types of valued resources for the collectivity.

Hierarchical Structure

In general, social structures and their resource(s) can be classified over a continuum of differential explicitness in resources, positions, authority,

---

[3] Rules and procedures exist beyond the social structure described here. In a larger society, the shared, understood, and largely consensual "ways of thinking and doing things" or "rules of the game" form culture or institutions (see Bourdieu 1972/1977; Meyer and Rowan 1977; North 1990; Scott and Meyers 1994; Lin 1994b). Also see Chapter 11.

rules, and agents. The formalization of a social structure is characterized by the extent to which these elements are made explicit, and inclusive and exclusive criteria are well understood in terms of valued resources, positions, authority, rules and procedures, and occupants.[4] It is impossible to identify the full range, and thus all types, of social structures in terms of their formality. In general, and stereotypically, the degree of formalization of social structures ranges from so-called formal organizations or hierarchical structures (e.g., firms, corporations, and agencies) to voluntary associations and clubs and to informal social networks.[5] We will focus on the more formally organized and hierarchical social structures. Differentiation between formal organizations and less formal structures such as social networks will emerge as the discussion warrants.

In hierarchical structures, positions are linked in a chain of authoritative command, where higher and more powerful positions not only dictate the behaviors of occupants of less powerful positions by instructing and socializing them as to how to interpret rules and procedures, but also dispose of these lower positions, discharge occupants, and reallocate embedded resources, as dictated by explicit rules and procedures or interpretations of the former by occupants in higher positions. The rules and procedures, in principle, are legalized in that they are usually enforceable, with the approval of and even enforcement by the larger community (e.g., the state); punitive actions can be taken against violations or deviations. The occupants are designated in contract relationships and can be dismissed under rules (Weber 1946, 1947).

A simple formal structure is therefore defined as a hierarchical structure consisting of a set of positions linked in authority (legitimately coercive) relations (command chains) over the control and use of certain valued resources. The relative rank ordering of positions in terms of access to valued resources can be determined by their vertical location in the authority hierarchy. A position higher up in the hierarchy, by definition, can exercise authority over lower positions. Just as important, the higher positions have more information about the locations of valued resources in the hierarchy – where specific types and amounts of resources are embedded. In other words, the higher the position in the hierarchical structure, the better information it provides of the structure's resources.

Lateral positions are defined as those endowed with authority over a similar amount of resources in a simple social structure. These positions

---

[4] It is theoretically possible to have a social structure with the specific criterion of "no criteria of exclusion and inclusion." This case, for our purposes here, is equivalent to no formal or rigid criterion.

[5] *Institutions*, in this volume, will be defined as sets of rules and procedures used by various social structures (see Chapter 11).

can also form relationships with each other because they offer opportunities for information exchanges about the location and availability of resources in different positions. Such information facilitates better control and manipulation of a position's resources, and access that ensures the maximal likelihood of preserving and/or gaining resources. Transactions over resources can take place among these lateral positions when they are authorized to do so, or when rules and procedures do not prevent such exchanges and are not interpreted as sabotaging higher authority in the command chain. Horizontal linkages become especially relevant when collective action is geared to massing or combining available resources in the structure.

The Pyramid of a Hierarchy

Another assumption about the macrostructure of resources is that there is a general tendency for the hierarchical structure to have a pyramidal shape in terms of position distribution: the higher the level in the command chain, the fewer the number of positions and occupants (Lin 1982). The inverse relationship between the number of positions and their command of other positions is assumed for most social structures. However, many evolving structures show a smaller bottom level than expected by this image, as industrialization and technological development continue to define or redefine the values of resources and to redistribute positions and occupants accordingly. For example, in most industrialized societies, there is only a small segment of agricultural production and positions at the bottom of the command hierarchy.

An important consequence of pyramid-shaped hierarchical structures is that authority is concentrated in a few positions and occupants. At the very top, only a few positions and occupants not only command the largest absolute and relative amounts of valued resources, but also have the most comprehensive information on the location of resources in the structure.

Transactions in Complex Social Structures

Any existing social structure reflects a complexity that involves multiple hierarchical structures over many different kinds of valued resources. For most collectivities, the highly valued resources are associated with economic, social, and political dimensions. For example, Weber (1946) identifies three dimensions of "power" distribution in a community: *classes*, *status groups*, and *parties*. Because other terms have also been used in the literature regarding resources distributed in society and among indi-

Table 3.1. *Dimensions of Valued Resources for Characterizing Structural Positions and Individuals*

Dimension	Positional	Individual
Social	Status (prestige)	Reputation
Economic	Class	Wealth
Political	Authority	Power

vidual actors, a clarification of how these terms are defined and used in this monograph is needed.

Valued resources are distributed in three dimensions (social, economic, and political) and can characterize structural positions and individual actors. These characterizations are specified in Table 3.1.

For example, a socially highly regarded structural position can be characterized as a high-status "group." Correspondingly, individual actors are considered as having better or worse reputations.[6] Positions in possession of valued economic resources are considered upper class, and individuals occupying these positions are wealthy actors. Positions higher up in a hierarchical command structure are seen as more authoritative, and individual occupants are labeled as powerful.[7]

In any event, the theory assumes that while the uneven distribution of various valued resources forms the basis of hierarchical structures, and each valued resource defines a particular hierarchy, these hierarchies have a tendency toward congruence and transferability. That is, there tends to be a correspondence of occupants among hierarchical positions across valued resource or status dimensions. An occupant in a position of relatively high standing with respect to one resource also tends to occupy a relatively high position with respect to other resources. For example, a person with relatively high standing (status) in the occupational structure is also likely to hold a high position in the class and authority dimensions.

---

[6] *Prestige* has been used in the sociological literature to represent both statuses of positions (e.g., occupational prestige) and statuses of individuals. To avoid this confusion, and for important theoretical reasons (see Chapter 9), I choose the term *reputation* as an indicator of social standing for individuals.

[7] Ambiguity concerning the term *power* remains. As used by Weber, it means general control over resources in a structural sense. For others (e.g., Emerson and Cook), power indicates the extent to which an individual actor, relative to other actors, controls alternative sources of resources. To avoid confusion, power is used in this volume as a characterization of individual actors or occupants.

When such convergence is not functionally complete (i.e., a one-to-one relationship), exchange of resources across dimensions is not only possible but, in most societies, is explicit and expected. For example, an occupant with power resources can negotiate and trade with an occupant with wealth resources to acquire some of the latter's wealth in exchange for lending power to the latter. The calculus of such transfers is usually institutionalized (with rules and procedures understood and practiced by individual actors) in a social structure.

Interaction and Homophily: Networking and Social Capital

Social networks represent a less formal social structure in that there is little or no formality in delineating positions and rules and in allocating authority to participants. In social networks, fluidity characterizes the occupants, positions, resources, and rules and procedures. Mutual agreement through persuasion rather than authority or coercion dictates the actors' participation and interaction, and defines the boundary and locations (positions) of participants' (nodes). A particular network may evolve naturally or may be socially constructed for a particular shared focus or interest regarding a resource (e.g., protection of the environment, women's rights). However, in general, a social network may be constructed for multiple interests in its different segments – different interests link nodes in different parts of the network. Being in a node of a network directly and indirectly provides potential access to other nodes (actors) in the social network. Resources embedded in these nodes become ego's social capital. As already pointed out, social capital reflects more than the mere personal resources of those nodes in the network. Since individual actors may be embedded in hierarchical structures and other networks, they bring to bear resources embedded in the positions of these hierarchies as well. These resources lie beyond the focus resource that might have been the initial reason for interacting. For example, individual actors may interact because of their shared interest in gun control or abortion issues, but they also bring to the interacting context their other personal and positional resources, such as their jobs and authority positions, wealth, and affiliations with religious institutions and political parties, as well as the networks and resources of their spouses, relatives, friends, and fellow workers.

Thus, interactions should be analyzed and understood not only as relationship patterns among individual actors or nodes but, much more importantly, as resource patterns linked in interaction patterns. The critical question then is: What patterns of resource linkage might be expected through interacting and networking?

The theoretical foundation for understanding interaction can be found in Homans's (1950) studies of small primary groups. He postulated in principle the reciprocal and positive relationships among three factors: interaction, sentiment, and activity. The more individuals interact, the more likely they are to share sentiments and the more they engage in collective activity. Likewise, the more individuals share sentiments, the more likely they are to interact and engage in activities. The critical hypothesis for us here is the positive relationship between sentiment and interaction. That is, the basis of interaction is sentiment – affection, respect, sympathy, and liking for each other (Homans 1950, pp. 37–40) and vice versa. In other words, interaction is based primarily on shared emotion.

An important extension of the sentiment-interaction hypothesis is the homophily hypothesis. Largely a theoretical induction from research on patterns of friendship (Lazarsfeld and Merton 1954) and associations (Laumann 1966), the principle of *homophily*, also known as the *like-me hypothesis*, is that *social interactions tend to take place among individuals with similar lifestyles and socioeconomic characteristics*. Research has shown that interactions tend to occur among individual actors occupying similar or adjacent and slightly different social positions.

If we assume that socioeconomic characteristics and lifestyles reflect resources embedded in individuals and their hierarchical positions and network locations, then the homophilous principle of interaction implies a positive relationship between individuals with similar resources and the amount of their interaction, since similarity of social positions/locations is presumably characterized by similarity of types and amounts of resources. From the resource perspective, this suggests that interactions tend to occur among actors at the same or adjacent social positions in the hierarchy.

Thus, the Homans sentiment-interaction hypothesis becomes a sentiment-interaction-resources hypothesis. That is, there are triangular reciprocal relationships among sentiment, resources, and interaction that thus link interactions not only to shared sentiment, but also to similarity in resources. (See Figure 3.1.) While the sentiment-interaction hypothesis and the homophily hypothesis do not insist on a particular cause-and-effect sequence among the three elements, an important consequence of these hypotheses is that individuals whose positions are situated closer to each other in social structures are more likely to interact.

We may further extend the homophily principle to occupants of similar positions in multiple resource structures (e.g., authority, status, or class) because, by the rules of congruence and transferability of resources, interaction may engage partners with different kinds of resources as long

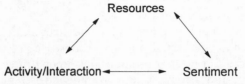

Figure 3.1 The homophily principle. (Modified from Homans 1950 and Lazarsfeld and Merton 1954)

as the values of their resources are equivalent. For example, a banker and a senator may have different resources, but they are both high in their respective resource structures, and thus are more likely to engage in interaction than, say, the banker and a local manager of a fast-food shop.

Concluding Remarks

This chapter has outlined the structural foundation for social capital, conceived as *resources embedded in a social structure that are accessed and/or mobilized in purposive actions*. It has defined resources and conceptualizes how resources acquire value in a society. It has suggested how such valued resources are embedded in hierarchical and network structures that are differentiated in terms of their degree of formalization of positions, authority, rules, and agents. Differential opportunity structures emerge because embedded resources in these social structures are differentially accessed by individual actors in their web of social relations and because the principle of homophily is the normative expectation. In this formulation, social capital is shown to have significant structural character – the embedded resources in hierarchies and networks, their capture at least in part contingent on the opportunity structure afforded by the normative principle of interactions, or homophily. In the next chapter, this structural foundation of social capital will be elaborated and complemented with the incorporation of possible action and choice elements in completing the conceptualization of social capital.

4

Resources, Motivations, and Interactions

The Action Foundation

As conceptualized in the previous chapter, social capital is rooted in social networks and social relations and is conceived as resources embedded in a social structure that are accessed and/or mobilized in purposive actions. Thus conceived, social capital contains three components intersecting structure and action: structure (embeddedness), opportunity (accessibility through social networks), and action (use). The previous chapter has articulated the structural and opportunity aspects of social capital. This chapter will add the component of action to complete the theoretical foundation.

"It's Not Just What You Know but Who You Know": The Microstructure of Resources

The saying "It's not just what you know but who you know" suggests that social capital should provide benefits for an individual who acts for a purpose. In this context, interaction is seen as a means to attain a goal of action. The task here is to understand how action is related to interaction and how agency is salient in the process of mobilizing social capital in a purposive action. I begin with a discussion of resources embedded in actors.

Individuals, like groups and organizations, gain and maintain valued resources to promote their well-being. They can mobilize and use such resources in purposive action to gain additional resources (see Chapter 1 for the discussion of neo-classical theories of capital). Just as important, possession of or access to resources protects and promotes an individual's standing in the social structure. Social recognition confers identity and reputation, providing recognized individuals with still more resources and a sense of worth and security within the structure. In general, two types of resources

41

can be defined for individual actors: personal resources and social resources.

Personal Resources as Human Capital

Personal resources are in the possession of individual actors who, as their owner, can use, transfer, and dispose of them without needing to receive specific authorization or be accountable to other actors or social positions.[1] Acquisition of personal resources can be pursued down many avenues. One major route is by way of inheritance or ascription. Resources may be declared the individual actor's by transfer from parents, kin, or other actors. By the institutional rules of the community, they are passed on from one individual actor to another. Another avenue is to acquire them by investing one's own resources or efforts. Education, for example, has been seen as an acquired resource through investment of parental or personal resources and personal efforts. Presumably, investment in education also leads to acquisition of other valued resources (e.g., power, wealth, and reputation) (see Chapter 1 on education as human and cultural capital).

A third way of acquiring personal resources is through exchange. Acquisition of personal resources may involve a direct payment (money) or exchange of resources (bartering) through which title to resources is transferred from one individual actor to another. It is possible to delay the payment or exchange; in this case, a personal credit or debt is incurred on either side, with the expectation that the credit slip (promise of future payment) will be honored. Nevertheless, in pure exchange there is no expected obligation beyond the payment of the debt itself and no expectation of further exchanges. Personal property, commodities, money, and labor are typical resources in such exchange.

Some personal resources are fully owned by an individual actor (e.g., education, wealth) in the sense that the individual actor is free to use and dispose of them.[2] But they are usually "owned" only by social contract, which designates an individual actor to be the user of specific resources – typical property rights designation (see Alchian 1965 and Alchian and Demsetz 1973 for a definition of property rights). As long as the contract is in force, the individual actor can exercise power in resource control and use. For example, an occupant of a position in a

---

[1] However, a larger or external community's (e.g., the state) sanction is necessary for such use and appropriation. See the references in footnote 2 in Chapter 3, in particular Willer (1985) on the legal sanctions for property rights.
[2] Some resources are more difficult to dispose of than others. For example, education seems permanent after acquisition and certification, even though discrediting or disqualification (disownership) may still be possible and legitimate under certain conditions.

hierarchical structure has the right to control and use the resources attached to that position. These ownership rights expire when the individual actor is detached from that position. Therefore, it is useful to distinguish positional resources from the more fully owned personal resources.

While positional resources are less permanent, they are much more powerful as far as the other resources they control are concerned. Being part of a hierarchical structure with authority and linkages offers opportunities for the actor-occupant to have access to other actor-occupants and borrow or exchange resources. In other words, through structural connections, positions in hierarchical structures gain control and use of resources beyond those that these positions are allocated. It is in this context that we need to go beyond personal resources and explore resources accessed through social connections, that is, social capital.

Social Resources as Social Capital

As already indicated, not all resources available to individual actors are in their personal (including contractual) possession. In fact, personal resources for most individual actors are very limited. More likely, individual actors access resources through social ties. We define *social resources*, or *social capital*, as those resources accessible through social connections. Social capital contains resources (e.g., wealth, power, and reputation, as well social networks) of other individual actors to whom an individual actor can gain access through direct or indirect social ties. They are resources embedded in the ties of one's networks. Like personal resources, social resources may include material goods such as land, houses, car, and money and symbolic goods such as education, memberships in clubs, honorific degrees, nobility or organizational titles, family name, reputation, or fame.[3]

Resources an actor can be linked to through her or his social networks[4]

---

[3] It is important to differentiate two types of social resources: social capital and cultural capital. Social capital is resources captured through social networks and social connections, whereas cultural capital is resources captured through social identification and reciprocal recognition. It is conceivable that some social resources, for certain actors, are captured through both identification (being a member of an ethnic group) and social networks (with ties to other members of the ethnic group), whereas other social resources for other actors are captured through either identification or social networks. Further articulation of the differentiation and integration of these two types of capital is beyond the scope of this volume. The focus here is on social resources captured through social relations – social capital.

[4] Individual actors' own knowledge of resources embedded in their ties may be only a subset of the actual types and amounts of their social capital. This is so for two reasons: they are unaware of all their alters' (direct ties') resources and/or of the ties and resources in their alters' networks. Thus, individual actors' social capital can be divided into two parts: (a) the portion that they are aware of and (b) the remaining unknown portion.

represent a repertoire of ego resources. Even if ego does not use or mobilize these resources, they have substantial symbolic utility. Letting others know about one's social capital may be sufficient to promote one's social standing. The symbolic utility occurs because such information imputes the potential power of ego by association. Spreading information about ego's having a millionaire friend provides better social recognition for ego in her or his social circle because the alleged potential is there for ego to activate the connection and draw on that resource if necessary.

Symbolic utility also occurs because such a connection reflects ego's social or cultural standing. Information about one's acquaintance with a movie star may not impute any power in action, but it can enhance ego's social recognition because it suggests that ego, through interactions with the movie star, could share and enjoy a lifestyle much admired in ego's social circle. Mentioning a tie ("So and so is a friend," "I talked to so and so yesterday") may be sufficient to promote ego's social standing. Of course, social capital can provide utility beyond its symbolic power. Actual use of social capital mobilizes it for a purposive action, a topic to be treated in Chapter 5.

Two important features of social capital deserve further clarification: (1) resources can be accessed through direct and indirect ties, and (2) such resources may be in alters' possessions (their personal resources) or in their social positions (their positional resources). First, social capital includes the resources accessed through indirect ties. Resources of alters (direct ties) represent a relatively small portion of ego's social capital. Often social capital activates chains of multiple actors. In order to gain access to a certain resource (say, information about a job), ego may go to someone who does not possess that information but who may know someone else who does. In this case, the initial contact's social networks become resources for ego. Thus, social capital does not come merely through direct connections or simple dyadic relationships. Both direct and indirect connections can afford access to resources. Through the direct and indirect ties of alters, actors' social capital extends as far as their social networks. That is, social capital is contingent on resources embedded in direct and indirect ties and accessible through these ties.

Second, resources accessed through social ties include both these alters' more or less permanent resources and the resources they control through their positions in a hierarchical structure, say an organization – their positional resources. In general, the positional resources of social ties are much more useful than personal resources to ego, because positional

Actors' self-reporting inevitably yields an incomplete and conservative estimate of their social capital's potential repertoire. Self-reporting may yield different estimates than sociometric methods. There is no true estimate because that if social capital is not within individual actors' cognitive maps, it may be inaccessible and not useful to them.

resources evoke not only the resources embedded in positions in an organization, but also the power, wealth, and reputation of the organization itself. Two equally competent professors who are respectively affiliated with an Ivy League university and a state four-year college, or two equally competent professional programmers, one of whom works for Microsoft and the other for a small local software company, will have quite unequal positional resources, even if their personal resources, including knowledge and earnings, are equal, because the positional and personal resources of their respective colleagues may be quite different in quality. Through these alters, ego gains access not only to their resources, both permanent and positional, but also potentially to resources through their connections in the organization, as well as the power, wealth, and status of the organization itself.

Furthermore, because each organization is located in a network of organizations, ego's social capital extends beyond the limits of the organization. Through the organization's linkages, both direct and indirect, to other organizations, and through the ties' connections to these other organizations' position occupants, ego's social capital may extend to include resources embedded in these other organizations.

Motives for Resources: Purposive Actions

Once it has become clear that individual actors have in their possession and access valued resources, it is then not difficult to understand human actors' motives for action and the consequences of different types of action. As stated in Chapter 2, both collectivities and individual actors take action for two primary motives: to protect existing valued resources and to gain additional ones. That is, it is assumed that actions are rational and are motivated to maintain or gain valued resources in order to survive and persist. The first motive dictates actions to preserve valued resources already at the individual's disposal. The second motive promotes actions to acquire valued resources not yet at the individual's disposal.

It is assumed that the motive to maintain valued resources promotes *expressive action*. Maintaining one's resources requires recognition by others of one's legitimacy in claiming property rights to these resources or sharing one's sentiments. The action, of course, can be seen as instrumental in that ego has a goal in acting – to solicit sentiment and support. However, the expected response is primarily expressive: acknowledging ego's property rights or sharing ego's sentiment. There is no action required beyond this public recognition and acknowledgment of others. Examples include a mother talking with another mother about her affection for her children, a woman talking to her mother about her husband's watching too much football on television, a man sharing his feeling of admiration for a woman with a friend, and a man complaining about his boss to his wife. In these cases, the act of communicating serves as both means and goal; alters are expected to sympathize and empathize with ego and to appreciate and reciprocate ego's feelings, thereby recognizing, legitimizing, and sharing ego's claims to their resources.

Further, it is assumed that the motive to seek and gain additional valued resources primarily evokes *instrumental action,* which hopes to trigger actions and reactions from others leading to more allocation of resources to ego. Thus, the action can be seen as a means to achieve a goal: to produce a profit (added resources). Likewise, instrumental action contains expressive elements in that alter must have sentiment for ego to take action on ego's behalf. However, action is required on alter's part, and the end result is expected to be a gain for ego. Examples include seeking a job, promotion, salary, or bonus increase; getting a loan; finding a babysitter; or looking for a job for one's son.

It should be noted that both types of action represent purpose or agency because motivations provide the drive to act. Of the two motivations for action – to maintain or to gain resources – it is assumed that the motivation to maintain and defend existing resources is the more important driving force. Losing resources in one's possession poses a greater mental and physical threat to ego's existence than not gaining additional resources. Thus, expressive action – action that seeks sentiment and support – is expected to take precedent over instrumental action (see Chapter 3).

These motivations for action result in two behavioral consequences: either actors can engage in activities by themselves that can produce better protection or gain resources, or they can engage one another to use one another's resources. It is the latter case that is of interest here for a theory of social capital. Purposive actions must therefore be understood in terms of interactions that allow actors to access and use one another's resources for their own purposes. We next examine the two types of interaction – homophilous and heterophilous – and assess their utilities for purposive actions.

Homophilous and Heterophilous Interactions

As explicated in the previous chapter, social interaction engages actors and thus intersects the resources embedded in the actors' structural positions and social networks. The extent to which the intersecting resources are similar or different in quality, type, and amount may be considered as variables ranging from identical to completely different. For simplicity's sake, two types of interaction have been be identified and defined: homophilous and heterophilous. The former characterizes relations between two actors who have similar resources, which can include wealth, reputation, power, and lifestyle. The latter describes relations between two actors with dissimilar resources. As described in Chapter 3, homophilous interactions prevail, since the homophily principle links sentiment, interaction, and similarity of resources in actors' reciprocal relationships.

While homophilous interaction has been much researched and examined, heterophilous interaction has received far less attention. The tendency has been to take heterophilous interaction as merely the opposite end of the continuum from homophilous interaction. Since there is a general tendency toward homophily in interaction, the logical deduction is that heterophilous interactions are less likely to occur. Given the hypothesized relationship between sentiments and interactions, the deduction has been that heterophilous interaction does not promote shared sentiment or that sentiment does not lead to heterophilous interaction.

Furthermore, heterophilous interactions demand effort, as the interacting partners, aware of the inequality in differential command over resources that can be brought to bear, need to assess each other's willingness to engage in exchange. The resource-poorer partner needs to be concerned about alter's intention or ability to appropriate resources from them. And the resource-richer partner needs to consider whether alters can reciprocate with resources meaningful to their already rich repertoire of resources. Thus, both partners in a heterophilous interaction have to make a greater effort in forging the interaction than those in a homophilous interaction. Heterophilous interactions therefore are relatively less likely to occur.

If this analysis is correct, one would also expect that when heterophilous interaction does occur, it requires more effort, probably at a greater cost, because of resource differentials and lack of shared sentiments. If homophilous interaction is the normative and ordinary interaction, then heterophilous interaction represents nonnormative and extraordinary interaction. What, then, motivates heterophilous interaction?

Action Guiding Interaction: Formation of Predictions

One clue explaining motives for heterophilous interactions is provided by the finding already referred to, that individuals prefer to associate

Table 4.1. *Initial Predictions of Effort and Return for Purposive Action and Interaction (without Taking Structural Constraints into Account)*

	Resources of Interaction Partners	
Motivation for Action	Similarity (Homophilous)	Dissimilarity (Heterophilous)
Maintaining resources (expressive)	Low effort/high return	High effort/low return
Gaining resources (instrumental)	Low effort/low return	High effort/high return

with others with somewhat better social status. The *prestige hypothesis* (Laumann 1966) shows that preferred partners for interactions are those occupying slightly higher social statuses. Empirically, such behavior has been well documented as the *prestige effect*. The implication is that such interaction is expected to enhance the prestige of the less advantaged actors. But the enhancement remains unclear, even though the term prestige hypothesis suggests a halo effect: a higher-status individual's prestige rubs off on the actor seen with him or her. Such a halo effect (e.g., being admired for knowing a movie star or a Nobel Prize winner) by itself does not represent a permanent gain, since termination of the interaction might also result in the loss of the halo. What needs to be considered, then, is what an interacting partner with more resources represents.

It should be obvious by now that the explanation to be offered is this: *actors access social capital, through interactions, to promote purposive actions.* Thus, the nature of embedded resources accessed in interactions becomes critical in the analysis of purposive actions and interaction patterns. This can be made clear by presenting the hypotheses in a typology of action and interaction, as shown in Table 4.1.

In this typology, the two motives for action are represented by two rows: maintaining resources or gaining resources. Two types of interaction relative to resources in the two columns are homophilous interactions, in which partners share similar resources, and heterophilous interactions, in which partners share dissimilar resources. Obviously, this is a simplification of many more gradations possible in reality, but it will serve for the purposes of our discussion here. Each cell represents the coupling of a particular purposive action and a particular type of interaction. Two variables can be used to describe each cell: how much effort is required for the interaction and how much return or payoff may result relative to the purposive action.

From the perspective of social interactions, the homophily principle points to the triangular relationships among sentiments, interactions, and shared resources. It provides a structural explanation for *least-effort* interactions; interactions tend to promote sentiment and shared resources and vice versa. It is expected, then, that the homophilous inter-action is the preferred and more frequent type of interaction; the least-effort homophilous interaction should be the expected pervasive pattern of interactions observed.

The purpose of expressive action, therefore, is consistent with this pattern of interaction. This type of action is likely to result in ego's seeking out other actors who have similar resources and a similar inter-est in maintaining and defending them. The more similar the partners' resources, the more likely they will share an understanding and concern for maintaining or defending such resources. Empathy and common concern promote interaction. Furthermore, the more homophilous the interacting partners are in terms of resources, the more socially equal they are. Thus, there is less concern regarding the possible intention or ability of alter to appropriate resources from ego. The cost of guarding and defending resources is reduced. The return, relative to the motiva-tion for action, is also expected to be better.

Defending one's resources requires the sentiments and support of those who are in the same social groups or those who are in a similar position (e.g., class) in the hierarchical structure. In other words, action taken to protect and maintain resources is consistent with normative patterns of interaction. At the extreme, then, normative interactions sustain main-tenance of resources among individuals without the need to stress the action component.

Gaining resources, on the other hand, implies a different type of inter-action. It is argued that the action to gain resources is better served, in terms of return, if the actor engages in heterophilous interactions – finding actors with dissimilar resources. In Chapter 3 it was pointed out that in macrostructures, social positions are characterized by the resources they control and manipulate. Interaction, then, represents not only the joining of two actors but also, much more important, the joining of two social positions that the actors occupy. Interacting with an actor who controlls more resources means interacting with a social position with more resources. A higher position in the hierarchical structure not only controls and manipulates more resources, but also has greater command and a better view of other positions in the structure. Access to such a position affords the possibility of borrowing that command or that view. If the resource an actor wants to gain is located in a social structure (e.g., in the hands of someone who occupies a position in that structure), then it follows that interacting with an alter who occupies a higher position in that hierarchy might have the benefit of finding that position (through alter's better view of the structure) or of mobilizing alter's commands for moving ego to link up with that position or even to occupy it.

Further, this benefit goes beyond the hierarchical structure in which alter holds an advantaged position. By the rules of compatibility and transferability across different hierarchical structures, alter may also exercise influence by providing information regarding other structural positions or by helping ego establish links to another actor in the structure where that actor holds an advantaged position, from which this third actor might exercise authority to help ego find resources or occupy a sought-after position.

While heterophilous interactions therefore may provide the social capital useful for attaining such a goal for an actor taking an instrumental action, the effort is more costly. That is, obtaining additional or better resources requires interacting, directly or indirectly, with actors in other (and better) positions so that more and better information or authority/influence may be obtained. It means seeking out actors in different social positions than ego's. Two factors make such efforts more difficult. First, the homophily principle suggests that a normative tendency is for actors of similar resources to engage each other. Finding and engaging others of dissimilar resources represents extraordinary interactions requiring greater effort.

Second, it should be clear by now that heterophilous interaction, as described here, goes beyond simply the reversal of homophilous interaction. It is more than merely interaction between dissimilar actors. From an actor's point of view, the payoff may come from interacting with another actor who is not only different but also has better resources. Since actors occupy hierarchical positions in society, ego would need to interact with someone who not only possesses more highly valued resources but also, more importantly, occupies a higher hierarchical position. Thus, as shall be made more explicit in the next chapter, heterophilous interactions have better returns if the partner occupies a higher, not lower, hierarchical position relative to ego. In such asymmetric interactions, while an actor seeking more resources may have much to gain, the payoff for the other partner (alter) in the interaction poses a serious problem: What favor can ego return to alter, who has better resources? Or why should alter respond by offering its resources as social capital to ego? Asymmetric exchanges, as heterophilous interactions imply, require further articulation, a topic I will treat in Chapter 9. Suffice it to state here that heterophilous interactions are costly and unusual.

Heterophilous interaction occurs, therefore, despite the fact that it requires greater effort to reach out beyond one's own social circles, and is more costly in commitments to reciprocity and the offer of one's resources for the initiating actors. In short, instrumental action requires a greater degree of agency to overcome the normative homophilous pattern of interaction.

Structural Constraint and Opportunity in Capitalization

The predictions based merely on action and interaction, as projected in Table 4.1, however, are tempered by necessary considerations of the structural positions and network locations the engaging actors occupy. More specifically, without an appreciation of the hierarchical structure and its constraints, heterophilous interaction by itself would make a poor prediction of instrumental return. Consider a bank president, who occupies a high-level position in the local community and beyond and who socializes with other highly positioned actors, as the homophilous principle would predict. Interacting with others with similar resources reinforces his or her position in the hierarchy, as the expressive action intends. However, when the bank president engages in instrumental action, would he or she need to engage others with dissimilar resources, as the heterophilous principle would predict? If valued resources are transferrable (see Chapter 4 on the transactions in complex structures), then we would expect the bank president to interact with others who may have different types of resources (e.g., power rather than wealth) but who nevertheless occupy a similar position in the complex hierarchical structure of the community – a homophilous interaction.

Likewise, actors occupying the lowest level of positions are not expected to garner as much return from heterophilous interactions as higher-level actors. As the distribution of positions and occupants in the pyramidal structure dictates, they are much more likely to engage in homophilous interactions (i.e., there are more actors like themselves in the structure, so that the opportunity for homophilous interactions is higher) and to find it much more difficult to engage others with higher positions (i.e., they have much less to offer in return for favors by those in higher positions). Thus, heterophilous interactions are less likely to produce the greater returns in their instrumental actions, as expected from Table 4.1.

It is therefore important to incorporate this hierarchical/structural dimension. The predictions presented in Table 4.1 may hold in general, but probably not for those who occupy elite positions in the structure.

For them, heterophilous interactions offer no greater return than homophilous interactions if multiple hierarchies implicating different types of valued resources are to be treated simultaneously. Structure does provide opportunities for some and constraints for others.

Concluding Remarks

This chapter, by specifying the motivations for action and the possible effort and return for such purposive actions in different types of interactions, and by bringing the action aspect and the structural aspect together, has set the stage for a formal presentation of a theory of social capital in the next chapter. Here we clarify the debate on action versus structure in the process of social capitalization: the process by which structural resources are turned into social capital. That is, does social capitalization represent purposive action on the part of the actor or does it simply reflect the structural opportunity present for an actor?

Classic capital theory and cultural capital theory (Bourdieu 1972/ 1977; Bourdieu and Passeron 1977) both see structural constraints or opportunities as decisive. Action is anticipated on the part of those in advantaged positions. For Bourdieu, the structural imposition is reflected in the dominant class's socializing other members of the society (e.g., through education) with the elite's values and norms, so that these others misrecognize the values and norms as their own. Individuals do use strategies of action to adopt and attain these values and norms, but such adaptation and action merely serve to reinforce the structural reproduction of the system that privileges the already dominant.

For most human capital theorists as well as some social capital theorists, the purposive action initiated by the actor seems to be the driving force behind the investment and mobilization of resources as capital. Actors' purposive actions may be constrained by their structural positions or network locations, but in this conception, even occupants of advantaged positions and locations cannot benefit from their positions/locations unless they initiate action to bring about desired results.

For Coleman, social capital is defined by the function it serves for a particular purpose and a particular actor (Coleman 1990, Chap. 12). If something embedded in the structure works for an individual for a particular action, then it is social capital. The same thing in another action and for another actor would not necessarily be social capital, as it may not serve the function. The concept has also been extended by Putnam (1993, 1995a, 1995b) and others to refer to participation in voluntary organizations, social clubs, and social groups, as it reflects trust in social institutions (Hardin 1998) and may be linked to the well-being of the society.

Granovetter (1974) points to the process of gaining information advantages through weaker ties and bridges. He does not specifically argue that actors are conscious of this advantage, or that they make efforts to use weaker ties or bridges. However, since normatively more frequent interactions tend to occur within one's own social circle (among persons with stronger ties), the implicit suggestion is that the use of weaker ties or bridges represents extraordinary effort – thus, purposive actions.

Burt's (1992) theory of structural holes says nothing about action. Yet, central to the utility of structural holes is an actor's calculation of profit, which is a joint function (multiplication) of investment and the "rate of return," as represented by structural opportunities. Burt analyzes structural opportunities in terms of structural holes and structural autonomy, expecting those with structural opportunities to take advantage of these resources and capital by taking action (investing) to generate a profit. Thus, for Burt, active manipulation of resources by the actor is assumed. In fact, he prefers the term *players* to *actors* to emphasize this point.

While these theorists hint at the action aspect, it remains implicit in their theories rather than being the focal point or the driving element. The theory of social capital offered here and elsewhere makes this action aspect more explicit (Lin 1982). From the resource perspective, action is important and is given equal significance relative to structure. Motivated action guides interactions. Instrumental action, in particular, motivates investing – seeking out and mobilizing – in relations and connections that may provide access to social resources. Making explicit the hints of purposive action suggested by Granovetter and Burt, the theory of social capital gives primacy to the propensity to act in order to gain access and mobilize better social resources. However, the effort at investment and mobilization is constrained by the extent of resources' availability and heterogeneity in the social structures in which actors find themselves. Actors are further constrained by their particular position in hierarchical structures and their location in the network. Given existing social structures, this constraint looms as large and significant. Thus, in any empirical study, structural effects must not be ignored or underestimated. In causal terms, however, it would be impossible to tease out the sequence in which either action or structure more significantly dictates access to social capital. Chapter 8 will propose the theoretical possibility that it is action that leads to social structures through the mobilization of social resources or social capital.

One puzzle that needs to be dealt with is how individual actors can use resources in the social structures for their own benefit rather than for the benefit of the social structures. As mentioned before, actors, as agents in social structures, are expected to take actions to maintain and promote the structural resources. How, then, can actors/occupants appropriate such positional resources for their own interests instead?

In general, social structure and individual actors reinforce each other: the structure rewards individual actors who support and recognize its valued resources, and individual actors strive to recognize and promote structural resources in order to gain status or better positions in the structure. However, actors/agents, empowered to interpret rules and procedures and to mobilize resources in the social structure, can and will trigger structural changes (Sewell 1992). Variations in their perception and interpretation of rules, and in their assessment of resource availability and needs, differ among agents due to their different experiences in socialization or professionalization. These variations bring about changes within a social structure as well as in a new structure to which the rules and procedures of an existing structure are supposedly transposed (Sewell 1992).

Furthermore, resources considered valuable by the social structure and its agents are not entirely identical. As both the collectivity and individual actors as agents strive to promote their own interests, and as the collectivity empowers the agents to interpret the rules and procedures and to mobilize resources, individual actors have the opportunity to promote their own interests. One way to promote self-interest is to mobilize and manipulate resources entrusted to the positions that actors occupy. A second way is to use linkages to other positions and their occupants, and to mobilize and manipulate their resources as well. These issues, directly implicating social change, will be dealt with in Chapter 11.

It is these structurally empowered relationships among positions and embedded resources that offer opportunities for the actors/occupants – the agents – to gain access to structural resources for their own interests. That is, these structural opportunities become social capital of the actors/occupants.

5

The Theory and Theoretical
Propositions

The discussions of the structure, interaction, and action aspects of social capital described in the previous three chapters have laid the groundwork for specifying propositions to guide research. This chapter will summarize the major principles presented so far and will then present the theory's principal propositions.

The Theory of Social Capital

The theory of social capital focuses on the resources embedded in one's social network and how access to and use of such resources benefit the individual's actions. Resources are defined as valued goods in a society, however consensually determined, the possession of which maintains and promotes an individual's self-interest for survival and preservation. The values are normative judgments rendered on these goods. For most societies, they correspond to wealth, reputation, and power. The theory focuses on those actions that are taken for the purpose of either maintaining or gaining valued resources.

Resources can be either ascribed or acquired. *Ascribed resources* are those one is born with, such as gender and race. Other resources are prescribed by inheritance, such as caste and sometimes religion, and may include parental resources. Resources can also be acquired, such as education, or prestigious or authoritative jobs. When resources are being invested for expected returns in the marketplace, they become social capital.

Capital can be classified into two types: (1) personal or human capital and (2) social capital.[1] Human capital consists of resources possessed by the individual, who can use and dispose of them with great freedom and

---

[1] As stated in footnote 2 of Chapter 4, social resources may also include cultural capital.

without much concern for compensation. Social capital consists of resources embedded in one's network or associations. Our focus here is on social capital, which is not the individual's possessed goods, but resources accessible through direct and indirect ties. Access to and use of these resources is temporary and borrowed in the sense that the actor does not possess them. A friend's bicycle is one's social capital. One can use it to achieve a certain goal, but it must be returned to the friend. One implication of the use of social capital is its assumed obligation for reciprocity or compensation.

Assumptions

The theory of social capital is framed in a set of assumptions about the macro-, meso-, and microstructures of society. For the macrostructure, the theory posits three assumptions. First, the theory begins with an image of the social structure, which consists of a set of positions that are rank-ordered according to certain normatively valued resources such as class, authority, and status. It further assumes that the structure has a pyramidal shape in terms of accessibility to and control of such resources. The higher the position, the fewer the occupants; and the higher the position, the better the view it has of the structure (especially down below). In terms of both number of occupants and accessibility to positions, the pyramidal structure suggests advantages for positions closer to the top.

A position closer to the top of the structure has greater access to and control of the valued resources not only because more valued resources are intrinsically attached to that position, but also because of the position's greater accessibility to positions at other (primarily lower) rankings. Thus, an individual occupying a higher position, because of its accessibility to more positions, also has a greater command of social capital.

With such an image of the social structure and an understanding of embedded resources, it is apparent that there is a direct relationship between the level of a position in the hierarchical structure and the amount of influence it may exert on other (lower) positions for instrumental purposes (obtaining additional resources), as well as the amount of information it possesses about the locations of resources in the structure. The influence factor derives from the ability of higher positions to cumulate resources at a higher rate than lower positions. Thus, any favor an individual at the higher position may provide can be expected to have a greater future payoff, since the higher position has more to offer the lower position than vice versa. The information factor is associated with asymmetric network relations across levels of positions. A higher position tends to have more information or a better view of the structure than a lower position; thus, it is more capable of locating the specific resources embedded in the structure.

Second, the theory assumes that while various valued resources form the bases of hierarchical structures and each valued resource defines a particular hierarchy, these hierarchies tend toward congruence and transferability. That is, there tends to be a correspondence among hierarchical positioning across resource dimensions. An occupant of a relatively high-standing position on one resource dimension also tends to occupy a relatively high position on another resource dimension. For example, a person with a relatively high standing on the occupational structure is also likely to have great wealth and power. When such convergence is not functionally complete (not isomorphic), exchange of resources across dimensions is not only possible but, in most societies, explicit and expected. For example, an occupant with power resources can negotiate and trade with an occupant with wealth resources to acquire some of the latter's wealth in exchange for lending power to the latter.

Third, the theory assumes that this hierarchical structure tends to be pyramidal, the upper levels having fewer occupants than the lower levels. An empirical structure may not actually look pyramidal because each such structure is evolving and shifting toward a redefined set of levels. For example, as industrialization progresses (defined as the process of developing technology to make machine tools and assumed to be observable in every modern society), the occupational structure deviates from the pyramidal structure as occupants shift from the agricultural to the nonagricultural sector. While the size of the agricultural population deceases and the size of the low-level nonagricultural sector increases, the occupational structure, in terms of numbers of occupants at various levels, tends to be vase-shaped. Similarly, as the level of education in a society rises, there is always a small trailing tail at the lowest level representing the "residual" groups consisting of the most poorly educated individuals.

For the meso- and microstructures, the theory makes two assumptions about interactions and actions. First, it assumes that social interactions are more likely to take place among individuals at similar or adjacent hierarchical levels – the principle of homophilous interactions. Following from the structural assumption about congruence and transferability of resources, expected or fair exchange involves partners who can offer as well as receive resources. Thus, the closer or more similar the social positions, the more likely it is that the occupants will interact with one another. The theory assumes that *two primary driving forces* account for most individuals' actions: maintaining valued resources and gaining valued resources. The first dictates actions undertaken to preserve and defend valued resources already at the individual's disposal, whereas the second promotes actions undertaken to add valued resources not yet at the individual's disposal. We may characterize them as expressive and instrumental actions, respectively.

Expressive actions are expected to result in interactions consistent with the principle of homophilous interaction. Recognition of the similarity of resources and of the need to reciprocate concerns about them and protect them constitutes the basis for satisfying interactions. This expectation is consistent with the observation that interactions tend not only to take place more often but also to be more satisfying among participants with similar socioeconomic characteristics, lifestyles, and attitudes (Homans 1950; Lazarsfeld and Merton 1954). These similarities are assumed to reflect the proximity of social positions in the hierarchical structure. In social systems where valued resources are distributed across all levels (i.e., where every individual in the system has some quantity of the resources), homophilous interactions are pervasive at all levels. In most empirical social systems, therefore, this pattern holds true.

Instrumental action, in contrast, may not result in interaction patterns consistent with the homophilous principle and the structural expectations. To gain additional or new resources, by definition, requires access to other social positions (especially those with more or better resources). That is, for the purpose of obtaining additional resources, more *effective* actions tend to be initiated toward others who have dissimilar (and presumably better) resources, consistent with the heterophilous principle of interactions.[2]

Thus, a theory linking individuals to structure must first distinguish the two classes of action: instrumental actions and expressive actions. Instrumental actions are those actions taken for the purpose of achieving certain goals. The distinctive feature of this class of actions is that the means and ends are separate and distinct. A typical example is the search for a job or a person. Expressive actions are taken for their own sake: the actions are both means and ends, and are integrated and inseparable. Confiding one's feelings is a typical example. The social capital theory varies in its propositions relative to instrumental and expressive actions.

---

[2] Instrumental actions can also be initiated by an occupant of a higher position toward an occupant of a lower position, since the latter provides many necessary services. Since the higher position commands and has greater access to resources than the lower position, the occupant of the lower position is normally obligated to respond to the action initiated by the higher-level occupant in the hope of receiving a reward. In this chapter, the focus will be on individuals who seek better resources. In Chapter 9, I will further elaborate the rationale for asymmetric exchanges.

Second, the theory must take into account the consistency or tension between action and interaction. An expressive action motivates the individual to seek out others with similar characteristics and lifestyles in order to share and confide so that the expected return, sympathetic and appreciative understanding and counseling, can be obtained. Since homophilous interaction is the normative type of interaction, the expressive action evokes normative interaction (the homophilous interaction). That is, there is a normative match between effort and return. On the other hand, an instrumental action motivates one to seek out others with dissimilar (and, it is hoped, better) characteristics and lifestyles in order to access information and influence to achieve the expected return of more and/or better resources. Thus, heterophilous interactions represent a potential mismatch between the extraordinary or "abnormative" effort and expected returns for the purposive (instrumental) action.

Because of the mismatch between instrumental action and normative patterns of interaction, a theory of social capital should pay special attention to the process by which instrumental action becomes successful through social capital.

Theoretical Propositions: Structurally Embedded Resources and Purposive Actions

The theory specified here also applies only to a class of actions that evoke other actors as intermediaries. Under certain conditions, an action may be accomplished without going through intermediaries. For example, in a perfect labor market system, where all job vacancies and their required skills are known to all who seek jobs, and recruitment of an applicant to fill the job depends entirely on the matching of required skills and each candidate's skills, there would be little need to use a contact; direct application should accomplish all goals. Similarly, if the searcher knows everyone else in the social system, there would be no need for him or her to go through a contact to locate someone else. A contact becomes a requirement only when the searcher does not know the target person directly. Thus, the theory applies in an imperfect market where the diffusion of information about the goal is less than perfect. I am assuming that this condition covers most if not all real market situations.

For the theory linking social capital to action, seven propositions are specified:

1. For the return of social capital (Proposition 1: the social-capital proposition)
2. For the access to social capital

- The advantage of structural positions (Proposition 2: the "strength-of-positions" proposition)
- The advantages of social ties (Proposition 3: the "strength-of-strong-tie" proposition and Proposition 4: the "strength-of-weak-tie" proposition)
- The advantage of network locations (Proposition 5: the "strength-of-location" proposition)
- The interaction between network locations and structural positions (Proposition 6: the location-by-position proposition)
- The interaction of structural positions and ties/locations (Proposition 7: the structural contingency proposition)[3]

The first proposition is the pivotal proposition expressing the expected return of social capital; it hypothesizes that better social capital accessed and used will tend to lead to a more successful outcome. The five other propositions hypothesize factors leading to better access and use of social capital. The strength-of-position proposition argues that the social position of origin has a positive effect on accessing and using better social capital. The strength-of-tie proposition posits that the use of weaker social ties (more heterophilous interactions) will have a positive effect on accessing and using social capital. The strength-of-position proposition reflects structural effects on instrumental action, whereas the strength-of-tie proposition may reflect action effects. It is also hypothesized that there will be interaction effects between position, tie, and location. In general, it is expected that the structural effect is stronger than the action effect. The relative strength of structure over action is more prominent near the top or bottom of the hierarchical structure. In the following section, these propositions will be explicated.

Return to Social Capital

(1) The Social-Capital Proposition: The success of action is positively associated with social capital. The primary proposition of the theory states that access to and use of better social capital leads to more successful action – the return to social capital. A simple strategy to accomplish a purposive action is to access an actor who possesses or can access more highly valued resources. Such access, as stated in Chapter 2, makes use of social capital for several important advantages. First, it makes use of the influence this intermediary may exercise on behalf of ego. The

---

[3] The earliest version of this theory and some of its propositions appear in Lin (1982), and subsequent versions and revisions appear in several other publications (Lin 1986, 1990, 1992a, 1995a, 1999a).

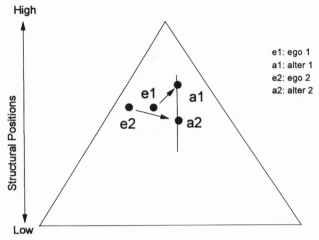

Figure 5.1 Relative effects of social capital.

better positioned the intermediary, and thus the better embedded and commanded resources, the more such influence should benefit ego. Second, the intermediary, given its advantageous view of the structure, may provide better information to ego. Third, a better-positioned intermediary, with its embedded and commanded resources, projects better social credentials, so that its willingness to serve as an intermediary assures or elevates ego's credentials. And, finally, the ability to access a better-positioned intermediary itself enhances ego's confidence and self-esteem in further interactions and actions (e.g., conduct in job interviews) that may be necessary to accomplish the goal of the action. Thus, the first and most important proposition for the theory is: *The success of action is positively associated with social capital.* It is argued that the relationship should hold for both expressive and instrumental actions.

Graphically, this proposition is depicted in Figure 5.1. The hierarchical nature of a social structure can be represented by the pyramid: levels of positions with varying degrees of valued resources can be plotted along its vertical axis. For two egos (identified as e1 and e2 in the figure), at approximately the same structural position, the proposition hypothesizes that e1 will have a competitive advantage over e2 as it accesses a social tie, a1, at a relatively higher position than that of the tie, a2, that e2 accesses.

Through direct and indirect ties, an individual actor gains access to a variety of resources; what measures can be suggested as indicators of social capital? Following Weber's argument, we may suggest three types of resources of social ties accessed as the contents of social capital: (1)

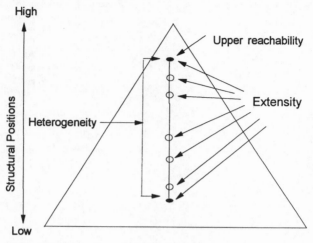

Figure 5.2 Measures of social capital.

wealth: economic assets, (2) power: political assets, and (3) reputation: social assets. Three summarizing characteristics can be suggested relative to each capital: (1) upper reachability: the best resource accessed through social ties; (2) heterogeneity: the range of positions whose resources are reachable through social ties; and (3) extensity: the number of positions that are reachable. These criteria and their measures are graphically depicted in Figure 5.2.

The first criterion of upper reachability seems straightforward: the resource of an uppermost position ego can reach in the hierarchical structure through social ties. As in Figure 2.2, ego is connected to other positions in the structure; the highest position ego can reach represents the upper-reachable social resource for ego. That position is characterized by the values of resources it possesses, usually reflecting relative status, class, or authority in the structure or community.

The second criterion, resource heterogeneity, reflects the vertical range of resources reachable by ego through social ties across positions in a structural hierarchy. As in Figure 1.2, this is represented by the range between the highest- and lowest-reachable resources through ego's ties. The resource heterogeneity criterion is not so obvious, but it is important. For example, an individual who does not know how to increase computer memory to run an application may not need to contact a high-status programmer; it should be sufficient to call on someone friendly who can quickly help. Nor is it necessary to call on a neighbor with many resources when ego needs a babysitter at the last minute. Getting one's basket emptied or floor swept at the office depends more on friendly relations with the custodians than on making demands on one's supervisor. Thus, having all social ties of high status may not meet many life needs. Thus, heterogeneity in the types, levels, and amounts of resources provided through social ties constitutes an important criterion of better access to social capital. The third criterion, extensity, simply reflects the diversity of positions, and their embedded resources, reachable by ego through social ties.

Actual measures of these economic, political, and social standings vary for each society or even each community. Therefore, identifying the locally meaningful measures of social capital for a given society is an empirical task. As long as such locally meaningful measures can be identified and examined, the proposed proposition is hypothesized to hold.

The correlations among the various measures of social capital, while generally assumed to be high, may also vary across societies and communities. To assess their correspondences for each society under study, and to exercise appropriate methodological controls to reflect the degree of convergence or distinction among the measures, is again an empirical task. Further, the relative utility of the social capital measures may depend on the purposes or motivations for action. As has been stated, action may be undertaken for expressive (maintaining resources) or instrumental (gaining resources) reasons. Whether the relative advantage among the social capital measures differs or not for different types of actions again may vary across societies and communities. In some societies, where the three measures of social capital largely overlap or correspond well, their utilities may also converge for both types of action. In other societies, when these assets are more segmented or independent, it becomes critical to assess their relative effects for the two types of actions.

The social-capital proposition is the primary proposition of the theory in that unless it can be verified in research, all other propositions become irrelevant. On the other hand, if this proposition is verified, then the stage is set for further propositions and elaborations. In the remainder of this chapter, we will focus on several other propositions concerning the etiology or causes of social capital – the factors determining the likelihood of achieving better social capital.

Accessing Social Capital

Who, then, is more likely to gain better access to social capital? We propose three possible factors: (1) the position of ego in hierarchical structures, (2) the nature of the tie between ego and the other actors, and (3) the location of the ties in the networks. These three factors lead to four theoretical propositions concerning access to social capital: (1) the strength of the ego's structural position, (2) the strength of the tie,

(3) the strength of the location of the tie, and (4) the joint (interaction) effect of the position, the tie, and the location.

Structural Advantage. The principle of homophily has been used to describe normative and expressive interactive patterns. This principle suggests that persons, for expressive reasons, tend to interact with others who are like themselves. When this principle is applied to the issue of who tends to attain better social capital, it should be obvious that those whose initial positions are relatively high in the social structure should have the advantage over others. The initial position may be inherited from parents or achieved by the individual. Once such an initial position is located, the normative interactive patterns for the position's particular occupant link it with others at similar or higher positions. The higher the initial position, the more likely the occupant will have access to more highly-valued resources. Thus, it is hypothesized that the level of the initial position is positively related to the social capital reached through a contact, known as the strength-of-position proposition.

(2) The Strength-of-Position Proposition: The better the position of origin, the more likely the actor will access and use better social capital. Figure 5.3 illustrates two egos, e1 and e2, with relative positions in the hierarchy that are predicted to access alters at different higher positions. Thus, e1 is said to have a better positional or structural advantage over e2 in access to better social capital.

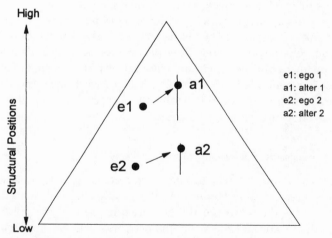

Figure 5.3 Relative advantages of structural positions for accessing social capital.

This proposition predicts a structural effect on social capital: those in better social positions will have the advantage in accessing and mobilizing social ties with better resources. *Position of origin* refers to both ascribed and attained positions of ego. *Ascribed position* is a position inherited by ego, usually from parents. *Attained positions* refer to social positions and social roles acquired and occupied by ego. Thus, the strength-of-position proposition predicts that those in better ascribed and occupied positions will also have a better chance of accessing and using social ties with better resources. This proposition is entirely consistent with the conventional structural theory; it reflects the structural advantage for actors and extends this structural effect to social capital. The haves will have more. It is argued that this relationship holds for both expressive and instrumental actions.

The strength-of-position proposition extends resources accessed beyond the homophily principle. Not only is an individual occupying a higher position more likely to have social connections with similar positions, but these other positions have their own connections whose social capital also becomes accessible to ego. By the same principle, these positions and their social capital should be similar to those with which ego has direct connections. Thus, these indirect connections further increase ego's propensity to access even wider resources. The strength-of-position proposition, therefore, suggests that the higher the individuals' own positions, the greater their likelihood of having access to better social capital.

Networking Advantages. The upshot of the strength-of-position proposition is that the structural opportunity for reaching better social capital is much better for those whose initial positions are relatively high. The next question is whether there is a mechanism by which persons at relatively low initial positions can reach better social capital. Or, when two actors occupy approximately the same position in the structure, would their actions make any difference in the outcome?

The proposal here is that access to social capital is also affected by ego's relationships with others in social networks. However, several principles would lead to different propositions. We will consider these in a logical sequence – from a structural perspective, to an opportunity perspective, to a choice perspective, and to a combination of these perspectives.

(3) The Strength-of-Strong-Tie Proposition: The stronger the tie, the more likely that the social capital accessed will positively affect the success of expressive action. The structural principle is straightforward: accessible resources are positively related to social ties to those alters with whom ego shares stronger sentiment. We may call this principle the

strength-of-strong-tie proposition. The strength of a relationship among those with social ties reflects their degree of intensity, frequency of intimacy (trustworthiness), reciprocity, and acknowledged obligations (Granovetter 1973). The stronger the relationship, the more likely the sharing and exchange of resources.

Mutual support and recognition go hand in hand with promotion of the ego and alter's resources, including their reputation. Thus, such a relationship is mutually tolerant and even encourages social debts and credits, as well as forgiveness of debt. Coleman (1990) describes any social structure with a higher than average density of obligations as a group with *closure*. The present proposition focuses on the likelihood of ego accessing others' resources because of the strength of ego's relationship with them. That is, even if alter has better resources, alter may not respond to ego's desire to gain access to them if their relationship does not reflect normative reciprocity, trust, and mutual obligations. Closer relationships are a necessary condition for getting access to social capital. There has been substantial argument (Bourdieu 1980, 1983/1986; Coleman 1990; Portes and Sensenbrenner 1993) for the effectiveness of dense, cohesive, interactive, reciprocatory, trustworthy networks as resources for participating actors.

These analyses suggest that stronger ties based on sentiment, trust, and sharing of resources and lifestyles support the maintenance and reinforcement of existing resources – consistency with expressive action. Thus, the proposition: *the stronger the tie, the more likely the social capital accessed will positively affect the success of expressive action.*

However, the modified principle of homophily (Figure 2.1) tells us that interaction, sentiments, and similarity in resources are positively related. Thus, stronger ties allow access to social capital that is similar or perhaps slightly different (e.g., better) than ego's own – the exact prediction made by the strength-of-position proposition. Once the principle of homophily is extended to resources, the access effects of stronger ties are accounted for. Thus, the strength-of-strong-tie principle reflects a structural advantage.

The interesting aspect of interaction and networking is that, unlike social positions, which are more or less fixed unless or until social change takes place (a topic to be dealt with in Chapter 11), strength of ties and location of resources in the networks are variable. An individual has weaker as well as stronger sentiments for the interacting partners. The strength of these partners' relationships with others also varies. Also, in networks, because of both direct and indirect ties, ego's location in the network varies. These variations in tie strength and network location suggest that further propositions need to be developed regarding how such variations may affect an individual's access to social capital. In other words, is there any benefit for ego if the strength of the tie is weaker rather than stronger and if ego's position is closer to the fringe than to the core of the network?

(4) The Strength-of-Weak-Tie Proposition: The weaker the tie, the more likely ego will have access to better social capital for instrumental action. Granovetter (1973, 1974) was among the first to theoretically examine issues involving the strength of weaker ties. Following Homans's conceptualization and the homophily principle, he envisioned social circles as being distinguished by denser and more reciprocally interactive partners. An individual embedded in a social circle tends to have characteristics homophilous with those of the circle's other members; these similarities also extend to information. In addition, knowledge about larger social structures is homophilous among members of a social circle. If individuals need different information, then they may be more likely to find it in different social circles than their own. To reach another social circle, ego would need to find ties that link the two circles. The ties between different social circles are *bridges*; without the linkage, the two social circles would be independent of each other.

Granovetter further argues that the tie between two individuals forming a bridge, for example, is weaker because each individual participates in a different social circle. There is also the implication, although he does not state it, that these bridging individuals tend to be on the margin of their respective social circles, as evidenced by their maintaining ties to other social circles, perhaps reducing the strength of their interactions with others in their own circles. Since stronger ties can be characterized by intensity, intimacy, frequency of contacts, acknowledged obligations, and provision of reciprocal services, individuals' chances of gaining better information are enhanced if they explore, among their ties, the weaker rather than the stronger ones, in order to find likely bridges to other social circles. Granovetter calls this strategy and benefit "the strength of weak ties."[4]

---

[4] The relational characterizations of the weak ties did not break any new ground, as they could be deduced directly from the homophily principle of interaction. Recall that the principle states that interaction tends to occur among actors with similar characteristics and lifestyles. The reverse statement is that interactions do not tend to occur among actors with dissimilar characteristics and lifestyles. If a social group or social circle is characterized by dense interactions and connections, then the homophily principle would predict that members must share similar characteristics and lifestyles, and therefore information as well. Since the connection with the other group is tenuous (only through a bridge), the homophily principle would also predict that the members of the two groups can be differentiated by their different characteristics, lifestyles, and therefore information.

The significance of the strength-of-weak-ties argument lies rather in its pointing out that the weak ties, because of their tenuous relationship, contribute to the flow of infor-

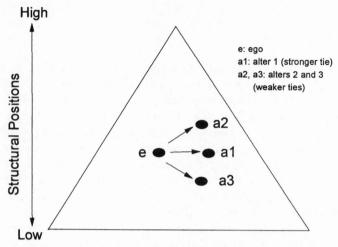

Figure 5.4 Relative advantages of weaker ties.

The benefit from weaker ties can be extended to social capital as well. The modified homophily principle suggests that dissimilarity of resources is related to less interaction and less sentiment (Figure 3.1). Thus, weaker ties characterized by less intimacy, less intensity, less frequent contact, fewer obligations, and weaker reciprocal services should also be associated with more dissimilar resources. As reflected in Figure 5.4, as ego reaches out for ties with weaker relations, the hypothesis on the strength of weaker ties suggests that ego would reach either toward the upper end (alter 2) or the lower end (alter 3) of the hierarchical structure. Weaker ties therefore allow access to wider resource heterogeneity. Thus, the

---

mation between the two groups. For several decades after the advent of social psychology in the 1920s and 1930s, the homophily principle in fact led much theoretical and research development by focusing on the strongly connected groups (e.g., primary groups, reference groups, small groups, and intimate relations) under the premise that stronger ties promote cohesion, satisfaction, and congruence of attitudes and opinions. These attributes were seen as desirable in sustaining members' relations as well as the group. That is, the focus was on the strength of strong ties. This development largely ignored bridges or weak ties because they were seen as the opposite of the strong ties that had all the positive features of social groups.

Granovetter's strength-of-weak-ties argument pointed out how weak ties might contribute to information flow. Through this bridge, and perhaps only through this bridge, a member in one group may learn and gain information about the other group. If that information is useful, then whoever has access to the bridge and uses it will gain an advantage over another member of the same group. Presumably the group also benefits from the information regarding the other group flowing through the bridge, even though this was not pointed out in Granovetter's original statements (1973, 1974).

modified strength-of-weak-ties proposition states that *the weaker the tie, the more likely ego will have access to heterogeneous resources.*

However, the weak-tie argument itself does not suggest that weaker ties will always link ego to better resources (upper reachability [alter 2 rather than alter 3] and extensity). After all, resource heterogeneity is only one criterion of better social capital (e.g., new and different information added to ego's repertoire of information). More critically, we need to modify the original strength-of-weak-tie hypothesis further in order to link it to the upper-reachability criterion for accessing social capital. Here we can employ an extension of the homophily principle.

Empirical observations (Laumann 1966) suggest that individuals prefer to associate with others of somewhat higher social status. Laumann calls this the *prestige principle*. Preference in association, of course, is different from actual behavior in interactions, but it does explain why empirical evidence shows that individuals tend to pursue interaction with others of similar or slightly higher, rather than lower, socioeconomic status.[5] That is, given a choice between alter 2 and alter 3 in Figure 5.4, ego will tend to prefer interacting with alter 2. Thus, we may further modify the strength-of-weak-ties proposition as follows: *the weaker the tie, the more likely ego will have access to better social capital (at least in terms of resource heterogeneity and upper reachability).*

The strength-of-weak-ties argument is now clear. The remaining issue is whether it is necessary to have the strength-of-weak-ties hypothesis in order to understand the advantage of network locations in getting access to social capital. To explore this question, we will now examine an alternative conceptualization.

(5) The Strength-of-Location Proposition: The closer individuals are to a bridge in a network, the better social capital they will access for instrumental action. Granovetter's discussion of the "bridge in the network" (1973) pointed to the utility of network locations in allowing information to flow from one social circle to another. It led to his formulation of the strength-of-weak-ties argument. However, he then shifted the argument from a focus on network location to one on social ties. The advantage was that the strength of ties, as measured by intimacy, intensity, frequency of contacts, and reciprocal services – especially other surrogate measures, such as role relationships (e.g., kin, friend, acquaintance) – could be readily studied in sample surveys, since such measures

---

[5] In actual behavior, individuals do interact with others of lower socioeconomic status. This is a given, because even when individuals interact with preferred others (those of higher status), these others are interacting with lower-status egos. What, then, is the motive for individuals to maintain interactions with lower-status others? One perspective on this topic will be discussed in Chapter 9.

could readily be assessed from respondents' self-reports. It would have been much more difficult to gather data on how individuals form ties in social networks. The problem is whether such measures, or even the notion of the strength of ties, captures the significance of network locations such as bridges.

A *social bridge* may be defined as a linkage between two individual actors in a social network, the absence of which would cause the breakup of a cluster into two separate clusters, each of which has two or more individual actors. In other words, a bridge is the sole link between two groups of actors. This definition can be relaxed somewhat in that two clusters may be linked through several bridges. Bridges serve the important function of making possible access to resources embedded in both groups.

The notion of a bridge is more explicitly explored by Burt (1992) in his theory of the *structural hole*, defined as "the separation between nonredundant contacts" and a "relationship of nonredundancy between two contacts." Burt further specifies that "the hole is a buffer, like an insulator in an electric circuit. As a result of the hole between them, the two contacts provide network benefits that are in some degree additive rather than overlapping" (Burt 1992, p. 18). An example of structural holes is provided in Figure 5.5. Three holes are represented here: between the cluster of ties around A and those around ego ("you") cluster, between ego's cluster and the cluster around B, and between A's cluster and B's cluster. While the structural hole indicates nonredundancies or near emptiness of linkages between clusters, the connections, if they do

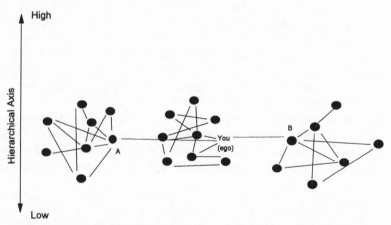

Figure 5.5 Structural holes (bridges) and strength of ties (horizontal clusters). (Adapted from Burt 1992, p. 27)

exist, between ego and A, ego and B, and A and B constitute bridges. The concept of structural holes focuses on the lack of access between clusters, while bridges emphasize access between clusters over the (nearly empty) holes. Thus, structural holes and bridges are two ways of describing similar network features and the strategic importance of certain locations.

Bridges allow individual actors in one cluster to have access to resources embedded in nodes in another cluster that otherwise would not be accessible. Burt argues that the benefit of bridges over structural holes is that they control the flow of information, very similar to Granovetter's argument. With no loss of generality, we may extend the benefit to include access to all social capital. Thus, this argument can be stated as the strength-of-location hypothesis: *the closer individuals are to a bridge in a network, the better the social capital to which they will have access.*

The strength-of-weak-tie argument can then be conceived as a surrogate proposition for the strength-of-location proposition. Since bridges tend to represent weak links between two clusters, using a weaker tie increases one's likelihood of gaining access to a bridge. This surrogate proposition is useful when it is difficult to rely on ego's cognition for complete mapping of a network. Rather than probing for all possible bridges in ego's network, ego's decision strategy can be simplified by looking for ego's weaker ties. This surrogate argument also simplifies the researcher's task. Rather than mapping an entire network for each ego, the researcher can use measures of the strength of ties instead. Of course, since this is a surrogate measure, evidence from research that tests the strength-of-location proposition may be weakened.

(6) The Location-by-Position Proposition: The strength of a location (in proximity to a bridge), for instrumental action, is contingent on the resource differential across the bridge. While the structural hole perspective shifts the formulation of social bridges from Granovetter's focus on the strength of ties to network locations, it also needs modification. Considering the vertical axis in Figure 5.6 as the hierarchy of a structure; then it is clear that ego's ("your") connection to A will be much more beneficial to members of ego's group than ego's connection to B, since A's cluster consists of positions richer in resources compared to those in ego's cluster, and B's cluster consists of poorer positions. This situation is a sharp contrast to the situation in Figure 5.5, where the three clusters are "flattened" to the same level in the hierarchy. The three structural holes and bridges remain the same as in Figure 5.6, but the relative benefit of resources accessed through the three bridges is minimal.

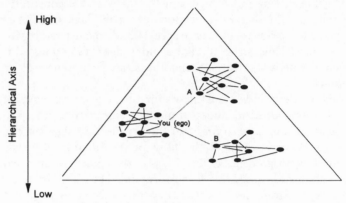

Figure 5.6 Differential advantages of structural holes (bridges) and weaker ties in a hierarchical structure.

Thus, the benefit of a strategic location such as the bridge in a social network depends on the resources accessed. Location near a bridge may not be very useful if the bridge simply leads to nodes that have similar or less highly valued resources. In other words, the relative advantage of proximity to a bridge in a network is contingent on the relative resourcefulness of the nodes to which that bridge provides access. This can be stated as an interaction proposition: *the strength of a location (in proximity to a bridge) is contingent on the resource differential across the bridge.*

Since differential resources among individual actors are best represented by their positions in the hierarchy, we can further specify this interactive proposition: *access to better social capital tends to occur for an individual actor who occupies a location closer to a bridge that links the actor to those in relatively higher hierarchical positions.* Thus, locational advantage is contingent on the resources of the accessible network. Since it is assumed here that better resources are embedded, by definition, in higher positions in a hierarchical structure, this means that the locational advantage in a network is contingent on the vertical extent of its accessible positions.

This location-by-position proposition does not entirely negate the significance of vertical bridges to lower as well as upper clusters. As seen in Figure 5.6, having bridges from ego to both A's and B's clusters increases resource heterogeneity for members in ego's cluster. However, since the strength-of-position proposition involves resource heterogeneity (the higher positions also have a greater vertical range in the resources accessible through their ties and networks) as well as upper reachability, we expect B to maintain the connection with ego so that it expands the heterogeneity of resources for members in B's cluster to ego's cluster and A's cluster.

In summary, the significance of network locations, whether conceived as bridges or as tie strengths, is contingent on the relative hierarchical structural positions of the individuals thus bridged or linked. The relative advantage of having bridges or weaker ties is a function of the relative vertical distance between ties or clusters of ties.[6]

Structural Contingency of Action Effects

The propositions just presented, especially the factors leading to better social capital, have identified two effects: effects due to positions of origin in the structure and effects due to networking (ties and locations) and their joint effects. While the strength-of-position proposition clearly reflects structural effects, the networking propositions reflect a mixture of opportunity and choice. Whether and to what extent opportunity and choice reflect purposive actions deserves some further consideration.

Both the strength-of-weak-tie argument and the strength-of-location argument, as discussed in Chapter 4, represent opportunity and choice, thus implicating action. However, there is little doubt that structure places constraints on opportunity and choice. Consider the strength-of-weak-tie argument. Toward the top of the hierarchical structure (see Figure 5.3), the vertical reach toward the upper ceiling is increasingly reduced. Thus, the likelihood of reaching up, as compared to reaching down, is decreased when the vertical link (weaker ties) is evoked. In fact, at the very top, any vertical link would be a downward link. Thus, stronger ties (horizontal ties) rather than weaker ties (vertical ties) should be more effective in accessing better social capital. In other words, as one's position in the hierarchical structure moves toward the upper ceiling, the homophily principle rather than the heterophilous principle becomes more effective.

At the same time, the strength-of-networking effect may also be constrained from below. At the low end of the hierarchy, as postulated, there will be more positions as well as more occupants. According to the structural theory postulated by Blau (1977), the probability of interaction is a function of group size. Thus, as the size of the population of positions and occupants increases, there is a greater likelihood of interaction

---

[6] Note that we do not postulate that the volume of the network, as reflected in the number of individual actors, is a determinant of better social capital. There is no theoretical reason to speculate that better social positions, resource-rich networks, or heterogeneous networks should be associated with a structure or network with a larger population.

among themselves if everyone is assumed to have the same propensity for interaction. Then it is conceivable that the social network becomes more homogeneous and less diverse as the size of the group increases. A derived hypothesis is that at the low end of the social hierarchy, the more homogeneous network increases the chances for interacting with strong ties and decreases the chances for interacting with weak ties. A conjecture can therefore be that the lack of the opportunity structure reduces the effect of networking as a way of accessing better social capital.

It is in the middle range of the hierarchical structure, therefore, that we should expect to detect the strength of networking effects. As the relative sizes of contiguous social positions are similar and the opportunity structure is extensive, the vertical reach should have the best probability of reaching upward. If this proposition is valid, we are also therefore predicting that action is most meaningful and effective when ego's position is in the middle range of the hierarchical structure. Actors at the lower level of the structure have little opportunity to exert meaningful actions. Similarly, but for different reasons, actors at the upper echelons have less incentive to take actions that would disrupt the structural effect (i.e., rocking the boat). This leads to the following proposition.

(7) The Structural Contingency Proposition: Networking (tie and location) effects are constrained by the hierarchical structure for actors located near or at the top and bottom of the hierarchy. Figure 5.7 illustrates this interaction between structure and action. Ego 1, near the upper ceiling, is shown to have limited opportunity to reach upward if

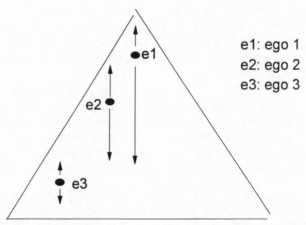

Figure 5.7 Structural constraints on networking effects.

he or she chooses vertical access. Ego 3, near the lower ceiling, is structurally constrained in opportunities to access vertically in either direction. Ego 2, somewhere in the middle range of the hierarchy, should have the advantages of both extensive upper reaches and opportunities to achieve such access.

Concluding Remarks

We now summarize the major points in the theory of social capital as a set of postulates (untested assumptions) and propositions as follows:

1. The structural postulate (Chapter 3): valued resources are embedded in social structures in which positions, authority, rules, and occupants (agents) usually form pyramidal hierarchies in terms of the distribution of valued resources, number of positions, level of authority, and number of occupants. The higher the level in the hierarchy, the greater the concentration of valued resources, the fewer the number of positions, the greater the command of authority, and the smaller the number of occupants.
2. The interaction postulate (Chapters 3 and 4): interactions usually occur among actors with similar or contiguous characteristics of resources and lifestyles – following the homophily principle. The greater the similarity of resource characteristics, the less effort required in interaction.
3. The network postulate (Chapters 3 and 4): in social networks, directly and indirectly interacting actors carry varying types of resources. Some of these resources are in their personal possession (personal resources or human capital), but most of the resources are embedded in others with whom each actor is in contact, directly or indirectly, or they are embedded in structural positions each actor occupies or is in contact with.
4. The definition (Chapters 2–4): these structurally embedded resources are *social capital* for the actors in the networks.
5. The action postulates (Chapter 4): actors are motivated to either maintain or gain their resources in social actions – purposive actions. Action to maintain resources can be called expressive action, and action to gain resources can be called instrumental action. Maintaining resources is the primary motivation for action; therefore, expressive action is the primary form of action.
6. The social-capital proposition: *the success of action is positively associated with social capital.*

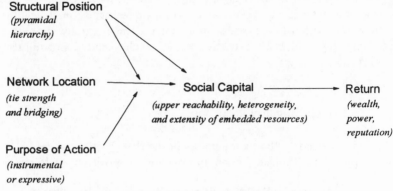

Figure 5.8 Model of the social capital theory.

7. The strength-of-position proposition: *the better the position of origin, the more likely the actor will access and use better social capital.*

8. The strength-of-strong-tie proposition: *the stronger the tie, the more likely the social capital accessed will positively affect the success of expressive action.*

9. The strength-of-weak-tie proposition: *the weaker the tie, the more likely ego will have access to better social capital for instrumental action.*

10. The strength-of-location proposition: *the closer individuals are to a bridge in a network, the better social capital they will access for instrumental action.*

11. The location-by-position proposition: *the strength of a location (in proximity to a bridge) for instrumental action is contingent on the resource differential across the bridge.*

12. The structural contingency proposition: *the networking (tie and location) effects are constrained by the hierarchical structure for actors located near or at the top and bottom of the hierarchy.*

A model based on these propositions is depicted in Figure 5.8.

These postulates and propositions have made it explicit that the proposed theory of social capital has four characteristics: (1) Its concepts are *relational* in nature and cannot be reduced to the individualistic or psychological level. (2) The theory is intrinsically interwoven within *a hierarchical structure.* In fact, it attains meaning only in the context of a hierarchical structure. (3) It entails *actions* on the part of the individuals, thus requiring a micro-level analysis. (4) Its development has been based on close reciprocal integration of *theorizing and empirical research*, thus avoiding pitfalls of infinite abstract-to-abstract deductions from assumed theories or mindless empiricism. These characteristics, I argue, place it in a unique position to address the macro–micro gap and development in sociology.

Finally, we should note that assumptions are made only to allow the theoretical propositions to be specified. Thus, assumptions may be exogenous (given) to the explication of a theory, but there is no guarantee that they are empirically valid. Theoretical development anticipates research not only on the validity of the propositions, but on the validity of the assumptions as well. That is, it is anticipated that when instruments become available, the assumptions themselves must be subject to research and empirical examination. There is nothing sacred about the assumptions. The theory itself is subjected to modification or even refutation when assumptions are invalidated. Theory guides research, and it must continuously be subjected to verification and possible modifications.

6

Social Capital and Status Attainment

A Research Tradition

This chapter[1] presents a research tradition reflecting the proposed linkage between social capital and instrumental action. Specifically, it investigates how social capital enhances the likelihood of getting better jobs. It thus falls within the general research paradigm known as the *status attainment process*.

Status attainment can be understood as a process by which individuals mobilize and invest resources for returns in socioeconomic standing. The theoretical and empirical work for understanding and assessing the status attainment process can be traced to the seminal study reported by Blau and Duncan (1967). The major conclusion was that even accounting for both the direct and indirect effects of ascribed status (parental status), achieved status (education and prior occupational status) remains the most important factor accounting for the individual's ultimate attained status. The study thus set the theoretical baseline for further modifications and expansions. All subsequent theoretical revisions and expansions must be evaluated for their contribution to the explanation of status attainment beyond those accounted for by the Blau–Duncan paradigm (Kelley 1990; Smith 1990). Several later lines of work, including the addition of sociopsychological variables (Sewell and Hauser 1975), the recasting of statuses as classes (Wright 1979; Goldthorpe 1980), the incorporation of "structural" entities and positions as both contributing and attained statuses (Baron and Bielby 1980; Kalleberg 1988), and the identification of comparative development or institutions as contingent conditions (Treiman 1970) have significantly amplified rather than altered the original Blau–Duncan conclusion concerning the relative merits of achieved versus ascribed *personal resources* in status attainment.

---

[1] A significant portion of this chapter was adapted from Lin (1999b) with permission.

In the last three decades, a research tradition has focused on the effects of social capital on attained statuses. The principal proposition is that social capital exerts an important and significant effect beyond that accounted for by personal resources. Systematic investigations of this proposition have included (1) developing theoretical explanations and hypotheses; (2) developing measurements for social capital; (3) conducting empirical studies verifying the hypotheses; and (4) assessing the relative importance of social resources compared to personal resources in the process of status attainment. These investigations have been carried out in North America, Europe, and Asia, in multiple political economies, and have involved scholars of many nations and cultures. The accumulation of and advances in theory and research have considerably expanded the intellectual horizon of sociological analysis in status attainment, and thus in social stratification and social mobility. It probably also represents the most prominent research area where explicit, systematic application and analysis of the theory and methods of social capital for instrumental actions has occurred. To a great extent, this research tradition has directly contributed to the development of the theory of social capital itself.

The purposes of this chapter are to (1) review the theoretical and empirical foundations of these lines of investigation; (2) summarize sampled studies and results; and (3) propose issues and directions for future research. Before proceeding with these tasks, I wish to identify the limitations of this review. It will focus on social capital – embedded resources in the networks accessed and used to attain statuses; as such, it does not review the effects of properties of social networks per se (e.g., density, centrality, bridging) unless they implicate accessed resources (what influence these characteristics may exert on the access and use of embedded resources). Second, the outcome of this focus is the status attained rather than whether a job search is successful. The latter has a substantial literature of its own and is better summarized elsewhere (e.g., Granovetter 1995). This chapter will touch on aspects of job searches to the extent that they affect attained statuses. Finally, only the literature available in English will be reviewed. I am aware of an expanding literature in Europe, but unfortunately, my language limitations do not allow for coverage here.

Formative Studies and Theoretical Foundations

Contributions of social network analysis to status attainment can be traced to the seminal study conducted by Mark Granovetter (1974), who interviewed 282 professional and managerial men in Newton,

Massachusetts. The data suggested that those who used interpersonal channels seemed to land more satisfactory and better (e.g., higher-paid) jobs. Based on this empirical research and substantiated by a review of job-search studies, Granovetter proposed (1973) a network theory for information flow. The hypothesis of the strength of weak ties states that weaker ties tend to form bridges that link individuals to other social circles for information not likely to be available in their own circles, and such information should be useful to the individuals.[2]

However, Granovetter never suggests that access to or help from weaker rather than stronger ties would result in higher-status jobs thus obtained (1995, p. 148). Clues about the linkage between strength of ties and attained statuses came indirectly from a small world study conducted in a tri-city metropolitan area in upstate New York (Lin, Dayton, and Greenwald 1978). The task of the participants in the study was to forward packets containing information about certain target persons to others they knew on a first-name basis so that the packets might eventually reach the target persons. The study found that successful chains (those packets successfully forwarded to the targets) involved higher-status intermediaries until the last nodes (dipping down in the hierarchy toward the locations of the targets) compared to the unsuccessful chains. Successful chains also implicated nodes that had more extensive social contacts (who claimed more social ties) and yet tended to forward the packets to someone they had not seen recently (weaker ties). The small world study thus made two contributions. First, it suggested that access to hierarchical positions might be the critical factor in the process of status attainment. Thus, the possible linkage between strength of ties and status attainment might be indirect: the strength of weak ties might lie in their accessing social positions higher in the social hierarchy, which have the advantage in facilitating instrumental action. Second, the study implicated behavior rather than a paper-and-pencil exercise, as each step in the packet-forwarding process required actual actions from each participant. Thus, the study results lend behavioral validity to the results of previous status attainment paper-and-pencil studies.

Based on these studies, a theory of social resources has emerged (Lin 1982, 1990). The theory begins with an image of the macrosocial structure consisting of positions ranked according to certain normatively

[2] On the surface, this hypothesis might be seen as simply the inverse of the long-known hypothesis that stronger ties are formed among those who share similar characteristics and lifestyles, known as the homophily principle or the like-me hypothesis (Homans 1950; Lazarsfeld and Merton 1954; Laumann 1966; Lin 1982). What the strength-of-weak-ties argument contributed, however, was a challenge to the taken-for-granted and attributed value given to strong ties, or the homophily principle: strong ties, which promote group solidarity, are socially valuable. By shifting our attention to the weaker ties, Granovetter alerted us that weak ties, which promote access to different and new information, are socially valuable as well.

valued resources such as wealth, status, and power. This structure has a pyramidal shape in terms of accessibility and control of such resources: the higher the position, the fewer the occupants; and the higher the position, the better the view it has of the structure (especially down below). The pyramidal structure suggests advantages for positions closer to the top, in terms of both number of occupants (fewer) and accessibility to positions (more). Within these structural constraints and opportunities, individuals act for expressive and instrumental purposes. For the latter (attaining status in the social structure being one prime example), the better strategy would be for ego to reach toward contacts higher up in the hierarchy. These contacts would be better able to exert influence on positions (e.g., a recruiter for a firm) whose actions might benefit ego's interest. This reaching-up process might be facilitated if ego uses weaker ties, since these are more likely to reach out vertically (presumably upward) rather than horizontally relative to ego's position in the hierarchy.

Three propositions have thus been formulated: (1) the social-resources proposition – social resources (e.g., resources accessed in social networks) exert influence on the outcome of an instrumental action (e.g., attained status), (2) the strength-of-position proposition – social resources, in turn, are affected by the original position of ego (as represented by parental resources or previous resources), and (3) the strength-of-ties proposition – social resources are also affected by the use of weaker rather than stronger ties.

Social Resources and Social Capital: A Theoretical Convergence

This theoretical development occurred in the late 1970s and early 1980s, when parallel but independent discussions on social capital (Bourdieu 1980, 1983/1986; Coleman 1988) were emerging as well. While social capital refers to a variety of features in the social structure, according to different scholars (e.g., community norms – Coleman 1990; group solidarity – Hechter 1983, Portes and Sensenbrenner 1993; participation in voluntary and civil organizations – Putnam 1995a, 1995b), it eventually became clear (Lin 1982, 1995a; Flap 1996; Tardos 1996; Burt 1997; Portes 1998) that social capital refers primarily to resources accessed in social networks. Further, the theory also focuses on the instrumental utility of such resources (capital as investment or mobilization). The convergence of the social resources and social capital theories complements and strengthens the development of a social theory focusing on the instrumental utility of accessed and mobilized resources embedded in social networks. It places the significance of social resources in the broader theoretical discussion of social capital and sharpens the definition and operationality of social capital as a research concept. The three propositions previously stated (i.e., social capital, strength of position, and strength of ties) remain valid in the framework of social capital, although other propositions have subsequently been proposed (see Chapter 5). The following discussion will reflect the merged notions of social capital and social resources and will examine the research conducted on the three propositions: (1) the social-capital proposition (Proposition 1 in Chapter 5): better embedded resources accessed in the social networks lead to better attained status; (2) the strength-of-position proposition (Proposition 2 in Chapter 5): the better the structural position of origin, the better the attained status; and (3) the strength-of-weak-ties proposition (Proposition 4 in Chapter 5): the weaker the ties, the better the attained status (in the instrumental action of a job search). At the empirical and research levels, social resources are used; at the general theoretical level, social capital is employed.

Research Models and Evidence

Research on the relationships between social resources and status attainment examines two processes, as illustrated in Figure 6.1. One process focuses on the access to social capital – resources accessed in the ego's general social networks. In this process, human capital (education, experiences), initial positions (parental or prior job statuses), and ego's social ties (e.g., extensity of ties) are hypothesized to determine the extent of resources the ego can access through such connections (network resources). Further, network resources, education, and initial positions are expected to affect attained statuses such as occupational status, authority positions, sectors, or earnings. We may describe this model as the *accessed social capital model*.

Another process focuses on the mobilization of social capital in the process of status attainment – the use of social contacts and the resources provided by the contact in the job-search process. As can be seen in Figure 6.1, contact status used is seen as the mobilized social capital in the status attainment process. It is hypothesized that contact status, along with education and initial positions, will exert a significant and important effect on the status of the job obtained. Contact status, in turn, is affected by education, network resources, and the tie strength between ego and the contact. Strength of ties may be measured either with a perceived strength (e.g., intimacy of the relationship) or with a role category (e.g., kin, friends, and acquaintances). We shall call this model the *mobilized social capital model*.

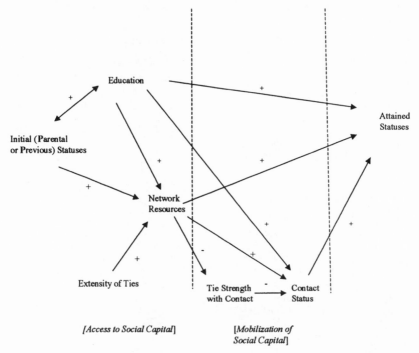

Figure 6.1 The social capital model of status attainment.

In both types of analysis, other factors may be added to the basic model, including age, gender, race/ethnicity, indications of job experience or tenure, the work sector, and the industry or organization, either as control variables or as opportunity/constraint factors. We turn now to a brief review of the literature, which will proceed first with the mobilized social capital model, as it received initial research attention, followed by the accessed social capital model and models incorporating both access and mobilization processes. A summary of the studies and findings appears in Table 6.1.

Mobilized Social Capital

The initial empirical examination of the mobilized social capital model[3] was conducted by Lin and his associates (Lin, Ensel, and Vaughn 1981;

---

[3] The fact that this estimation procedure studies only a subsample of labor force participants who use personal contacts in job searches raised concern about the selectivity bias on the estimations. It has been shown that in surveys of community labor populations,

Table 6.1. *Summary of Studies and Findings on Social Capital and Status Attainment*

Study	Social Resources Effect (Outcome Var.)	Position Effect	Tie Effect
Mobilized social capital model			
Lin, Ensel, and Vaughn (1981, USA)	Yes	Yes	Yes
Marsden and Hurlbert (1988, USA)	Yes	Yes	No
Ensel (1979, USA)	Yes	—	—
DeGraaf and Flap (1988, the Netherlands)	Yes	—	—
Moerbeek, Utle, and Flap (1995, the Netherlands)	Yes	Yes	—
Wegener (1991, Germany)	Yes	—	—
Requena (1991, Spain)	No	—	—
Barbieri (1996, Italy)	Yes	Yes	No
Hsung and Sun (1988, Taiwan)	Yes	—	—
Hsung and Hwang (1992, Taiwan)	Yes	Yes	No
Bian and Ang (1997, Singapore)	Yes	—	Yes*
Volker and Flap (1999, East Germany)	Yes	Yes*	No
Bian (1997, China)	Yes	—	No
Accessed social capital model			
Name generator methodology			
Campbell, Marsden, and Hurlbert (1986, USA)	Yes	—	—
Sprengers, Tazelaar, and Flap (1988, the Netherlands)	Yes	Yes	Yes*
Barbieri (1996, Italy)	Yes	Yes	—
Boxman, DeGraaf, and Flap (1991, the Netherlands)	Yes	—	—
Boxman and Flap (1990, the Netherlands)	Yes	—	—
Burt (1992, USA)	Yes	—	—
Burt (1997, 1998 USA)	Yes*	—	—
Position Generator Methodology			
Lin and Dumin (1986, USA)	Yes	Yes	Yes*
Hsung and Hwang (1992, Taiwan)	Yes	—	—
Volker and Flap (1999, East Germany)	Yes	Yes	Yes
Angelusz and Tardos (1991, Hungary)	Yes	No	—
Erickson (1995, 1996, Canada)	Yes	—	Yes*
Erickson (1998, Canada)	Yes	—	—
Belliveau, O'Reilly, and Wade (1996, USA)	Yes	—	—
Joint accessed/mobilized model			
Boxman (1992)	Yes	—	—
Flap and Boxman (1996, 1998, the Netherlands)	Yes	—	—
Volker and Flap (1997, Germany)	Yes	—	—
Lai, Lin, and Leung (1998, USA)	Yes	Yes	Yes

—: not reported.
* Conditional confirmation; detail in text.

Lin, Vaughn, and Ensel 1981). The study used data from a representative community sample in metropolitan Albany, New York, of more than 400 employed men, and confirmed that contact status exerted effects on attained status beyond and after accounting for parental status and education effects. It also confirmed that contact status was affected positively by the father's status and negatively by the strength of ties between ego and the contact. The results provided the initial confirmation of all three propositions of the social capital theory. Ensel (1979) extended the investigation to both men and women in a study of employed adults in New York State. While confirming that contact status significantly affected attained status, he found that male contacts were much more likely to reach higher-status contacts than female contacts. Further, women were more likely to use female contacts in job searches, while men overwhelmingly used male contacts. When women did use male contacts, their disadvantage in reaching higher-status contacts as compared to men was significantly reduced. This study was one of the first to provide direct evidence that men, being positioned advantageously in the hierarchy, had better social capital than women. Secondly, women's disadvantages in mobilizing male contacts, and thereby accessing better social capital, accounted in part for their inferior status attainment. Further replication and extension of the model were done by Marsden and Hurlbert (1988), who analyzed the transition to current jobs for 456 men in the 1970 Detroit Area Study. This confirmed that contact status (occupational prestige and sector) exerted the strongest effects on attained prestige and sector, respectively. The authors also found that the contact's prestige and position in the core sector were related to the prestige and sector of the prior job, respectively, confirming the strength-of-position proposition. On the other hand, the authors did not confirm the strength-of-tie proposition; contact status was not associated with the strength of ties between ego and the contact.

Extension of the model to other societies quickly followed. De Graaf and Flap (1988) lent further support to the social resources proposition in their analyses of 628 males in a 1980 West German survey and 466 males in a 1982 Dutch survey. They did not examine the strength-of-position or the strength-of-tie propositions for social resources. The Netherlands Family Survey of 1992 provided data on male–female com-

---

anywhere from 20 percent to over 61 percent of the job seekers indicate the use of personal contacts (for a summary, see Granovetter 1995, pp. 139–141). Yet, studies of selectivity bias have revealed no major differences in the characteristics of those who used personal contacts compared to those who used formal channels or direct applications in job searches. Younger and less experienced workers do show a slightly greater tendency to use personal contacts. Thus, most studies have incorporated age and/or work experience as controls to account for possible bias.

parisons in the social capital effect. Moerbeek, Ultee, and Flap (1995) used father's occupation as the indicator of social capital when the father was mentioned as the social contact, and found that it exerted a positive and significant effect on the statuses of first and current/last jobs for both men and women. Wegener (1991) analyzed a 1987 data set from Germany of 604 men and women aged forty-two and thirty-two, and found that contact status significantly affected the prestige of the job found, confirming the social resources proposition. However, the strength-of-ties proposition and the strength-of-position hypotheses were not examined. Barbieri (1996), reporting a study of 500 newly hired persons in the administrative area of Milan, Italy, confirmed the social-resources proposition by finding that contact status significantly affected present job status, having already accounted for effects from father's status, education, and first and previous job statuses. Further, he found that father's status indirectly affected contact status through education, lending some support to the strength-of-tie proposition. When Barbieri subdivided the sample into those who used strong versus weak ties, he found no advantage of using weaker ties in the association between contact status and attainted status. In fact, there was some evidence that stronger ties increased the association between contact status and statuses of first and previous jobs. Requena's (1991) study in Spain provided the only disconfirming evidence for the social resources proposition, as it showed that greater social resources did not provide better jobs, even though they did affect income attainment. He speculated that the lack of social-resources effects was due in part to the rigid bureaucratization of Spain's employment policies and practices.

Systematic tests of the theory have been carried out in Asia as well. A series of studies were conducted by Hsung and others in Taiwan, which is also a capitalist state. One study (Hsung and Sun 1988) surveyed the labor force in the manufacturing industry, and another (Hsung and Hwang 1992) examined the labor force in a metropolitan area (Taichung). Both studies supported the social resources proposition that contact status significantly affects the status of obtained first and current jobs after accounting for father's education and occupational status, education, and, in the case of the current job, prior job status. Hsung and Hwang (1992) also found modest support for the strength-of-position argument, but father's education and occupational status had only a modest effect on contact status for the first job and no significant effects on the current job's contact status. For strength of ties, a composite measure (closeness with contacts, frequency of visits, frequency of calls, and content of the relationship) indicated only a slightly negative relationship with the first job's contact status and no relationship with the current job's contact status. In addition, in 1994, Bian and Ang (1997) conducted a study of 512 men and women in Singapore that strongly confirmed the social resources proposition: contact status significantly affected obtained status. Helper status was strongly related to the current job's occupational status, along with age, education, and prior job status. For all respondents, weaker ties reached higher-status contacts. However, the weakest ties (not intimate at all) had no effect on contact status, a finding similar to that of a 1988 Tianjin study that will be described shortly. For those who reached helpers indirectly, the association between tie strength and contact status was negative. However, stronger ties between the intermediary and the helper were more likely to result in reaching a higher-status helper.

A major extension of the research paradigm has examined the propositions in different political economies, such as state socialism. Bian (1997), in a 1988 study conducted in Tianjin, China, including 1,008 men and women, found that helper's job status (measured by the hierarchical level of his or her work unit) was strongly associated with attained work unit status in the job change, along with education and prior job status. The overall effect of the tie strength between ego and the helper on the helper's status was insignificant. Further analyses showed that medium-strength ties reached helpers with better status; this was true for the tie strength between ego and intermediaries, as well as between intermediaries and helpers. Moreover, in a retrospective panel study conducted by Volker and Flap (1999) in Leipzig and Dresden, two cities in the former German Democratic Republic, the occupational prestige of the contact person had strong and significant effects on both the first job and job prestige in 1989. Thus, the social resources proposition was confirmed. However, strength of ties (measured by the intensity of the relationship between ego and the contact) had no effect on contact statuses or on attained occupational status and income. Neither father's education nor occupational prestige affected contact status for the 1989 job search. However, education had a significant effect on contact status. Since the father's status had direct effects on education, these results confirmed the indirect effect of the strength of positions, mediated through education.

Accessed Social Capital

Two methods are used to measure accessed social capital: name generators and position generators. The *name generator* method is the more common method and has been used extensively in the network literature. The general technique is to pose one or more questions about ego's contacts in certain role relationships (e.g., neighborhood, work), content areas (e.g., work matters, household chores), or intimacy (e.g., confi-

Table 6.2. *Position Generator for Measuring Accessed Social Capital: An Example*

Here is a list of jobs (*show card*). Would you please tell me if you happen to know someone (on a first-name basis) who has each job?					
Job	1. Do you know anyone who has this job?*	2. How long have you known this person (no. of years)?	3. What is your relationship with this person?	4. How close are you to this person?	5. His/her gender	6. His/her job
Job A						
Job B						
Job C						
(etc.)						

* If you know more than one person, think of the one person whom you have known the longest.

dential, most intimate interactions). Such questions generate a list of contacts ranging from three to five or as many as volunteered by ego. From these lists, relationships between ego and contacts, and among contacts, as well as contacts' characteristics, are generated. Social capital measures are constructed to reflect the contacts' diversity and range of resources (education, occupation) as well as characteristics (gender, race, age). There are a number of problems associated with the use of name generators to measure social capital, including variations in distributions being affected by the content or role and number of names. As a result, the data tend to reflect stronger ties, stronger role relations, or geographically limited ties (Campbell and Lee 1991).

Position generators, first proposed by Lin and associates (Lin and Dumin 1986), use a sample of structural positions that are salient in a society (occupations, authorities, work units, class, or sector) and ask respondents to indicate contacts (e.g., those known on a first-name basis), if any, in each of the positions. In addition, relationships between ego and the contact for each position can be identified. Thus, instead of sampling content or role areas, the position generator samples hierarchical positions. It is content free and role/location neutral. Instead of counting and measuring data from specific names (persons) generated, the position generator counts and measures access to structural positions. An example of the position-generator instrument is shown in Table 6.2.

The name-generator methodology has been employed in research over a longer period of time, while the position-generator methodology has emerged in more recent studies. The following section will report on the studies and results for each methodology on accessed social capital and status attainment.

Name-Generators Studies. Campbell, Marsden, and Hurlbert (1986) examined the associations between network resources and socioeconomic statuses with name-generator data from the 1965–1966 Detroit Area Study and found that the resource compositions of networks (mean and maximal education, mean and maximal prestige) were significantly associated with attained statuses such as occupational prestige and family income. In the Milan study, Barbieri (1996) also constructed three measures for social capital from name-generator data and found them to affect present job status after accounting for parental statuses, experience, human capital (years of schooling), and first and previous job statuses. Further, social capital was affected by father's status, confirming the strength-of-position proposition.

Several studies have assessed the associations between accessed social capital and attained statuses among certain labor populations. Access to social capital by the unemployed was the focus of a study conducted by Sprengers, Tazelaar, and Flap (1988). Among a group of 242 Dutch men aged forty to fifty-five who were unemployed in or before 1978, those with better social capital were more likely to find jobs within a year after unemployment, especially those with access to social capital through weak ties. Those with better social capital did not find a better occupational status or a higher income when they found reemployment. However, better social capital increased optimism about job opportunities, which in turn increased the intensity of the job search, leading to more and better jobs. Further, it was found that the more restricted the labor market, the more intense those with greater social capital tended to be in job searches. After a year of unemployment, those with better social capital among strong ties (relatives) also tended to have a better chance of being rehired in the next one to three years. The study also found that those with better education, former occupations, and higher incomes also tended to have better social capital, confirming the strength-of-position hypothesis. Focusing on 1,359 top managers of large companies in the Netherlands, Boxman, De Graaf, and Flap (1991) found that both education and social capital (measured with work contacts in other organizations and membership in clubs and professional associations) had direct effects on income. The job-search activities of 365 persons in the Netherlands who finished vocational training were also studied by Boxman and Flap (1990) in 1989. Data were obtained from job seekers and employers, as well as from contacts used by the job seekers. Preliminary analyses showed that for income, the more important predictors were gender (in favor of men), social capital, career perspective, and company-specific skills.

Early promotion and better bonuses were the outcomes assessed by Burt (1992) for managers in a large electronic components and computing equipment firm. Using the extent to which each ego was embedded in a constrained network (fewer contacts, more dense relations, and more contacts related to a single contact) as a measure of social capital, he found that there was a negative association between structural constraints and early promotion. That is, he suggested that access to diverse resources in one's networks enhanced the opportunity to locate useful information and influence for promoting one's position in the firm. For men in senior positions in the investment banking division of a large American financial organization, a similar negative association between constrained networks and bonuses was found (Burt 1997).

Position-Generators Studies. Lin and Dumin (1986) analyzed the data from an Albany, New York, study in which twenty occupations were sampled from the U.S. 1960 census listing of occupations, with all occupations ranked according to job prestige scores. At equal intervals on the job prestige scale scores, occupations were identified. From this group, the most popular (frequency of occupants) occupation was selected. Each respondent was asked if he had any contact (person he knew on a first-name basis) in each of the positions. If more than one contact was indicated, the respondent was asked to focus on the most familiar one. For each accessed position, the respondent identified the contact's relationship (relative, friend, or acquaintance). From the data matrix, Lin and Dumin constructed two social resources access measures: the highest status accessible (the position accessed with the highest prestige score) and the range of statuses accessed (the difference between the highest and lowest accessed statuses). Analyses showed that the two measures were positively and significantly related to current occupational status. Further analysis showed that respondents' original positions (father's occupational prestige score or white–blue and high–low occupational groupings) and these two measures were positively and significantly related, confirming the strength-of-position hypothesis. When Lin and Dumin analyzed the relationships between the three types of ties (relatives, friends, acquaintances) and the access variables, they found that friends as well as acquaintances provided the best access to both the highest-status position and the range of accessed statuses.

Hsung and Hwang (1992) also incorporated network resources in their Taichung study, as cited earlier. Adapting the position-generator methodology with twenty occupations, they failed to find significant effects for the highest status accessed and for the difference between the lowest and highest occupational statuses accessed. However, they did find significant effects on the first job status of a measure of the "total amount of network resources," which was based on the sum status scores of all occupations accessed. This measure, however, did not have any effect on current job status. Volker and Flap (1999), in their Germany study, used the position-generator methodology to ask respondents to identify, among thirty-three occupations, whether they knew anyone in any of the occupations, and if so, what their relationships were (relatives, friends, and acquaintances). For 1989 occupational status, the effect of the highest status accessed was positive and significant, controlling for fathers' education and occupation, the respondents' own education and sex, and the prestige of their first job. This variable also had a positive and moderately significant ($p < .10$) effect on 1989 income when 1989 occupational prestige was added to the equation along with all other independent variables. This result confirmed the social resources proposition. Further, Volker and Flap found that both relatives and acquaintances accessed better occupations (upper-white-collar or higher prestige) than friends. On the other hand, acquaintances accessed a greater range (the difference between the highest- and lowest-prestige jobs) of occupations than either relatives or friends. Since the highest occupational prestige accessed turned out to be the best predictor of attained status, the effects of weak ties were not found (as relatives and acquaintances were almost equally likely to access high-prestige occupations). The father's occupational prestige was positively related to the highest occupational prestige accessed in general, as well as for each group of occupations accessed through relatives, friends, and acquaintances. Thus, the strength-of-position proposition was confirmed. In pre-1989 Hungary (1987–1988), Angelusz and Tardos (1991) also used the position generator to identify "weakly tied" relations or resources. This variable was found to be significantly associated with wages, after accounting for the effects of sex, education, residence, and age.

In her study of the private security industry (161 guard, investigation, and security companies) in Toronto in 1991–1992, Erickson (1995, 1996) used Wright's (1979) class dimensions (control of property, control of organizations, and control of skill) to select nineteen job positions. Data were gathered from 155 employees, 46 supervisors, 80 managers, and 112 owners. Erickson found that social capital (diversity in accessing various positions) contributed to job autonomy and authority, which in turn generated better job returns. The major conclusions are that (1) accessed social capital helps people to rise to higher positions (in comparisons between mangers versus lower-level employees and owners versus employees) and (2) social capital pays off even if people do not use a contact to get a job (see Recruitment and Social Capital in the next section). In another study on social capital, Erickson (1998) differentiated two types of social capital: global and local. Local settings refer to geographic areas (neighborhoods), ethnic areas (ethnic communities and enclave economies), or organizations (schools, voluntary organizations, social movements, or firms). In a telephone survey of 352 participants in the Toronto Local Employment and Trading System (LETS), Erickson asked the respondents to identify contacts in a list of thirty occupations both inside and outside the LETS system. Analyses showed that local social capital was associated with income in the LETS system (the local economy), while global social capital was not associated with income in the general economy, pointing to the fact that social capital's effect is more contingent in the global economy system.

Joint Effects of Accessed and Mobilized Social Capital

Since there are two types of social capital in the process of status attainment, a logical step would be to examine accessed and mobilized social capital in a single study. The theoretical question posed is the extent to which accessed social capital facilitates social capital: that is, whether having more accessed social capital increases the likelihood of mobilizing better social capital. The structural opportunity and advantage implied in this hypothesis is apparent. However, it is also to be expected that the correspondence will not be overwhelming: not all persons accessed with rich social capital are expected to take advantage of or be able to mobilize social capital for the purpose of obtaining better socioeconomic status. An element of action and choice should also be significant. Several studies have lent support to this hypothesis.

For example, in their study of vocational training graduates, Boxman and Flap (Boxman 1992; Flap and Boxman 1996) showed that contact status (mobilized social capital) affects attained occupational status, whereas accessed social capital does not. The Germany study (Volker and Flap 1996) is another study in which both accessed and mobilized social capital were measured. It was found that the highest occupational prestige accessed using the position-generator methodology was significantly and positively related to the status of the contact person used in the 1989 job search, but its direct effect on 1989 job prestige, while positive, was only modest in significance ($p < .10$). The contact person's prestige had a much stronger effect. In fact, its direct effect on 1989 job prestige was stronger than education once the prestige of the first job was also incorporated (and was the most significant predictor).

Lai, Lin, and Leung (1998) also examined the joint effects of accessed and mobilized social capital on status attainment using the Albany data (Lin, Ensel, and Vaughn 1981). Incorporating both the network resources measures from the position generator (Lin and Dumin 1986) and the contact resources (contact status in the job search) in structural equation models, they showed that current job status is significantly and directly affected by education (achieved status) and by contact status.

Contact status, in turn, is affected by parental statuses (ascribed status), education, network resources, and weaker ties with the contact. Thus, it is clear that mobilized social capital directly influences status outcome and mobilized social capital is affected by accessed social capital, along with ascribed and achieved statuses.

Issues and Research Directions

Research has provided consistent support for the proposition that social capital, in the form of social resources, makes a significant contribution to status attainment beyond personal resources. This association persists across societies (different nation-states and political economies), industrialization and development levels, labor market populations (recent graduates, new hires, job changers), different economic sectors (industries, organizations, positions in organizations), and status outcomes (occupation, authority, sector, promotion, bonuses). The association remains significant across differential conceptualization (accessed versus mobilized capital) and measurement (name generators versus position generators). Yet, there remain important issues to be conceptualized and studied in the future. In the following subsections, a number of these issues will be briefly identified and discussed.

Informal and Formal Job Search Channels

It is clear by now that the use of informal channels by itself offers no advantage over other channels, especially formal channels, in attained status. In fact, if anything, informal channels tend to be used by the disadvantaged: women, the less educated, and the less skilled. The statuses attained therefore tend to be lower. Yet, among those who use informal channels, social resources (contact statuses) make a major difference. Several issues remain. First, is it really true that the advantaged do not need to use informal channels, as they possess greater human capital and can apply directly to high-status positions? The evidence is mixed. For some jobs that have specific requirements (dealing with technology and hardware, for example), credentials regarding skills and training in the formal application may be sufficient to obtain positions. However, for other critical jobs (high-level managerial and human-interfaced positions), formal credentials are often insufficient to convey the social skills and resources so essential for occupants' performances. The necessary informal or shadow channels through which such information is conveyed, yet not detected in survey instruments, remain an important methodological challenge. Secondly, for the disadvantaged, social capital is restricted (the strength-of-position argument). Within this restricted range of resources, there is little information on whether the disadvantaged are also less likely to mobilize the optimal resources available to them, thus creating double jeopardy. Knowledge about the choice behaviors of the advantaged and the disadvantaged will be helpful in sorting through the structural constraints and choice constraints.

Strength of Ties or Network Locations?

While the social resources proposition and the strength-of-position propositions have been consistently confirmed (see Table 6.1), much ambiguity has resulted regarding the strength-of-ties proposition. Strength of ties in and of itself should not be expected to exert a direct effect on status outcomes (Granovetter 1995), and much research evidence points to the absence of a direct association (e.g., Bridges and Villemez 1986; Marsden and Hurlbert 1988; Forse 1997). The modified proposition that weaker ties might access better social resources also lacks consistent empirical support (see Table 6.1). Yet, social capital is theorized to contain both structural effects and agency effects; further specifications of network or tie choices within structural constraints may eventually turn out to be meaningful. Several lines of investigation have provided some leads. For example, it has been argued that the effect of strength of ties on social resources accessed or mobilized may be contingent on the original status. Some studies have pointed to the ceiling effect of tie strength: at or near the top level of the hierarchy, it is strong ties that tend to yield successful job attainment (Lin, Ensel, and Vaughn 1981; Erickson 1995, 1996). Also, the weakest ties are clearly not useful (Bian 1997; Bian and Ang 1997), since ties with no strength offer no incentive for exchanges. On the other hand, the strongest ties, by the same token, may be useful despite the restricted range of resources accessed. There ties, by definition, represent commitment, trust, and obligation and therefore the motivation to help. Willingness and effort to search for other ties using these strong ties may be critical under institutional uncertainties or constraints (e.g., under state socialism: Rus 1995, Bian 1997; or tight market situations: Sprengers, Tazelaar, and Flap 1988). Organizational constraints and opportunities may also condition the relative utility of weaker or stronger ties (Lin 1990).

Another source of possible clarification suggests a possible modification in the conceptualization of the strength of ties in network terms. For example, strength of tie may be reflected in the length of the links between ego and the alter whose resources are eventually accessed. If each link is assumed to be of equal strength, then the strength of the tie between ego and the alter may become an inverse function of the length of the links between them: the longer the chain of connection, the weaker the tie. While the multiple links necessarily weaken the degree of obligations, trust, and reciprocity between ego and the ultimate alter, such a chain also extends the reach for resources not present in the proximal areas of ego in the networks. To the extent that heterogeneous or rich resources are present in distant parts of the network, the chain length or weaker ties may in fact become useful. Further analysis along this line (e.g., Bian 1997) will clarify the utility of both the bridge effect and the strength-of-tie effect.

Other considerations point to locations in the social networks. The utility of social ties may be more dependent on the locations of the actors in the social networks or on the hierarchical structure rather than the strength of ties (e.g., Lin and Dumin 1986; Angelusz and Tardos 1991; Burt 1997). Positions at or near strategic locations, such as bridges or structural holes, may provide a competitive advantage to actors accessing heterogeneous and thus rich resources.

These findings and considerations have led to further articulation of the propositions for the theory of social capital, as reflected in Chapter 5, where network positions, in conjunction with structural positions, provide the key to predict how likely an instrumental action is to lead to better social capital.

Further Development of the Position Generator

In order to ascertain the causal sequence, the time framework of the contacts needs to be specified. For example, the generator may wish to ask, "When you were looking for the first (or current) job, did you know of anyone who had this kind of work?" Also, it is important to sample the positions from a meaningful hierarchy in a given society. In addition to occupational status or prestige, work units, sectors, authority, or autonomy may confer important statuses in certain societies. Catering to the significance of meaningful statuses/classes in a given society is thus an important consideration in identifying the positions in the generators (Erickson 1995).

Inequality of Social Capital

Differential access to social capital deserves much greater research attention. It is conceivable that social groups (gender, race) have different access to social capital because of their advantaged or disadvantaged structural positions and social networks. Thus, for example, inequality of social capital offers fewer opportunities for women and minorities to mobilize better social resources to attain and promote careers. For the disadvantaged to gain a better status, strategic behaviors require accessing resources beyond their usual social circles (e.g., women) using male ties (Ensel 1979) to find sponsors in the firm (Burt 1998) and to join clubs dominated by men (Beggs and Hurlbert 1997); or for blacks to find ties outside their own neighborhood or those employed (Green, Tigges, and Browne 1995); or for scholars of Mexican origin to find ties of non-Mexican origin or to establish ties with institutional agents such as teachers and counselors (Stanton-Salazar and Dornbusch 1995; Stanton-Salazar 1997). Systematic data on inequalities in social capital will provide an explanatory framework for inequality in social stratification and mobility and offer behavioral choices to overcome such inequalities. The next chapter, in fact, will describe one such effort.

Recruitment and Social Capital

The relationships between social capital and status attainment apply to both the supply and demand sides of the labor market. So far, research literature has primarily concentrated on the supply side – the status attainment process from job seekers' perspective. The demand side of the model – the recruitment process from the organization's perspective – has only begun to emerge (Boxman and Flap 1990; Boxman, De Graaf and Flap 1991; Erickson 1995, 1996; Burt 1997; Fernandez and Weinberg 1997). There are reasons to believe that social capital is important for firms in selective recruitment, as firms must operate in an environment where social skills and networks play critical roles in transactions and exchanges. This is especially true of certain types of positions. Thus, we may anticipate that certain positions require more social capital than other positions in a firm. First, top-level executives are expected to possess rich social capital, as they need to deal with and manage people both within and outside the firm. In fact, we may postulate that at the highest level of management, social capital far outweighs human capital for occupants. Thus, it can be hypothesized that firms such as IBM and Microsoft are more likely to recruit experienced managers with social skills rather than computer expertise for their CEOs, and that top universities need presidents who have the social skills to negotiate with faculty, students, parents, and alumni, and to raise funds rather than produce distinguished scholarships. Second, we should expect positions that deal with persons (e.g., nurses) rather than machines or technologies (e.g., programmers) to be filled with occupants who have better social capital. Third, positions at the edge of the firm are more likely to be filled by those with better social capital than others (e.g., salesperson, public relations personnal, or managers at remote sites; Burt 1997). Firms with more needs for such positions, therefore, should be expected to use informal sources in recruitment more extensively. Such hypotheses will help empirical specifications and testing.

Social Capital versus Human Capital

The relationship between social capital and human capital is theoretically important. Some scholars (Bourdieu 1983/1986; Coleman 1990) have proposed that social capital helps produce human capital. Well-connected parents and social ties can indeed enhance the opportunities for individuals to obtain better education, training, and skill and knowledge credentials. On the other hand, it is clear that human capital induces social capital. Better-educated and better-trained individuals tend to move in social circles and clubs rich in resources. The harder question is: given both, which is more important in enhancing status attainment? Several studies cited in this chapter suggest that social capital may be as important as or even more important than human capital (education and work experience) in status attainment (Lin, Ensel, and Vaughn 1981; Marsden and Hurlbert 1988), while others show the opposite (Hsung and Sun 1988; DeGraaf and Flap 1988; Hsung and Hwang 1992). Industrialization probably is not the explanation, as the former group includes studies conducted in the United States and the latter in the Netherlands and Taiwan. More likely, there is an association between specific educational institutions and methods of job allocations and searches. As Krymkowski (1991) showed in a comparative analysis of data from the United States, West Germany, and Poland in the 1970s, both West Germany and Poland showed stronger associations between social origins and education and between education and occupational allocations than the United States. Yet, there is no clear evidence that the educational system in Taiwan resembles the West German and Dutch systems more than it does the U.S. system. The contrasting results from these countries thus remain to be explained.

Still more intriguing are the possible interactions between human capital and social capital. Boxman, De Graaf, and Flap (1991) found that human capital had its greatest effect on income when social capital was low, and human capital had its least effect on income when social capital was high. Further, in the study of Dutch managers, Flap and Boxman (1998) found that for top managers, social capital led to higher income at all levels of human capital, but the returns on human capital decreased at higher levels of social capital. If these patterns can be confirmed, they would suggest that human capital supplements social capital in status attainment. That is, when social capital is high, attained status will be high, regardless of the level of human capital; and when social capital is low, human capital exerts a strong effect on attainment. Or, given certain minimal levels of human and social capital, social capital is the more important factor in accounting for status attainment.

Concluding Remarks

This brief chapter can only provide an abbreviated presentation of the rich and sizable research literature on social capital and status attainment. Many studies are currently being conducted in many parts of the world and have not been covered here. Nevertheless, it should be apparent that this research tradition has contributed significantly to the development of the social capital theory itself, as well as providing detailed and varied empirical data for its verification and continuous evolution. The research enterprise truly exemplifies the importance and fruitfulness of the continuing interplay and reciprocal feedback between theory and research.

7

Inequality in Social Capital

A Research Agenda

This chapter[1] examines a critical issue in social capital research – inequality in social capital, or the extent to which social capital is unequally distributed across social groups in a community or population. First, I will consider some general issues and approaches to the analysis of inequality in all types of capital. These considerations will lead to formulations of research agenda, and data from urban China will then be used to illustrate them. The chapter will conclude with a brief statement about the future research agenda.

Theoretical Considerations

Social inequality is a major research issue; its etiology demands attention. From the capital theoretic perspective, we may make the initial proposition that inequality in different types of capital, such as human capital and social capital, brings about social inequality, such as in socioeconomic standing and quality of life. Given this proposition, we may further explore the processes leading to inequality in capital. In this formulation, the plan is to identify the specific mechanisms that lead to inequality in capital, which in turn affects social inequality. Thus, the research task is twofold: identification and verification of mechanisms leading to inequality in capital, and demonstration of the linkage between inequality in capital and social inequality among social groups. The initial proposition, linkage between capital inequality and social inequality, has been the guiding theory regarding different types of

[1] I want to acknowledge Marc Magee's assistance in this analysis. The study reported here was supported in part by a grant from the Chiang Ching-Kuo Foundation. An earlier version was presented at the twenty-eighth Sino-American Conference held on June 12–14, 1999, at Duke University.

99

capital (Chapters 1–6). This chapter explores the formulation of processes accounting for inequality in capital, including social capital.

It is argued that capital inequality may result from two processes: capital deficit and return deficits. *Capital deficit* refers to the consequence of a process by which differential investment or opportunities result in relative shortage (in quantity or quality) of capital for one group compared with another. For example, families may invest more in the human or social capital of their sons compared to their daughters. Or different social groups may be embedded in different social hierarchies or social networks that facilitate or constrain their members' capital acquisition. *Return deficit* is the consequence of a process by which a given quality or quantity of capital generates a differential return or outcome for members of different social groups. For example, males and females, with a given quality or quantity of social capital, receive differential returns in status attainment – such as positions in organizations, occupational prestige, or earnings.

Inequality in capital between social groups may be due to capital deficit, return deficit, or both. Consider the problem of gender inequality in the labor market. A substantial literature suggests that a gendered labor market accounts for differential earnings for males and females in different occupations (Treiman and Terrell 1975; Bose and Rossi 1983; Bielby and Baron 1986; Jacobs 1989; England, Farkas, Kilbourne, and Don 1988; Reskin 1988, 1993; Kilbourne, England, Farkas, Beron, and Weir 1994; Reskin and Roos 1990; England 1992a, 1992b; Tomaskovic-Devey 1993). Yet, little theory or research has refined the empirical finding of a gendered occupational structure, and has systematically explored the mechanisms that account for different group members' differential allocations in structural positions, and the subsequent returns or rewards to members of different social groups (see Tam 1997 for a competing argument). From the capital theoretic perspective, we may offer two possible explanations for these possible relationships.

The capital deficit explanation focuses on the differential acquisition of capital. One process may be differential investment: it hypothesizes that families invest differentially in capital for male and female children. We may speculate that in most societies, families anticipating a labor market and an economy that provide differential returns for males and females wish to be competitive by investing more capital in sons than in daughters. Thus, it may be expected that males are favored over females for both education (human capital) and extensity of social networks (social capital). A second process may be differential opportunities: prevailing social structure and institutions (rules and practices or culture; see Chapter 11) differentially afford opportunities for males and females in developing capital. Male children are encouraged and rewarded for extensity and heterogeneity of social ties, while female children are constrained or even punished for doing so. These two processes result in differential capital deficit; females will acquire less capital in terms of quality and quantity. Capital deficit, in this formulation, is expected to account for the differential placements and rewards received by males and females.

Return deficit explanation, on the other hand, focuses on the return to capital – in the labor market, for example. The argument is that it is the return to capital in the labor market that differentiates males and females. In this case, it may be assumed that even when males and females have relatively equal (quality or quantity of) capital, they have different status outcomes in the labor market. That is, the labor market differentially rewards males and females for their capital. Given the same quality or quantity of capital, males will generate greater rewards than females in the labor market, such as positions in the organization, occupational titles or prestige, and earnings. Three different explanations may be offered for this scenario. In one, females may not use or mobilize the appropriate capital for the instrumental action of attainment in the labor market. For example, they may not use the best social ties and thus the best possible social capital in the attainment process, either because they are cognitively unable to identify the best possible social ties and social capital or because they hesitate to mobilize such social capital due to perceived lack of resources or capacity to return the favor. Alternatively, the appropriate social ties are mobilized, but for real or imagined reasons, these ties are reluctant to invest their capital on ego's (the female's) behalf. These ties may suspect that employers would be more resistant to female candidates and would not take their recommendation or influence seriously. Such wasted influence would be a cost rather than a prize for their investment in the candidate. Not "putting out" may also be the cultured or institutionally expected understanding, as even for the females and their families, less effort is expected from social ties on behalf of ego. A third explanation for a return deficit may be the differential responses from the labor market's structure itself: employers respond differentially to male and female job/promotion candidates even if they present similar human and/or social capital – a bias shared by organizations in an institutional field (an institutional field is a social community in which the organizations share a set of prevailing values and practices; see Chapter 11 and Lin 1994b).

In summary, we can propose the following mechanisms for social inequality from the perspective of capital theories:

1. Capital deficit is due to (a) differential investment or (b) differential opportunity.

2. Return deficit is due to (a) differential mobilization of appropriate capital resulting from cognitive deficiency or reluctance to mobilize; (b) differential effort by intermediary agents; or (c) differential responses by organizations and institutions to the mobilized capital.
3. Return deficit may or may not occur independent of capital deficit. Certain social inequalities may be due to capital deficit distributed in different social groups. Other types of inequality may be due mainly to return deficit: social groups may have a similar quality and quantity of capital and yet may generate differential returns. For still other types of inequality, both capital deficit and return deficit may account for inequality among social groups. These mechanisms may also vary in different communities or societies.

The preceding can thus be seen as hypotheses regarding inequality in different types of capital (e.g., human, institutional, and social capital), among different social groups (e.g., gender, race/ethnicity, religion), for different labor markets (e.g., economic, political, educational), and for different societies. The remainder of the chapter employs a recently collected data set from urban China to illustrate how such specification and analysis can be undertaken to shed light on the inequality in social capital between males and females. While the focus will be on social capital, the data also permit some analysis of the two groups' human and institutional capital. The data cannot be used for specification and analysis of all the possible mechanisms mentioned previously. However, it is hoped that the analysis will demonstrate how fruitful such a "decomposed" approach can be in shedding light on the critical issue of inequality in social capital and its consequences for male and female attainment in the urban Chinese labor market.

The Study, Sample, and Data

Three research questions are asked in this exploratory study: (1) Do males and females have different social capital? (2) If so, is this difference due to capital deficit, return deficit, or both? (3) What are the consequences of inequality of social capital for males and females in getting ahead in the labor market? The data used here are derived from a 1998 survey of eighteen cities. Fifteen of these cities were sampled from a stratified probability sample of all cities. Stratification was based on region (coastal, central, and interior) and economic status (high, medium, and low). Three additional cities were sampled from three outlier regions (Pingliang, Ge'ermu, and Tacheng). Appendix 7.1 presents the cities and the sample sizes from these sites. City-level data were also collected for multilevel analyses. However, the present study, a preliminary analysis, concerns only individual-level data.

The sample consists of 3,050 respondents, aged nineteen to sixty-nine inclusive, who were participating or had participated in the labor force of these eighteen cities at the time of the survey. The basic characteristics of these respondents appear in Table 7.1. The sample consists of 43.5 percent males and 56.4 percent females. The average age is forty-one,

Table 7.1. *Summary of Sample Characteristics (N = 3,050)*

Variable	Percentage or Mean			Gender Significance Test
	Sample	Males	Females	
Gender – male	43.5%			
Age	41.3	42.0	40.9	ns
Martial status				
Single	6.7%	7.5%	6.2%	ns
Married	90.0	91.0	89.1	.08
Divorced or widowed	3.3	1.5	4.7	.00
Residence at 16 years of age				.00
Big city	52.0%	48.6%	54.6%	
Medium-sized city	22.7	23.8	21.9	
Town	11.4	11.5	11.3	
Countryside	13.9	16.2	12.2	
Education				.00
Less than high school	33.4%	31.4%	35.0%	
High school	41.4	37.4	45.0	
College or more	25.2	31.3	20.4	
Experience (number of years)	21.6	22.3	21.1	.00
Tenure (number of years)	14.7	15.0	14.4	ns
On-the-job training				
Number of types				.00
No.	67.4%	64.0%	70.0%	
1	28.0	30.5	26.1	
2	3.7	4.5	3.0	
3	.9	.9	.8	
4	.1	.1	.1	
Number of certificates				.03
No.	71.7%	69.3%	73.6	
1	25.1	26.7	23.8	
2	2.9	3.5	2.4	
3	.4	.5	.3	
Communist Party membership				.00
No	73.0%	63.8%	80.1%	
At time of current job	21.3	28.16	16.0	
At time of first job	5.7	8.06	3.9	

(continued)

Table 7.1 *(continued)*

Variable	Percentage or Mean			Gender Significance Test
	Sample	Males	Females	
Current job characteristics				
Work unit ownership				.00
State	80.8%	81.8%	80.0%	
Collective	12.7	9.2	15.5	
Joint venture	2.7	3.8	1.7	
Private	1.2	1.4	1.1	
Self	2.6	3.8	1.7	
Rank of position				.00
No	75.6%	64.7%	84.1%	
Group leader	5.2	6.4	4.2	
Section level	2.05	2.4	1.8	
Section chief	2.2	2.9	1.6	
Department level	6.3	9.3	3.9	
Department chief	6.1	9.9	3.2	
Division level	1.5	2.4	.8	
Division director	1.0	1.8	.4	
Bureau level	.1	.2	.0	
Occupation				
Professional	27.8%	25.8	29.9	.00
Managerial	2.2	2.3	2.2	ns
Office	17.5	18.4	16.8	ns
Commercial	7.0	6.0	7.7	ns
Service	4.7	2.9	6.1	.00
Farm	.1	.2	.1	ns
Manufacturing	21.4	26.1	17.8	.00
Monthly salary	663.7	739.2	603.1	.00
Year-end bonus	1,114.4	1,231.5	1,024.1	.00

ns: not significant.

and there is no significant difference in age between the male and female respondents. Nine of ten respondents were married, 6.7 percent were single, and 3.3 percent were divorced or widowed. About half (52 percent) of the respondents lived in large cities when they were sixteen years old. Female respondents were slightly more likely to have lived in large cities than males.

Deficit in Human and Institutional Capital

This study examined three types of capital: human, institutional, and social. Human capital is indicated by education, work experience, tenure, and on-the-job training. Education is measured by years of education. As can be seen in Table 7.1, about a third of the respondents had less than high school education, 41 percent of them had high school education, and a quarter of them had college or higher education. Males were better educated than females. Males also had somewhat longer work experience (an average of 22.3 years) than females (21.1 years), but there was no difference in tenure or in number of years at the current work unit. Males were also more likely to have received on-the-job training (in terms of the number of different types of training and the number certificates received from training) than females. In short, then, males showed substantial advantage over females in human capital.

Institutional capital is capital associated with the identification and association of prevailing ideology and power (Lin 1994b, 1995b; see also Chapter 11). It is indicated by membership in the Communist Party, ownership of the work unit, and rank of the current position. Party membership was coded as (1) not a member, (2) a Party member when entering the current job, and (3) a Party member when entering the first job. As can be seen in Table 7.1, a significantly higher percentage of males (36.2 percent) than females (19.9 percent) were Party members, and male Party members had been in the Party relatively longer than females.

Until recently, ownership of the work unit differentiated workers in the Chinese dual labor market (Lin and Bian 1991; Bian 1994). However, in the 1990s, a more diverse and marketized labor market emerged. A small but increasingly significant market was created by joint ventures (although most of the Chinese partners in these firms were state or collective enterprises or institutes), private firms, and household (self) enterprises. Of these types of work units, collectives are most disadvantaged, as they do not have the security and status of the state work units or the economic and market benefits of the joint ventures. Currently, private and household enterprises tend to be small in both size and scale of economy. As can be seen, a significantly larger percentage of females (15.5 percent) than males (9.2 percent) were employed in the collectives.

Rank of current position is another indicator of institutional capital, since these positions command differential resources in the state and collective enterprises where over 90 percent of the respondents work. Again, there was a significant difference in the ranks occupied by males and females. Over four-fifths (84 percent) of the females held no rank titles compared to less than two-thirds (64.7 percent) of the males. Close to a quarter (23.6 percent) of the males held ranks at and above departmental level compared to less than one-tenth (8.3 percent) of the females.

In short, then, males held an overwhelming advantage over females in institutional capital.

Measures of Social Capital: The Position Generator

The third type of capital studied was social capital. I employed the position-generator method for measurement (for a review of this method, see Chapter 6). Two types of social capital were constructed: general social capital and political social capital. The instrument used is reproduced in English in Appendix 7.2.

For general social capital, thirteen occupations were sampled from a full list of all occupations to represent different levels of socioeconomic status (SES) (see Bian 1994 and Lin and Ye 1997 for the occupational socioeconomic scale development and status scores for various occupations in China). These were university professor (SES score of 91), mayor (83), head of a bureau (76), lawyer (72), journalist (68), head of an enterprise (67), chief of a section (60), elementary school teacher (58), worker (45), administrative personnel (45), electrician (44), farmer (30), and housemaid (11). The position generator question was: "Of your relatives, friends, and acquaintances, is there anyone who has the jobs listed in the following table?" If the response was "yes," the respondent was asked if she or he knew this person at the time when she or he was looking for the current job. If the response was again affirmative, the respondent received a score of "1" for that position and was asked a series of questions concerning the relations between the respondent and the position occupant. If the respondent knew more than one occupant of the position, we asked him or her to think of the first occupant who came to mind. Information regarding indirect access (access through intermediaries) was also obtained but was not used in the present study.

From these data, three variables were constructed: (1) the number of positions accessed, (2) the prestige score of the highest accessed position, and (3) the range of the prestige scores of positions accessed (the difference between the highest and lowest prestige scores among accessed positions). These were indicators of access to general social capital.

Since political connections may remain significant in state socialist China, the instrument also listed three Party cadre positions: (1) provincial or city Party secretary, (2) Party secretary of a bureau, and (3) Party secretary of a factory or institute; these positions formed a political power hierarchy. Again, three variables were constructed: (1) the number of positions accessed, (2) the rank score of the highest accessed position, and (3) the rank scores range of positions accessed. Variations of the three scores, as will be seen, were very limited, but results suggest that they were meaningful.

Deficit in Social Capital for Females

Table 7.2 presents the basic statistics on the two types of social capital variables. First, we summarize general social capital. As can be seen, the average number of accessed positions was 6.7 out of 13 sampled positions, with males accessing an average of 7 positions and females 6.5, for a statistically significant difference. The highest prestige among accessed positions was 75 (about the position of the head of a bureau), with males again having a significant advantage over females (76 versus 74.2). The range of prestige scores between the highest and lowest prestige scores of accessed positions was 40, with males advantaged over females (41.3 versus 39). It is clear that males had significantly better general social capital than females on all three indicators.

Table 7.2. *Access to Two Types of Social Capital*

Variable	Sample Gender	Percentage or Mean		Sig.
		Males	Female	
General social capital				
Number of positions accessed	6.7	7.0	6.5	.00
Prestige of highest accessed position	75.0	76.0	74.2	.00
Range of prestige of positions accessed	40.0	41.3	39.0	.00
Accessed positions (prestige score)				
University professor (91)	34.8%	39.4%	31.4%	.00
Mayor (83)	9.7	12.5	7.6	.00
Head of bureau (76)	23.8	29.0	20.0	.00
Lawyer (72)	28.0	32.6	24.6	.00
Journalist (68)	27.4	31.2	24.6	.00
Head of enterprise (67)	61.5	65.3	58.6	.00
Chief of a section (60)	81.7	85.5	78.8	.00
Elem. school teacher (58)	75.1	74.6	75.5	.56
Worker (45)	94.4	95.1	93.9	.18
Administrative personnel (45)	70.8	72.8	69.3	.04
Electrician (44)	79.5	83.6	76.3	.00
Farmer (30)	72.3	73.9	71.0	.09
Housemaid (11)	25.5	24.7	26.1	.39
Political social capital				
Number of positions accessed	.62	.72	.55	.00
Prestige of highest accessed position	.59	.69	.52	.00
Range of rank of positions accessed	.11	.15	.08	.00
Accessed positions (rank score)				
City secretary (3)	4.0%	5.5%	2.8%	.00
Bureau secretary (2)	8.4	11.5	6.1	.00
Factory secretary (1)	49.9	56.1	45.2	.00

The most accessible position was worker (94 percent of the respondents), followed by chief of a section (82 percent), electrician (79 percent), elementary school teacher (75 percent), farmer (72 percent), administrative personnel (71 percent), and head of an enterprise (62 percent). There was a sharp drop in accessibility from over half of the respondents to less than a third of the respondents. The next cluster of accessed positions included lawyers (28 percent), journalists (27 percent), housemaids (26 percent), and heads of bureaus (24 percent). The least accessible position was mayor, accessed only by 10 percent of the respondents. This pattern reflected the differentials in social contacts among a representative sample of urban respondents who showed, not surprisingly, greater contacts, and therefore access, to others who occupied positions either similar to their own or slightly higher or lower than theirs, in the prestige hierarchy's middle rankings.

The advantage of males over females was reflected in most of the sampled positions. As shown in Table 7.2, male respondents were more likely than females to access every position except elementary school teachers, workers, farmers, and housemaids, all of which were on the lower half of the prestige ranking scale. Thus, the males had an advantage in reaching positions similar to or better than theirs in the prestige hierarchy.

As for political social capital (also shown in Table 7.2), males had the advantage over females on all three variables. They accessed more cadre positions, higher-ranked cadres, and a larger range of positions. At each hierarchical level, males also had greater access.

To assess whether the three variables for each type of social capital could be considered as a cluster, or indicators of a single dimension perhaps called "access to social capital," we performed a factor analysis on the three variables. The analysis (principal component and varimax rotation), as shown in Table 7.3, resulted in a three-factor solution for each type of social capital.

For general social capital, the first factor had an eigenvalue of 2.47, while the second and third factors had very small eigenvalues. These results strongly suggest a single dimensionality among the three variables. When we restricted solutions for factors having eigenvalues greater than 1.0, the factor loadings of the three variables on the single factor were all very high (.84, .96, and .92). Thus, a factor score was constructed with differential weights assigned to the three variables where the range variable received the greatest weight (.13 for number of positions accessed, .63 for the range variable, and .25 for the highest prestige of an accessed position). When separate analyses were conducted for males and females, similar patterns emerged. Thus, the decision was to

Table 7.3. *Factor Structures of Access to Social Capital*

Variable		Sample	Males	Female
General social capital		(N = 2,713)	(N = 1,147)	(N = 1,566)
Factors eigenvalues	Factor I	2.47	2.46	2.48
	II	.00	.01	.00
	III	−.08	−.08	−.08
Factor loading on Factor I*				
Number of positions accessed		.84	.83	.85
Range		.96	.96	.96
Highest		.92	.92	.91
Factor scoring on Factor I*				
Number of positions accessed		.13	.11	.14
Range		.63	.64	.62
Highest prestige		.25	.25	.25
Political social capital		(N = 2,811)	(N = 1,188)	(N = 1,623)
Factors eigenvalues	Factor I	2.44	2.52	2.36
	II	−.01	−.01	−.01
	III	−.03	−.02	−.03
Factor loading on Factor I*				
Number of positions accessed		.98	. 98	.98
Range		.73	.77	.67
Highest rank		.98	.98	.98
Factor scoring on Factor I*				
Number of positions accessed		.51	.54	.47
Range		.03	.03	.03
Highest rank		.46	.42	.50

* Principal component, minimal eigenvalue of 1, and varimax rotation.

use the same scoring weights to construct a general social capital score for all respondents.

For political social capital, a three-factor solution also showed concentration of variance explained in the first factor and similarity in the solution patterns for both males and females. Factor scores of the three variables on the first principal factor again yielded almost identical patterns for males and females. However, unlike general social capital, where the range variable carried the strongest weight or coefficient in the score, the number of positions accessed and the highest rank had high coefficients. This is understandable, as the range was extremely limited and overlapped substantially with the other two variables.

It is clear that inequality between urban Chinese males and females in social capital as of 1998 was due at least in part to capital deficit. This capital deficit by females prevailed in all three types of capital: human capital, institutional capital, and social capital.

Further Analysis for Social Capital Deficit

How, then, is social capital related to the other two types of capital – human capital and institutional capital? Would such relations account for the relative deficit of social capital for females? Human capital and social capital, as conceptualized (see Chapter 2), are expected to be related. It would be interesting to assess whether such a relationship varies for males and females. As argued elsewhere (Chapter 11), institutional capital is significant in the labor market for both organizations and individuals as they attempt to match and interact with the larger society's prevailing values and practices. In Chinese society, even in the 1990s, the Communist Party held much of the valued resources and exercised power over much of the population. Whether such institutional capital was differentially related to social capital for males and females, especially to political social capital, deserves research attention.

Kin versus Nonkin Ties

In addition to these two types of capital, the nature of social ties evoked in accessing social capital was considered. The question posed was: do different types of social ties lead to differential access to social capital? As conceived by the network location scholars (see Chapters 3 and 5), ties that serve as bridges in the networks might be more useful in accessing better-embedded resources in the social structure. No direct measure was possible in the survey instrument to assess whether each position accessed was a bridge in the shared networks. However, the survey did ascertain the relationship between the respondent and the occupant of the position accessed (see Appendix 7.2). A simple kin versus nonkin classification was constructed. I use this measure to represent stronger versus weaker ties. In the Chinese context, kin ties represent extensive yet strong ties (Lin 1989). This does not argue that only kin ties are strong; even in the Chinese context, other social ties (e.g., coworkers, school alumni, regional ties) may also be strong (Bian 1997; Ruan 1998). Thus, this measure is a relatively weak and conservative estimate of tie strength. The initial hypothesis is that, following Granovetter's argument (1973, 1974), *weaker ties (i.e., nonkin ties) tend to access better general social capital.*

However, the cultural context of Chinese society presents an alternative consideration. Much has been said about the significance of familial ties among the Chinese (Fei, 1947/1992). Some have ventured to suggest that familial ties constitute the meaningful core social structure in a Chinese society (Lin 1989). Because the Chinese definition of family

extends beyond the immediate nuclear family to include multiple generations and multiple clan and marital linkages, it may well be that such
extensive networks provide sufficient access to many parts of the society.
Further, in a society where formal institutions block many forms of
legitimate access to resources, trust is paramount when interpersonal
relations are evoked for utilitarian purposes. There is evidence (Bian,
1997) that stronger ties rather than weaker ties are preferred when
seeking effective help in job searches. Thus, accessing power positions
(Party cadres) in a state socialist system may signal informal access
to resources that cannot be accessed through formal channels and
processes. Such relationships are better if they remain informal and
"invisible" so that exchanges can continue in the constrained structure.
To maintain such informal ties would probably require commitments to
relations (see Chapter 9) beyond casual exchanges and transactions.
Thus, stronger ties might network well here. Given these considerations,
it may be postulated that in Chinese society, kin ties present a certain
advantage in political exchanges. We therefore propose the alternative
hypothesis that *kin ties rather than nonkin ties access better political
social capital*. We will submit these two alternative hypotheses to empirical examination.

In Table 7.4, the relative advantages or disadvantages of kin versus
nonkin ties in accessing the positions are examined. In general social
capital (the first thirteen rows of Table 7.4), females were more likely
than males to use kin ties to access most positions. The only exceptions
were elementary school teachers and housemaids, where males used kin
ties as much as or more than females for access. In other words, males
were more likely than females to use nonkin ties to access most positions. When it came to accessing elementary school teachers and housemaids, males were just as likely to use kin ties – probably their spouses.
Since we know that males are advantaged in accessing social capital,
these data strongly hint that nonkin ties are more likely to access better
social capital. This speculation is confirmed when we examine the zero-
order correlations between the use of kin ties and the three variables of
general social capital. As can be seen in the next three rows of the table,
all coefficients were negative, indicating that the use of kin ties was negatively related to the number of positions accessed, the range of prestige
scores among accessed positions, and the highest prestige score of an
accessed position. Thus, we conclude that nonkin ties are more advantaged in accessing the general social capital. If nonkin ties represent
weaker ties, then this result confirms the strength-of-weak-tie argument
proposed by Granovetter.

The lower panel of Table 7.4 examines the relationship between the
use of kin ties and access to political social capital. While there was no

Table 7.4. *Access to Social Capital by Kin*

		Percentage Using Kin Ties		Gender
	Sample	Males	Females	Sig.
General social capital				
Accessed positions (prestige score)				
University professor (91)	34.5%	33.2%	35.7%	.41
Mayor (83)	15.1	14.8	15.6	.85
Head of bureau (76)	22.4	19.2	25.8	.04
Lawyer (72)	15.0	12.4	17.5	.04
Journalist (68)	13.4	8.6	18.0	.00
Head of enterprise (67)	11.5	8.8	13.9	.00
Chief of a section (60)	13.3	10.8	15.3	.00
Elem. school teacher (58)	26.1	26.4	25.9	.79
Worker (45)	19.2	16.4	21.3	.00
Administrative personnel (45)	15.8	12.1	18.9	.00
Electrician (44)	13.7	10.9	16.0	.00
Farmer (30)	74.4	70.1	77.1	.00
Housemaid (11)	21.1	27.5	16.6	.00
Association (*r*) between	Percent Using Kin Ties			
Number of positions accessed	−.26***	−.20***	−.29***	
Range of prestige scores	−.16***	−.11***	−.18***	
Highest prestige score	−.20***	−.17***	−.21***	
Political social capital				
Accessed positions (prestige score)				
City secretary (3)	13.6%	14.1%	13.0%	.88
Bureau secretary (2)	11.4	7.3	17.2	.02
Factory secretary (1)	5.4	3.8	6.9	.01
Association (*r*) between	Percent Using Kin Ties			
Number of positions accessed	.05*	.04	.08*	
Range of prestige scores	.05*	.05	.07*	
Highest prestige score	.07**	.05	.10**	

* $p < .05$; ** $p < .01$; *** $p < .001$.

difference between males and females in using kin ties to access city secretaries, females were again more likely to use kin ties to access bureau and factory secretaries. However, in contrast to the negative association between kin ties and better general social capital, there were positive correlations between kin ties and access to political social capital. These associations were much more pronounced for females than for males. If kin ties represent stronger ties, then there is some evidence that, perhaps for females, stronger ties may have a slight advantage than weaker ties in their accessing political social capital.

Patterns of Capital Deficits

Next, I conducted a multivariate analysis in which access to social capital was regressed on the nature of social networks (percentage of kin ties in the access to social capital), human capital (education), and institutional capital (party membership) simultaneously. Different equations were constructed for the two types of social capital (general and political) and for males and females. Also, for each equation, age, marital status (married), and household size (logged) were controlled for. As presented in Table 7.5, access to social capital for both males and females was affected by human capital (education), as expected. Institutional capital (Party membership) had only a slightly positive effect on social capital. Network effects were significant but, as shown earlier, were more complex. Use of kin ties had negative effects on general social capital, whereas use of kin ties had positive effects on political social capital. Also, the network effects were more significant for females than for males.

We may summarize the findings thus far regarding the distribution of social capital for females and males – the issue of capital deficit. There was a substantial capital deficit for females. Males showed access to a

Table 7.5. *Determinants of Access to Social Capital (Partial Regression Coefficients, with Standardized Coefficients in Parentheses)*

Exogenous Variable	Access to General Social Capital		Access to Political Social Capital	
	Males ($N = 1{,}004$)	Females ($N = 1{,}393$)	Males ($N = 997$)	Females ($N = 1{,}389$)
Age	.10	.05	.01**	.01**
	(.06)	(.03)	(.10)	(.12)
Married	.79	.98	.03	.07
	(.02)	(.02)	(.01)	(.05)
Household size (log)	−1.26	2.79**	−.03	.00
	(−.04)	(.08)	(−.02)	(.00)
Education	2.84***	3.1***	.10***	.10***
	(.21)	(.19)	(.19)	(.19)
Party membership	1.01	1.67*	.04	.05
	(.04)	(.06)	(.05)	(.06)
Percent accessed	−7.28***	−11.36***	.11	.21**
through kin	(−.11)	(−.20)	(.04)	(.11)
Constant	27.92	28.24	.39	.31
R^2	.07	.09	.05	.06

$p < .01; p < .001.$

greater number of occupational and political positions, to higher positions in the hierarchies, and to a greater variety of positions. Social
capital was found to be significantly related to human capital. Because
males had higher educational attainment than females, there was a corresponding advantage in their social capital as well. There did not seem
to be much difference in whether institutional capital (Party membership) affected social capital for females and males. Weaker ties (nonkin
ties) facilitated access to general social capital, and stronger ties (kin ties)
enhanced access to political social capital. Females seemed to rely more
on such network ties to access social capital than males. Whether
such differential access to social capital translated into advantages or disadvantages in generating returns in the labor market will be examined
next.

Return on Social Capital

The next analytic tasks were to assess the effects of social capital on
status attainment. Four attainment variables were used: (1) work sector
(work unit ownership), (2) rank of position, (3) job prestige, and (4)
monthly income (logged). As seen in Table 7.1, the work sectors in which
the respondents were currently employed included the state sector, the
collective sector, joint-venture enterprises, private enterprises, and the
self-employed. Working in the state was a distinctive advantage (Lin and
Bian 1991; Bian 1994) and was considered by many as the primary target
of status attainment, rather than job or income per se. While the rapid
transformation since the late 1980s in the social stratification system and
in the reconstruction of state enterprises might have affected the work
preferences of workers, the state sector – especially with its dominance
in agencies, organizations, and institutes – might still offer advantages
over the emerging private and joint-venture sectors in areas such as job
security, housing discounts, health care, and pensions.

Rank of position (also seen in Table 7.1) reflects an array of positions
along a hierarchical structure. For the present analysis, these positions
were converted into an ordered set ranging from "1" for no title to "9"
for bureau or higher level. The occupational groupings, as shown in
Table 7.1, were also examined as dummy variables. In both multinomial
and logistic regression analyses, these groupings showed linear relationships (in terms of estimate coefficients), in either ascending or descend-
ing order, with other key variables (e.g., sector, rank, and income),
farming, and manufacturing alternately showing the lowest coefficients.
Thus, for parsimony, it was decided that the current job of each respondent would be converted into a prestige score, according to the scheme

developed by Lin and Ye for China (1997). Two measures of income were used: the current monthly salary and the current monthly income, which included both salary and bonus.

These variables are seen as a sequential set of statuses of attainment: an individual first enters a work sector, assumes a ranked position in the organization, occupies a job, and earns an economic return. The analyses will focus on each of these attainment variables as the endogenous (dependent) variables in the sequence. As the analysis proceeds to later endogenous variables in the sequence, preceding endogenous variables also become exogenous variables. The first set of analyses assesses the effects of human capital (education, training, and certificates), institutional capital (Party membership), and social capital (general and political) on landing in one of the work sectors in the current job. Since there were five sectors (state, collective, joint venture, private, and self-employed), multinomial logistic regressions were employed to estimate the odds-ratio likelihood of being in a particular sector given these exogenous variables. As shown in Table 7.6, the state sector is the (missing) reference sector. Thus, these estimates showed the relative effects of human capital, institutional capital, and social capital on each of the other sectors compared to those in the state sector. Separate analyses were conducted for males and females. Age and urban residence at age sixteen were also controlled for.

Experience and tenure were both highly correlated with age (.94 and .54). In the Chinese context, most workers still enjoy lifetime employment; and experience and tenure do not add any additional asset to

Table 7.6. *Determinants of the Sector of the Current Job (Multinomial Logistic Regression Coefficients, with State Sector as the Comparison Group)*

	Sector							
	Collective		Joint		Private		Self	
Exogenous Variables	Male	Female	Male	Female	Male	Female	Male	Female
Age	−.01	−.02*	−.02	−.09**	−.08*	−.02	−.05*	−.06*
Urban	.09	.04	1.21**	1.36	1.67	1.52	.88	.84
Education	−.44**	−.57**	.11	−.41	−.68*	−.73	−.30	−.57*
Training	.12	−.09	.34	.80	.97	−18.12**	−19.53**	.52
Certificates	−.45	.16	−.33	−.47	−1.59	—	—	−1.13
Party membership	−.24	−.20	−.06	−.10	.33	—	−1.14*	−.59
General social capital	.00	−.01	−.00	.02	.00	−.01	.01	.00
Political social capital	−.42*	−.13	.08	−.24	.38	.02	−.41	−1.15*
Constant	.82	2.47	−3.49	−.49	.29	−.80	−.29	1.01

* $p < .05$; ** $p < .001$.

seniority, as represented by age. Since age, training, and certificates are already in the equations, experience and tenure were excluded, as their inclusion would have simply created multicolinearity biases to the estimates.

Since most of the respondents were in either the state or the collective sector, the analyses for the remaining sectors (i.e., joint ventures, private enterprises, and self-employed) were based on small sample sizes, with unreliable estimates. Nevertheless, the patterns seem consistent. As expected, education had a negative effect in any sector other than the state sector. This effect was most pronounced for those in the collective sector. Training also showed some negative effects for those in private or household enterprises compared with those in the state sector. However, due to small sample sizes, these effects were unreliable. Party membership also had a slight but consistently negative effect on being in any sectors other than the state sector. Social capital had slight negative effects, especially for males in the collective rather than the state sector and for females in the household enterprises sector. Thus, we found moderate but consistent negative effects of human capital, institutional capital, and social capital for those not in the state sector.

Our analyses now turn to three sequential endogenous (dependent) variables: being in the state sector, the rank of the position, and job prestige. As can be seen in Table 7.7, I employed a path-analytic strategy in the analyses since these three dependent variables were considered in a causal sequence, with the assumption that entering work sectors preceded holding a rank or a position, and gaining jobs with certain prestige which, in turn, resulted in differential earnings. Again, analyses were conducted separately for males and females.

The first two columns in Table 7.7 present the results of logistic regression analyses pertaining to entrance into the state sector compared to other sectors. Being in the state sector was highly associated with education. Training and certificates were correlated with education (.24 and .21) and did not show any significant marginal effects. Being a Party member was also significantly associated with being in the state sector. Social capital showed positive but marginal effects, except for females. Females benefited from political social capital in entering the state sector. Thus, there is little evidence that females entering the state sector suffered a return deficit in social capital.

The third and fourth columns in Table 7.7 examine the effects of these variables on gaining higher-ranked positions. In addition, sectors were entered as an exogenous variable in the ordinary regression analyses (the state sector was used as the reference sector). As can be seen, both males and females generated returns from human capital (education and age), with the benefit more pronounced for males than for females. Institu-

Table 7.7. *Determinants of Sector, Rank of Position, and Job Prestige (State Sector as Reference)*

Exogenous Variables	State Sector[1]		Rank of Position[2]		Job Prestige[2]	
	Male	Female	Male	Female	Male	Female
Age	1.02***	1.02**	.05***	.02***	−.15*	−.04
			(.21)	(.11)	(−.07)	(−.01)
Urban	.61**	.70**	.03	.08	−2.66*	−4.78***
			(.01)	(.02)	(−.06)	(−.09)
Education	1.34***	1.60***	.52***	.27***	3.73***	5.48***
			(.28)	(.19)	(.26)	(.23)
Training	.84	1.05	−.04	.25*	2.34	1.47
			(−.01)	(.11)	(.07)	(.04)
Certificates	1.14	.91	.37	.19	−2.69	1.92
			(.10)	(.07)	(−.07)	(.04)
Party membership	1.61***	1.49**	.93***	.75***	1.91	2.09
			(.28)	(.28)	(.06)	(.04)
General social capital	1.00	1.01	.01	−.00	.06	.03
			(.04)	(−.01)	(.04)	(.01)
Political social capital	1.24	1.29**	.16*	.23***	.77	.22
			(.06)	(.11)	(.03)	(.01)
Sector (state sector as reference)						
Collective			.29	.06	−3.00	6.20***
			(.04)	(.01)	(−.04)	(.09)
Joint			−.14	−.28	1.38	5.48
			(−.01)	(−.03)	(.01)	(.03)
Private			−.49	.01	.02	9.48
			(−.02)	(.00)	(.00)	(.04)
Self			−.13	−.13	2.59	17.66***
			(−.01)	(−.01)	(.02)	(.10)
Rank					1.70***	1.02*
					(.17)	(.06)
Constant			−3.33	−.97	35.24	30.93
R^2			.27	.22	.18	.11

[1] Logistic regression estimates (odds ratios).
[2] Partial regression coefficients, with standardized coefficients in parentheses.
* $p \leftarrow .05$; ** $p \leftarrow .01$; *** $p \leftarrow .001$.

tional capital (Party membership) benefited males and females equally. Political social capital had a positive effect on the ranking of the position, especially for females.

The last two columns in Table 7.7 estimate the effects of these variables, plus the rank of the position, on job prestige. Again, both males and females benefited from education. Social capital no longer had any direct effects; rather, their effects on job prestige, especially the effect of political social capital, were mediated through being in the state sector and the position ranking – also institutional capital. Position rank benefited males more than females in getting more prestigious jobs. While being in the state sector (in contrast to being in the collective sector) ben-

Table 7.8. *Determinants of Salary*[1]

	Monthly Salary (Logged)			
	Model 1		Model 2	
Exogenous Variables	Male	Female	Male	Female
Age	−.00	−.00	−.00	−.00
	(−.02)	(−.00)	(−.01)	(−.00)
Urban	.01	.07*	.04	.10*
	(.01)	(.04)	(.02)	(.06)
Education	.08***	.19***	.07***	.18***
	(.14)	(.25)	(.11)	(.23)
Training	.04	.06	.01	.03
	(.04)	(.05)	(.01)	(.03)
Certificates	.03	.11	.05	.13
	(.02)	(.08)	(.04)	(.09)
Party membership	.02	.05	.00	.05
	(.02)	(.04)	(.00)	(.03)
Sector (state sector as reference)				
Collective	−.28***	−.06	−.29***	−.03
	(−.12)	(−.03)	(−.13)	(−.02)
Joint	.46***	.78***	.45***	.74***
	(.13)	(.14)	(.13)	(.13)
Private	.09	.28	.23	.27
	(.02)	(.04)	(.04)	(.04)
Self	−.08	.21	−.08	.28*
	(−.02)	(.04)	(−.02)	(.05)
Rank	.04**	.04**	.04**	.04*
	(.11)	(.08)	(.12)	(.07)
Job prestige	.00**	−.00	.00*	−.00
	(.08)	(−.01)	(.08)	(−.01)
General social capital			.00**	.01***
			(.09)	(.09)
Political social capital			−.04	.07*
			(−.04)	(.06)
Constant	5.78	5.05	5.63	4.89
R^2	.11	.15	.12	.16

[1] Multiple regression coefficients (standardized coefficients in parentheses).
* $p \leftarrow .05$; ** $p \leftarrow .01$; *** $p \leftarrow .001$.

efited males in getting more prestigious jobs, females seemed to get better jobs if they were in the collective sector. Since the collective sector is a peripheral sector in comparison to the state sector, it is clear that institutional capital was a more effective mediating factor in political social capital effects on job prestige for males but not for females.

Finally, we turn to income (monthly salary and income logged). In Table 7.8, the first two columns examine effects of human capital and institutional capital on salary for males and females. While females seemed to benefit more from human capital (education), males tended to benefit more from institutional capital. Both rank and job prestige showed much stronger effects on salary for males than for females. Being in the joint-venture sector generated the best returns for both males and females. However, being in the state sector, in contrast to being in the collective sector, greatly benefited males but not females. When the two social capital variables were added to the equations (the third and fourth columns), both males and females generated returns from general social capital. Females, however, gained added, though moderate, benefits from political social capital. Analysis for income (salary and bonus), as shown in Table 7.9, yielded results that were almost identical to those obtained for salary alone.

In summary, there is some evidence that females do not particularly suffer a return deficit on social capital in entering the state sector, gaining higher-ranked positions, or earning higher wages. In fact, they enjoy a slight edge in generating return from political social capital, getting into the state sector, and gaining higher-ranked positions and better wages. These findings do not imply that females have gained equality in rank, occupations, or wages. In fact, they fared much worse than males on these status measures in the stratification system (see Table 7.1). These findings merely suggest that females need to mobilize political social capital effectively to close these gaps somewhat.

What accounts for the effects of political social capital for females? As we already understand from Table 7.2, females suffered a deficit in both general social capital and political social capital compared to males. While social capital was associated with human and institutional capital, there was no evidence that females gained any advantage over males because of these other types of capital. In fact, females suffered from capital deficits in these two domains as well. The clue to females' ability to deflect these deficits somewhat lies in the nature of social ties accessing political social capital. As shown in Table 7.4 and discussed earlier, kin ties constitute a positive factor in accessing political social capital, and more females use kin ties than males.

In further exploring these social ties to access political social capital, it was suspected that access to factory and bureau secretaries was a key, as females were much more likely than males to use kin ties to access these key positions (Table 7.4). The data in Table 7.10 show that, especially in accessing factory secretaries, these ties tended to be through a spouse and a sibling's spouse for females. Thus, females may have gained some benefit through such strong ties in accessing local political resources, as these family ties helped some female workers move up in the work unit ranks and gain a break in wages.

Table 7.9. *Determinants of Income*[1]

Exogenous Variables	Monthly Income (Logged Salary and Bonus)			
	Model 1		Model 2	
	Male	Female	Male	Female
Age	−.00	−.00	−.00	−.00
	(−.02)	(−.02)	(−.02)	(−.02)
Urban	.01	.08*	.03	.11**
	(.01)	(.05)	(.02)	(.06)
Education	.08***	.19***	.07**	.18***
	(.14)	(.25)	(.12)	(.23)
Training	.07	.05	.04	.02
	(.06)	(.04)	(.04)	(.02)
Certificates	.00	.12	.03	.15
	(.00)	(.09)	(.02)	(.11)
Party membership	.02	.07	.01	.06
	(.02)	(.05)	(.01)	(.04)
Sector (state sector as reference)				
Collective	−.28***	−.08	−.30***	−.06
	(−.12)	(−.04)	(−.13)	(−.03)
Joint	.48***	.77***	.46***	.73***
	(.13)	(.13)	(.13)	(.13)
Private	.08	.24	.22	.24
	(.01)	(.03)	(.03)	(.03)
Self	−.11	.15	−.11	.22
	(−.03)	(.03)	(−.03)	(.04)
Rank	.04**	.04**	.04***	.04*
	(.12)	(.08)	(.12)	(.07)
Job prestige	.00**	.00	.00**	.00
	(.08)	(.01)	(.09)	(.00)
General social capital			.01**	.01***
			(.10)	(.10)
Political social capital			−.04	.06*
			(−.05)	(.06)
Constant	5.81	5.13	5.63	4.95
R^2	.13	.15	.13	.17

[1] Multiple regression coefficients (standardized coefficients in parentheses).
* $p \leftarrow .05$; ** $p \leftarrow .01$; *** $p \leftarrow .001$.

Summary and Discussion

A critical issue for social capital research is the extent to which inequality in social capital contributes to social inequality across social groups. This chapter conceptualizes this issue by proposing the analysis of two processes from the capital perspective: capital deficit and return deficit. Capital deficit is the extent to which different social groups, for reasons

Table 7.10. *Access to Factory and Bureau Secretary by Tie Relationship*

| | Percentage of Positions Accessed | | | |
| | Factory Secretary | | Bureau Secretary | |
Tie Relationship	Males (N = 710)	Females (N = 759)	Males (N = 137)	Females (N = 99)
Kin ties				
Father	.70%	.53%	.73%	4.04%
Mother	.00	.13	—	—
Siblings	.42	.26	.73	2.02
Spouse	.14	1.05	—	—
Parents of spouse	.14	.13	—	—
Siblings of spouse	.42	.40	—	—
Spouse of siblings	.00	.53	—	1.01
Son	.00	.00	—	—
Daughter	.00	.00	—	—
Son-in-law	.00	.00	—	—
Daughter-in-law	.00	.13	—	—
Relatives on father's side	.42	.13	2.19	2.02
Relatives on mother's side	.42	.66	1.46	2.02
Son's children	.00	.00	—	—
Daughter's children	.00	.00	—	—
Other relatives	1.13	1.71	2.19	6.06
Nonkin ties				
Workmate	10.42	5.93	9.49	6.06
Supervisor	66.20	70.75	57.66	50.51
Subordinate	4.08	1.98	6.57	3.03
Neighbor	2.25	3.24	2.19	6.06
Good friend	4.37	2.90	4.38	5.05
Ordinary friend	8.45	7.91	12.41	12.12
Other	.23	.26	—	—

of investment or opportunities, have come to possess a different quality or quantity of capital. Return deficit is the extent to which a given quality or quantity of capital generates differential returns for different social groups due to differential mobilization strategies, agent efforts, or institutional responses. Since it is assumed that social inequality results from inequality in capital, it becomes important to understand inequality in capital. These formulations help clarify the mechanisms by which inequality in various types of capital, including social capital, emerges for different social groups, and how it potentially affects social inequality among members of different groups.

Data from urban China residents were used to explore these mechanisms for male and female attainment in the labor market. With the position-generator instrument used to measure both general and political social capital, the results confirm that Chinese female workers suffer a deficit in social capital as well as human and institutional capital. Males show access to a greater number of occupational and political positions, to higher positions in hierarchies, and to a greater variety of positions. Social capital is found to be significantly related to human capital. Because males have higher educational attainment, they have a corresponding advantage in social capital as well. There does not seem to be much difference in whether institutional capital (Party membership) affects social capital for females and males.

On the other hand, there is some evidence that females do not particularly suffer from a return deficit in social capital upon entering the state sector, gaining higher-ranked positions, or earning higher wages. In fact, they enjoy a slight edge in generating returns from political social capital, entering the state sector, gaining higher-ranked positions, and earning higher wages. These findings do not imply that females have gained equality in rank, occupations, or wages. In fact, they fare much worse than males on these status measures in the stratification system. These findings merely suggest that females need to mobilize political social capital effectively to close these gaps somewhat.

One clue to why females are able to bridge the gap is due to the nature of the ties used to access social capital. Females seem to rely more on kin ties to access social capital than males do. Since weaker ties (nonkin ties) facilitate access to general social capital, females thus become disadvantaged in accessed capital. However, stronger ties (kin ties) enhance access to political social capital due to the need for trust and commitment in such relations in China. Thus, some females, relying on their spouses and the spouses of kin, might be able to gain better access to political social capital, which helps to overcome their disadvantages in entering the state sector and gaining higher-ranked positions and better wages.

As mentioned in Chapter 6, differential access to social capital deserves much greater research attention. It was suggested that social groups (gender, race) have different access to social capital because of their advantaged or disadvantaged structural positions and social networks. For the disadvantaged to gain a better status, strategic behaviors require them to access resources beyond their usual social circles (Ensel 1979), find sponsors in the firm (Burt 1998), and join clubs dominated by males (Beggs and Hurlbert 1997); find ties outside their own neighborhood or those who are employed (Green, Tigges, and Browne 1995); or find ties across ethnic boundaries (Stanton-Salazar and Dornbusch 1995; Stanton-Salazar 1997). This study, in a limited way, illustrates the viability of the capital perspective in analyzing social inequality.

The notions of capital inequality, capital deficit, and return deficit help us to decompose and clarify the mechanisms by which inequality of capital (especially social capital) comes about between social groups and the consequences of these inequalities for social inequality. At the same time, they help to isolate the cultural and institutional nature of such inequalities for a given society and demonstrate the strategic significance (i.e., for females to use kin ties to access political social capital) for the disadvantaged within such institutional contexts. The research agenda outlined and the empirical study explored in the present chapter suggest that systematic empirical investigations equipped with specific measures and designs to flush out institutional and cultural variations can be fruitful in advancing understanding of capital inequality and social inequality for different social groups, on different social inequalities, and in different communities and societies.

Appendix 7.1. *Sampled Cities and Number of Respondents in the Urban China Study, 1998*

City	Sample	1996 Relative Labor Force (10,000)
Beijing	300	326.58
Taiyuan	150	144.09
Shenyang	300	304.36
Dandong	150	113.11
Shanghai	400	560.02
Nanjing	150	160.92
Anqing	100	33.73
Nanchang	150	44.29
Wendeng	100	34.99
Huaihua	100	30.81
Guangzhou	200	240.23
Nanchong	100	96.79
Chongqing	300	324.18
Yuxi	100	21.78
Xi'an	150	165.21
Pingliang in Gansu	100	19.71
Ge'ermu in Qing Hai	100	4.62
Tacheng (in Xinjinag)	100	7.66

Appendix 7.2. *Position Generator of Social Capital*

Of your relatives, friends, and acquaintances, is there anyone who has the jobs listed in the following table? If yes, what is your relationship to them? If no, through whom are you most likely to find people holding such jobs? What is your relationship to this person?

Occupation	Do you know people in the position? 1. Yes 2. No	Did you know the person when you were looking for your present job? 1. Yes 2. No	What is his/her relationship to you?	If you do not know such a person, through whom are you most likely to find him or her?	What is this person's occupation?	How long have you known each other?	Do you know each other well?
Elementary school teacher							
Journalist							
Administrative personnel of public or private enterprises							
Electrician							
Chief of a section							
Head of public or private enterprises							
University professor							
Farmer							
Head of a bureau							
Lawyer							
Housemaid							
Mayor							
Provincial or city party secretary							
Party secretary of a bureau							
Party secretary of a factory							

Part II

Conceptual Extensions

8

Social Capital and the Emergence of Social Structure

A Theory of Rational Choice

This chapter[1] focuses on the problem of how rational actions lead to social structure. So far in this monograph, the social capital theory has been developed and research undertaken to understand the meaningfulness of actions within the context of social structure. That is, the theory has addressed the issue of actions while acknowledging and recognizing the a priori existence and effect of social structure. What I propose to explore in this chapter is the plausibility that actions may lead to social structure. That is, I seek to develop some theoretical arguments to answer the question of whether rationality based on resource maintenance or defense, as well as resource expansion and gain, allows us to better understand the rules of interaction and the formation of primary social groups (e.g., the primordial group). And further, whether consideration of social capital's relative utility to personal capital offers the theoretical plausibility that rational actions may indeed lead to the emergence of social structure beyond the primordial group.

This chapter sketches a theory proposing how actions may lead to the emergence of social structure. I choose to theorize this process because it should theoretically (logically) precede processes dealing with interdependence and mutual causation between structure and action. Once the issue of action leading to the emergence of structure is explicated, interdependence and interaction between the two should follow (action affects structure and structure affects action). By focusing on the issue of an emerging social structure, I hope to shed light on other critical issues involved in action theory: what rationality is, what principles guide action and interaction, and why social structures (group and collectivity) are not only possible but inevitable from such action and interaction principles.

---

[1] A significant portion of this chapter was adapted and revised from Lin (1994a) with permission.

My basic arguments are three. First, rational action is seen as having multidimensional motives regarding valued resources. At least two are considered fundamental: minimization of loss and maximization of gain. These are independent, though empirically correlated, calculations, with the former claiming priority over the latter (see Chapter 4). Second, these calculations, and the problem of succession, lead to rules of resource transfers and the primacy of the primordial group. Interactions and collective action in the primordial group are guided primarily by the sentiment to retain and defend resources and secondarily by the need to gain resources. Third, in general, the utility of social capital (resources embedded in social ties) substantially exceeds that of personal or human capital. This calculation, in the face of the scarcity of valued resources, propels the extension of interactions beyond one's primordial group. Once such ties and exchanges are formed, certain collective rules follow. These rules, beyond interacting actors' original intents and interests, constitute the basis for social structure formation.

This chapter will follow some fundamental propositions concerning action and interaction in the proposed social capital theory (Chapter 5) to describe the primordial group's formation and significance. It will then specify the relative utilities of human and social capital, and argue that social capital's relative utility constitutes a motive for interaction and exchange with actors outside the primordial group. The chapter concludes with some further discussion on the nature of the emerging social structure. These explorations are speculative in nature and will be inevitably brief here. The purpose, nevertheless, is to present the key arguments and outline a set of propositions so that further elaboration and evaluation are possible.

Before we begin, it is useful to locate this problem in the context of theorization about social structure and action.

Sociological Theorizing

One way to categorize theorization in sociology is to capture how a theory specifies its causing and consequent concepts relative to two levels of society: structure and actors. If these two levels constitute a dichotomy, a simple typology may look like the one presented in Table 8.1. This typology identifies four types of theory. A macrotheory specifies both cause and effect concepts at the structural level, while a microtheory posits a relationship between them at the actor level. A structural theory links causal structural concepts to effectual actor-level concepts, and an action theory hypothesizes structural effects of actor-level concepts.

Table 8.1. *A Typology of Sociological Theorization Based on Macro–Micro Specification*

	Causal Concepts	
Effectual Concept	Structure	Actors
Structure	Macrotheory	Action theory
Actors	Structural theory	Microtheory

This is a simplification, because it is possible to specify a more complex theory that involves cause or effect concepts at both structural and actor levels or concepts implicating more than two levels (e.g., individual actors, organizations, and society; see Hannan 1992). For example, a theory concerning an actor's psychological well-being (an actor-level effect concept) may be specified as a consequence of both her or his network support (a structural-level concept) and her or her self-esteem (an actor-level concept) (see, e.g., Lin, Dean, and Ensel 1986). Likewise, a theory may concern the income level as a consequence of the education level (an actor-level concept), the nature of the firm (an organization-level concept), and the industrial sector (an economy or society-level concept) (see, e.g., Kalleberg and Lincoln 1988).

Given these precautions, the typology in Table 8.1 informs us of the fundamental theoretical process within which a particular theory positions itself. My sense is that of the four types, action theory is the most challenging and controversial. It is challenging because its causal concepts clearly intersect those primarily and usually identified as under the domains of other scientific disciplines: economics, psychology, or cultural anthropology. Rational choice theory, for example, extensively borrows the economic assumptions concerning optimization or maximization of choices relative to self-interest (Coleman 1990). Psychological and personality characteristics lay claim to concepts such as *well-being, distress,* and *attitudes* (see the discussion of shame in Elias 1939/1978 and that of emotion in Scheff 1992). Norms, values, and traditions can hardly be dissociated from collective and socialization experiences (Marini 1992). An action theory does not wish to disown these potential sources of action (or *spring of action,* as Coleman 1990 calls it). It merely considers them as factors exogenous to the theory. The theory nevertheless needs to demonstrate that it involves more than a simple derivation from concepts already claimed theoretically by other disciplines.

Action theory is also controversial because its principal proposition concerning the causal linkage from action (the actor-level concept) to structure seems to suggest that the whole can be explained by its inter-acting parts. In general, trans-level causation is harder to demonstrate theoretically than same-level causation. Structural theory, however, has at least the advantage of the omnipresence of structure over actors. Thus, when it is claimed that an actor's job-seeking behavior is dictated by the tightness of the labor market, it is hardly possible to place such actions outside the context of the labor market.[2] Action theory, on the other hand, does not have this advantage because it is generally assumed that the structure is more than the sum of actions and interactions of actions (see the argument of structural or organizational robustness in Hannan 1992). Further, once a structure is in place, it becomes theoretically dif-ficult to rule out the continuous interaction between structure and action. An action theory faces the constant challenge to demonstrate whether and how effects of action remain when or after structural effects are taken into account. Abell (1992, p. 186) correctly points out that the primary puzzle for a rational choice theory is to demonstrate how "interdependent individual actions produce system (or collective) level outcomes."

Principles of Action: Minimization of Loss and Maximization of Gain

The theory begins with two simple assumptions about motives for action: actions are primarily driven or motivated by the innate need for survival, and survival is seen as dependent upon the accumulation of valued resources. These assumptions regarding the motives (springs) for action require no further elaboration. What needs to be explored are the prin-ciples for action – choices and priority among choices. Again, for sim-plicity, I assume that action is driven by the desire to defend (maintain) resources or to seek (expand) resources.[3] Action driven by resource defense is a calculation for minimizing resource loss (relative loss to cost). Action driven by resource expansion, on the other hand, is a calculation for maximizing resource gain (relative gain to cost). Based on leads from previous sociological theories (the homophily principles and predomi-nance of expressive needs) and research evidence (see Marini 1992 for a review of evidence supporting the claim that in routine behavior, defend-ing against loss may be a greater concern than seeking gain) regarding the relative significance of assessing losses and gains, I now propose that defending resources has higher priority than expanding resources.[4]

---

[2] This is not to argue for or claim the proposition's validity.
[3] This assumption is consistent with the purposive action approach.
[4] This is valid only if the actor has some resources to begin with.

Proposition 1: Defense and maintenance of resources is the ultimate motive for action. Thus, *the first principle of action is a
calculation of minimizing (resource) loss.*

Proposition 2: Gaining and expanding resources is the next
primary motive for action. Thus, *the second principle of
action is a calculation of maximizing (resource) gain.*

These propositions present two important arguments. First, minimization of loss and maximization of gain are two different functions
rather than inverse functions of each other.[5] They may involve different
choices (what kind and how much of a resource) and therefore different
preferences. Second, they form a ranked action set rather than a
dichotomy. A series of actions may manifest two motives: minimizing
loss and maximizing gain. Given the opportunity, actions are taken to
fulfill both motives. However, when the actor must make a choice, preference is given to maintaining resources: the higher priority is given to
the calculation that minimizes loss.

Recognition and Profit: Principles of Interaction

How would these two action principles implicate interactions? They
would, first of all, suggest that interactions are engaged primarily for
minimizing resource loss and secondarily for maximizing gain. An interaction following the principle of loss minimization strives to defend loss
of resources to another actor. The best possible outcome is that there is
no loss. If both actors employ the minimization principle, one local equilibrium is that both actors accept the no-loss outcome for both actors.
In social terminology, this outcome is a *mutual recognition* of each
other's claim to their respective resources – property rights.[6] Recognition
therefore is a cost to each actor in that ego abandons any challenge to
the alter's sovereignty over its resources.[7] It is a minimal cost.

This is a local equilibrium, because it is very constrained. First, it
assumes that only two actors engage in the interaction. When multiple
actors (three or more) are engaged, a coalition is likely to result and the
local equilibrium becomes increasingly difficult to maintain. Second, it
is seldom the case that the two actors bring equal resources to bear in
the interaction. Thus, recognition itself becomes a variable rather than

---

[5] Empirically, they may be negatively correlated.

[6] *Trust* may be an alternative term. However, I believe recognition may be evoked without
trust, which has a stronger affective meaning. See Chapter 9 for further discussion of
recognition.

[7] Note that this would be considered a mere stalemate or a worst outcome if the principle of maximization is evoked.

a constant. That is, recognition may occur with unequal costs to the two parties. One actor may be willing to give more recognition to the alter in that ego not only disclaims the alter's sovereignty over resources, but also commits itself to come to the defense of the alter, should its sovereignty be challenged in interactions with other actors. Or recognition may be maintained only after an actor has also agreed to give up some resources to the alter. Thus, at a minimum, there are two types of recognition. In the first instance, where mutual recognition is achieved with minimal cost to each actor (Pizzorno 1991), we may consider the recognition as approval or social approval (Lindenberg 1992). In the second instance, recognition implicates legitimation – certain generally accepted rules for responsive actions to ensure recognition. Third, seldom do actors use the pure minimization principle in a series of actions. Recognition may be a temporary outcome – until one or more actors proceed to evoke the principle of maximization of gain.

Thus, in realistic situations, recognition usually comes as an outcome with unequal costs to parties, an issue I will address in more detail in the next chapter. Nevertheless, I argue that it is the fundamental principle for interactions, for it guarantees the minimal survival of an actor and is consistent with the first principle of action (Proposition 1).

Proposition 3: *Interaction, following the minimization principle of action, seeks recognition of one's claim to resources.*

The element of recognition, I argue, is consistent with some concepts acknowledged or developed by several rational choice theorists (Pizzorno 1991; Lindenberg 1992). What is made explicit here is that recognition in interactions can be understood when action is motivated by the principle of minimization of loss rather than maximization of gain.

I will skip further discussion of interactions based on the principle of maximization of gain, for they would merely reflect the usual economic calculations as developed extensively in the literature. What needs to be studied at this point is how these principles of action and interaction offer clues to the emergence of social structure.

Succession and Transfer of Resources: The Primacy of the Primordial Group

Human actions are further compounded by additional innate but prominent life circumstances: finality of life and reproductivity of life. Survival of an individual actor is limited in time. One possible consequence of an actor's exit might be that all resources associated with the actor revert back to a pool for other actors to compete for. However, this strategy would mean a total loss of resources to the actor after lifelong efforts (actions and interactions) to maintain and expand them.

Alternatively, the resources may be transferred to another actor(s). An extension of the primacy of the principle of minimization of loss (Proposition 1) suggests that the actor prefers to transfer claimed resources to another actor deemed most suitable as a surrogate. Suitability is reflected in the extent to which the surrogate is easily identified with the actor in continued recognition and legitimation relative to other actors. Reproductivity of life, in most societies, offers an easy rule to identify the surrogate. Thus, for most societies, the primordial group, the family, becomes the immediate and natural extension of the actor.[8]

The primacy of the primordial group for succession and transfer of resources further incorporates noneconomic considerations into actions. Restriction of succession within a primordial group reduces the range of the surrogate's choices. Depending on the rules of succession, the choice may be reduced to zero degree (e.g., the oldest son as the successor). Thus, recognition and legitimation considerations are given increasing priority over competence and skills that are useful in maximizing gains – the economic calculation. It is clear that the existence of the primordial group, as it prevails throughout human history, makes any theory based on economic calculations alone unattainable.

This last conclusion does not lead to another conclusion: that actions are not rational. If rationality is defined as the process of reasoning by way of calculation over choices, then it is clear, as argued earlier, that recognition and profit provide rational bases for interaction choices.

Human Capital, Social Capital, and Social Network

The need to minimize loss and maximize gain establishes two building blocks to understand interactions beyond the primordial group. However, we need to introduce another building block: consideration of

---

[8] Elsewhere (Lin 1989), I discuss rules of transfer and types of resources transferred. There are variations in transfer rules within the context of family. For example, inheritance rules vary across societies, and there is no uniformity regarding unigeniture, primogeniture, or even-distribution principles, even though there seems to be a strong tendency toward male primacy. In the most interesting case, the Chinese traditional system uses split rules: primogeniture for authority inheritance but even distribution among sons for property inheritance. The resulting conflict and chaos, as well as the diminishing pooled resources, cannot be explained by any economic principles. Nor is the family group (predominantly the primordial group in most systems) the only primordial group. A primordial group can be and has been constructed on other bases (e.g., ethnic, religious, and gender identities). These variations, however, do not affect subsequent arguments in the chapter.

the relative utility of two kinds of resources, human capital and social capital.

Human capital is resources in the possession of the actor who can make decisions (exercise authority) about their usage and disposition. These possessed goods can also be transferred to designated successors as the actor sees fit. Social capital is resources attached to other actors. Interactions and relations with other actors offer the possibility that such resources can be borrowed for ego's purposes. In return, the borrowed resources must be returned, replaced, or reciprocated. In the most primitive terms, borrowing a neighbor's cutting instruments during a harvest is one example of access to and use of social capital. Once the harvest is over, the instruments are returned (either intact or replaced) to the neighbor. More important, the expectation is that the neighbor may borrow ego's resources, such as his son, to help him harvest as well.

Because of the constraints attached to the use of social capital, as well as the energy and resources required to maintain relations and reciprocal transactions, sentiment dictates a preference for the accumulation of personal capital rather than social capital. That is, the relative cost (temporality in use, obligation for return or replacement, and commitment for reciprocity) for using human capital is much lower than that for using social capital. How do we account, then, for the use of social capital and therefore the maintenance of social relations? That, of course, is the critical and pivotal issue in any theory linking actions to structure.

The pinnacle argument, for me, rests with two central theoretical propositions:

> Proposition 4: *The accumulation of social capital is much faster than that of human capital.* That is, *accumulation of human capital tends to be additive* in nature, whereas *accumulation of social capital tends to be exponential.*
>
> Proposition 5: *When interactions outside of one's primordial group are intended to gain resources, they are used more for accessing social capital than gaining human capital.*

Human capital is accumulated by actions taken by the actor and members of his or her primordial group. Each action generates a given amount of additional resources. Therefore, there is a tendency to expand the primordial group (e.g., the extended family) so that the generation and accumulation of resources can accelerate.

Social capital, on the other hand, is generated by creating and maintaining social ties. A relation with a social tie suggests a linkage and therefore access to the tie's resources: social capital for ego. Further, once a tie is accessed, not only do his or her resources become social capital to ego, but the alter's social ties also offer possible social capital. Con-

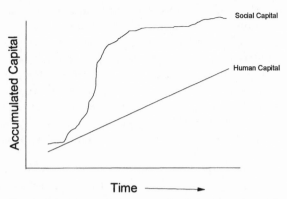

Figure 8.1 Accumulation rates for human and social capital.

ceivably, social capital might be accessible through ego's network of direct and indirect ties. The extent of access to such social capital, of course, depends on how much resources are at the disposal of the social ties, as well as on the nature and extent of the ties. As these ties extend into a network of both direct and indirect ties, the pool of social capital grows exponentially. Thus, by using the networking principle, the potential pool of social capital becomes extended quickly. The hypothesized rates are depicted in Figure 8.1.

Further considerations need to be taken into account in developing possible models of exponential accumulation of social capital. The free rendition in Figure 8.1 is entirely conjectural. The slope of the S-shaped curve is based on the assumption that interactions and networking extend slowly at first, probably among a small number of actors with similar resources, and then quickly, to larger numbers of actors with dissimilar and better resources as the network extends through indirect ties. It plateaus and reaches an upper limit, because the function must be constrained by an efficiency factor (it may be a function of the number of intermediary links, associated negatively with recognition and legitimation and positively with the cost or multiplicity of reciprocal obligations).

While the relative cost of accumulating and using social capital is high, there are conditions in which such cost is more than compensated for and exceeded by the relative advantage in the speed of accumulating social capital. The calculation tipping in favor of social capital approaches inevitability for most actors due to the likelihood of two limiting conditions for the accumulation of human capital: the ultimate limiting size of the primordial group and the scarcity of materials for resources.

As mentioned earlier, one way to speed up the accumulation of human capital is to expand the primordial group, whose membership shares the interest in resource production and transfers. However, as the size of the primordial group increases, it also creates problems for the maintenance of centralized authority over resources and competition for the succession to resource entitlement. To maintain the primordial group's expansion, more and more resources must be generated so that there is sufficient sharing among members. So long as there are plenty of raw materials for resource production, the primordial group's expansion can continue.

However, it is inevitable that multiple groups seeking resources increase in size to the point where they have to compete for materials. Competition for scarce materials can be and is ended at a primitive level by one group taking physical possession of other primordial groups and turning the members of these groups into resource-generating instruments – enslaved laborers. However, unless the ability to take possession of another group is overwhelming in terms of relative size or superiority of instruments (technology), there is always a risk that the confrontation will result in the enslavement of ego's group instead.

An alternative to enslavement in the face of material scarcity is access to and use of social capital, even though such use, as discussed, incurs a greater cost than the use of human capital. Once such a rational decision is made, interactions with actors beyond one's primordial group not only take place, they are actively sought for their access to social capital. Such access is also entirely consistent with the motives for actions (minimizing loss and maximizing gain) and the principles of interactions (recognition and profit). Social capital can be mobilized to accomplish both purposes.

The Emergence of Structure

Such access comes at an important cost – willingness and preparedness to reciprocate in terms of recognition and profit. There must be a commitment to provide one's own resources as social capital to others. To ensure stable access to social capital and to demonstrate reciprocity, interactions are routinized – that is, social relations are formed. The maintenance of social relations is likewise based on the two rational principles specified in Propositions 1 and 2. Social capital is used primarily and is relied on to maintain, sustain, and defend one's resources. It is used secondarily to gain additional resources. Legitimation guides reciprocity and the calculation process. The calculation is complicated by the fact that routinized social relations directly and indirectly involve multiple actors and their primordial (and extended) groups. While such relations promote access to social capital, recognition and legitimation of relations and obligations quickly increase the complexity of calculations. That is, sharing social capital and an increasing need for legitimation rules go hand in hand. In subsequent actions, an actor's calculation must take into account whether the action is consistent with the obligation to defend and/or expand the resources of the interacting actors.

The multiplicity and complexity of routinized social relations demand increasing rules of recognition and legitimation. These rules recognize the basic right to human capital (property) and, at the same time, specify responsibilities and obligations for actors in the interacting network to contribute resources. Recognition, in fact, is an important way to overcome a possible cost of unequal exchanges – why someone in a higher social position and with richer resources would be engaged in repeated exchanges with someone in a lower social position and with poorer resources. I will elaborate on this function further in the next chapter.

Collectivity and Public Capital

Once such social relations and sharing of resources are established and maintained, a collectivity is formed. A *collectivity* is an aggregation of actors and primordial groups bound together for the sharing of social capital. A collectivity can also decide to produce further resources that belong to the collectivity rather than to specific actors – the *public capital*. The persistence of a collectivity depends on a set of formal and informal rules governing actors relative to each other and to the access and use of shared resources. These rules establish differential obligations and rewards for member actors.

Differential obligations are necessary because the collectivity's continued existence depends on the maintenance and gain of shared resources. Obligations include two types: (1) recognition and loyalty (sentiment) to the collectivity and its rules and (2) amount and type of performance (work) in the production of shared resources, especially public capital. The loyalty factor minimizes the loss of public capital, and the performance requirement maximizes the gain of such resources. *Differential rewards* are necessary because actors are evaluated as differentially fulfilling their obligations to the collectivity. Thus, more rewards are given to those who demonstrate a high degree of loyalty and/or a high level of performance. Rewards can be symbolic as well as material. Material rewards include the designation and allocation of resources to the actor-occupants (the gaining of human capital) and the authority to access and use shared resources (public capital). Symbolic rewards include public commendation of the actor-occupant and assurance of the transfer of such honors to the actor's future generations. Another increasingly important reward system concerns rules and procedures for allocating enforcing agent positions in the collectivity. This will be discussed further.

These obligations and rewards, while required for the continued existence of a collectivity, both complement and compete with the primitive obligations actors have for themselves and their primordial groups. They are complementary because the shared resources in the collectivity supplement human capital, so that shortage of human capital no longer need always be a threat to survival. They are competitive because energy allocation for resource production and loyalty commitments can be taxing.

There is the inevitable conflict of interest, however. Since primitive motives drive the actors to maintain and gain human capital rather than public capital, willingness to perform and be loyal to the collectivity and collective goods depends on at least two important factors: (1) how important the public capital is to the actors and (2) how collective obligations and rewards, in terms of loyalty and performance, synchronize with primary obligations and rewards. The more positive the two evaluations, the more likely the actors will be willing to perform and be loyal to the collectivity and the collective goods. In the extreme situation, an actor may be willing to make the ultimate sacrifice, his or her own life, in order to preserve shared resources for the primordial group and the collectivity.

If the two factors are not seen as matched, two outcomes are likely. The actor may choose to leave the collectivity, at the risk of losing public capital but in the hope of finding another collectivity better matched to the interest of ego and his or her primordial group. Alternatively, there is an increasing likelihood that the actor will become a free rider, who takes and treats shared resources as human capital. There are, of course, risks associated with both of these choices. Leaving increases the problem of protecting oneself and finding resources for survival. Free riders may run the risk of punishment (deprivation of human and public capital) established by the collectivity, which will be discussed later.

As the size of the collectivity increases, interactions become fragmented (localization of networks) and shared resources become segmented (localization based on shared resources and characteristics). At the collective level, obligations and rewards must be continuously revised to cover the increasing number of actors and their need for public capital. As a result, the proportion of collective obligations and responsibility overlapping with individual actors and their primordial groups decreases. Routinized recognition and legitimation will decrease in their utility to bind actors to the collectivity.

Social Contracts

To ensure that collective obligations and rewards are perceived as matched with those of member actors, structural problems of fragmentation and segmentation are overcome, loyalty and performance are exercised, and exits and free rides are minimized, a collectivity can develop and employ three strategies: (1) cultivate actors through education and acculturation to *internalize* collective obligations and rewards (Bourdieu and Passeron 1977; Marini 1992); (2) engage in mass campaigns promoting the *identification* of the actors with the attractiveness of shared resources and the collectivity (Putnam 1993); and (3) develop and enforce rules for *forced compliance*. Kelman's (1961) discussion of the three processes (internalization, identification, and compliance) implies that these strategies form points along two axes. Compliance can be achieved with maximal speed but a minimal span of effect. When control is present, compliance is quickly achieved (e.g., war prisoner's behaviors). But when it is absent or lifted, such behaviors will also quickly change or disappear. Internalization, on the other hand, takes the longest time to achieve, but the consequent behaviors presumably persist with minimal control. Discussion of the employment of these strategies is beyond the scope of this chapter. What needs to be emphasized is that each of these strategies entails the development of rules of engagement for actors in the collectivity. Further, agents and agencies of enforcement must be developed.

These enforcing actors are used to administer and manage activities as well as enforce the collectivity's rules. They are rewarded according to the evaluation of their performance. The emergence and necessity of these enforcing agents generates further relationships between actors and the collectivity. These agents assume authority over individual resources and act on the collectivity's behalf. While they are expected to defend and expand individual actors' resources as well, their ultimate rewards come from demonstrating loyalty to the collectivity and to public capital expansion.

As scarcity of resources increases and the collectivity grows in size, the enforcing agents gain prominence among members, as the collectivity's survival increasingly depends on the agents' enforcement of rules. One important means of integrating actors, shared resources, and rules is to specify positions (corporal actors) with defined roles relative to types and amounts of resources; to execute the rules; and to designate actors as occupants of the positions. Thus, a hierarchy among actors will emerge not only because of differential obligations and rewards, but also because of differential allocation and the opportunity to be enforcing agents.

These obligations, rewards, and opportunities form the basis of agency relative to the positions they occupy.

Sources of Tension in Social Systems

Space does not permit further elaboration of the relationships between corporal (enforcing) actors and natural actors, the formalization of legitimation and profit rules in the realized social system, and the perpetual tension between loyalty and profit for a social system and its individual and corporal actors. However, I can point out several sources of tension in social systems that can develop. The most obvious one is the tension between human capital and public capital. Because of the ultimate survival instinct and the cost of accessing public capital, there is a much stronger tendency for a natural person to strive for human capital. A social system needs to strike a balance between providing opportunities for the participants to maintain and gain reasonable amounts of human capital and enforcing their willingness to produce and maintain public capital.

A second source of tension is the balance between mobility and solidarity. Mobility represents the opportunity to move up in the social hierarchy, whereas solidarity is the need to share sentiment and legitimacy with regard to other participants' interests and resources.[9] Mobility encourages actors to break away from their social circle of shared interests and resources in order to gain more or better resources in the social system. Solidarity relies on identification with others who share similar

---

[9] I define *solidarity* as the degree of sentiment and legitimacy regarding one another's resources, as expressed by a collectivity's actors. This conception is somewhat similar to Hechter's (1983) conceptualization. Hechter, using a rational-choice perspective, suggests that the solidarity of a group become possible when two elements are present: (a) dependence relations between individuals and the group, as determined by access to alternative sources for resources, and (b) a monitoring capacity of the group in terms of both monitoring individuals' behaviors and sanctioning behaviors via leadership. Thus, Hechter's work can be seen as an attempt to specify further the interactions linking individuals to obligations and reciprocity and thereby to various market, authority, and norms systems that Coleman (1986a, 1986b) suggested but never specified. The first element identified by Hechter is a direct application of the dependence-power theory advanced by Emerson and Cook (Emerson 1962; Cook, Emerson, Gillmore, and Yamagishi 1983; Yamagishi, Gillmore, and Cook 1988). It emphasizes the significance of networking among individuals and issues of resources deemed valuable to individuals. It can follow from the basic argument of individuals seeking maximal resources through interactions with multiple actors. However, this resource-dependence or power argument, I would argue, is not a necessary condition for solidarity, which for me reflects more a mutual sentiment and thus a predisposition among members to reinforce and defend one another or shared resources. The second element, the monitoring capacity of the group via leadership, creates a component that hints at the legitimation process.

resources and sentiments. Overemphasis on mobility tends to break down social identity and group cohesion. Overemphasis on solidarity fragments sectors of the structure and creates potential class identification and conflict. Striking a balance between the two is critical for the survival of the social system.

Still another source of tension is related to the system's size. One consequence of increasing size is decreasing shared resources relative to the amount of resources unique to member actors. Thus, the value attached to the commonality of shared resources decreases among the members. This creates a tendency for member actors to form subsets of relations with others who share resources of common interest and value. Special interests and lobbying efforts by the subsets of actors and collectivities competing for rules in their favor can tip the legitimacy of the rules regarding the distribution of shared, especially public, resources available to the system. As shared resources become relatively more scarce, these competitions, if unchecked or unresolved, may lead to fragmentation of loyalty. Loyalty then shifts to groups or clusters within the system rather than embracing the structure as a whole, endangering the identity and continued existence of the system as a whole. How to maintain the structure while it continues to grow in size and faces increasingly shared resources is an issue no open social system can avoid (see a similar discussion in Coleman 1986a, 1986b).

Concluding Remarks

In this chapter, I have proposed two types of rational principles for action, minimization of resource loss and maximization of gain, with the former claiming primacy. This position, in support of the primacy of action and the viability of rationality as a theoretical argument, challenges the exclusive use of the economic profit-maximization (or even profit-optimization) approach as the sole basis of accounting for human actions, interactions, and the functioning of social organizations. Further noneconomic but quite rational calculations naturally and logically flow from issues fundamentally linked to the nature of human life, such as reproduction and succession, sovereignty of property, and the need for recognition of such sovereignty – issues that any theory of human society cannot ignore but that the economic approach does.

Consideration of these issues does not relegate sociology's significance to psychology or cultural anthropology. Claims to property rights, recognition, transfer of resources, and succession are clearly all socially driven. They describe social life and social activities and are meaningful only in interactive and networking contexts.

Not only does rationality for action spring from the innate nature of human life, but principles of interactions cannot afford to ignore two different types of resources: personal and social. A model that considers only transactions of human capital will never be able to account for the links between actors and social structure, because social networks and social capital are at the core of the micro–macro link. Concepts of power, dependence, solidarity, social contracts, and multilevel systems do not make sense until social capital is brought into consideration.

This chapter demonstrates how several simplified propositions concerning principles of action and interaction thus conceived can explain the emergence of social structure from bases of action and interaction: an action theory of society. The propositions and theoretical arguments presented here, I believe, provide building blocks for further analysis of the formation and development of social institutions and organizations. For example, considerations can be extended to multiple social contracts and the subsequent hierarchical structure subsuming these contracts by way of variations in the social (recognition), political (legitimation), and economic (profit) rules.

Once a social system is in place, it inevitably becomes the dominant aspect of social life. Its imposition on individuals is increasingly pervasive. Therefore, we must necessarily take structural effects as given when we describe observable social systems. I agree with Hannan's observation (1992) that organizations take on characteristics that are unintended and unpredictable from individual actions. However, the principle of the *robustness* of social systems, I believe, is derivable from the same principles guiding individual actions and interactions. That is, principles of loss minimization and gain maximization, rules of resource transfer and succession, and the primacy of social (public and shared) capital over human capital guide institutions and organizations to establish rules in their authority, opportunity, and sociocultural structures. Collective interest supersedes individual interest, just as primordial group interest supersedes individual actor interest. Loyalty supersedes performance in reward/punishment rules as recognition supersedes profit for individual actors. While the principles are similar, the primacy of collectivity over individuals forges structural variations not accountable from individual action and interactions.

Ultimately, a viable social theory must integrate both individual and structural elements. A comprehensive and balanced treatment of these two elements, I suspect, is the challenge sociologists must accept in order to offer theories that are both analytically and descriptively valid. In the next chapter, I will continue the line of theorization commenced in this chapter and pursue the issue of why recognition, rather than resource gain, is an important element in exchanges.

9

Reputation and Social Capital

The Rational Basis for Social Exchange

This chapter continues the dialogue on action and social structure initiated in the previous chapter. As has been pointed out, the multiplicity and complexity of routinized social relations in a collectivity demand increasing rules of recognition and legitimation that recognize the basic right to human capital (property) while at the same time specifying responsibilities and obligations for actors contributing resources. Thus, recognition was also suggested as an important process for individual actors overcoming possible costs to unequal exchanges – why someone higher in social position and richer in resources would be engaged in repeated exchanges with someone lower in social position and poorer in resources. How this process operates at the interactional level has not been articulated. What needs to be understood is that unequal transactions in exchanges can and do occur because there are payoffs for the actors who give more resources than they receive and why this is somewhat related to recognition. This chapter will focus on this issue. I will set aside the legitimation issue and concentrate on the social process of recognition and its significance in exchange – a process of repeated interactions between actors and the fundamental building block of a collectivity.

Exchange: Social and Economic Elements

Exchange, a central concept in sociological analysis, can be defined as a series of interactions between two (or more) actors in which a transaction of resources takes place. By this definition, exchange has two central components: it requires a relationship between the actors, and it leads to resource transaction. Thus, exchange is social in that the relationship can be seen as interactions (Simmel 1950) in which the action of one actor during the process takes into account the action of the other actor(s) (Weber 1947, pp. 111–115). The process can be seen as economic, since transaction of resources is typical of economic acts. Therefore, an elementary exchange, evoking a relationship between two actors and a transaction of resource(s), contains both social and economic elements. It is useful here to refer to the *relational* aspect of the exchange as *social exchange* and to the *transactional* aspect as *economic exchange*.

This distinction between exchange's social and economic elements is often blurred in the research literature due to the common co-occurrence of both elements. This is especially true of the use of the term *social exchange*. That social exchange is more than social interaction is reflected in the understanding that social exchange contains the added element of resource transactions. As a result of this common usage, social exchange as a concept has been employed by scholars who have selectively focused on one of the two elements in their theoretical or research schemes.

The focus on the economic element in the discourse on social exchange can be traced to Weber. While pointing to four types of action (goal-oriented, valued-oriented, effectual, and traditional action), he concentrated his analytic effort on instrumentally rational (or rational goal-oriented) actions, which are based on the calculation of alternative means to the end (Weber 1968, p. 25). Value-oriented action is determined by a conscious belief in the value (for its own sake) of some ethical, aesthetic, religious, or other form of behavior independent of its prospect. Both types of action are based on consciously regulated comparison and choice – that is, on rationality (Misztal 1996, p. 54). The theoretical embedding of the transactional aspect of exchange in rationality of action was thus identified.

This line of argument was brought home forcefully by George Homans (1958), who clearly stated this position: "Interaction between persons is an exchange of goods, material and nonmaterial. An incidental advantage of an exchange theory is that it might bring sociology closer to economics – that science of man most advanced, most capable of application, and, intellectually, most isolated" (p. 597). For Homans, social behavior or exchange[1] focuses on the gain (value) and cost for an actor in the transaction; "the problem of the elementary sociology is to state propositions relating the variations in the values and costs of each man to his frequency distribution of behavior among alternatives, where the value (in the mathematical sense) taken by these variables for one man determine in part their values for the other" (p. 598). Thus, the interest of two actors in continuing the interactions or the relationship is con-

---

[1] Homans sees social behavior "as an exchange of activity, tangible or intangible, and more or less rewarding or costly, between at least two persons" (1958 and 1961, p. 13).

tingent on the relative utility or payoff to each in each transaction. Interest in the relationship diminishes as the relative payoff (the marginal utility) decreases. It is logical, therefore, for Homans to argue that "the principles of elementary economics are perfectly reconcilable with those of elementary social behavior, once the special conditions in which each applies are taken into account" (1961, p. 68).

Blau's (1964) work on exchange also reflects this emphasis. While admitting that social exchange may follow from social attractions, a primitive psychological tendency left as exogenous,[2] the major theoretical focus of his analysis is the linkage between transactions in exchanges and distribution of power. When an actor (ego) is unwilling or unable to reciprocate[3] transactions of equal value in an exchange with another actor (alter), one choice available to ego to maintain the relationship with the alter is to subordinate or comply with the alter's wishes – the emergence of a power relationship (p. 22). Collective approval of power gives legitimacy to authority, the backbone of social organizations. Thus, in Blau's theoretical scheme, patterns of transactions dictate patterns of relationships, and this fundamental microstructural process evokes, though not necessarily explains, the much more complex macrostructural (organizational) process.

Coleman (1990) carried this analysis further in his theory of social action, in which social exchange is a means by which actors with differential interests and controls over resources (events) negotiate (through the relative value of the resources they control, or power) with each other to maximize their control over interested resources (a new equilibrium) (pp. 134–135). The mechanism between exchanges and power seems quite similar to Blau's scheme, but the focus is on an actor's maximization of gain (control over desired resources) in this process.

By now, the sociological explication of the process of exchange seems to have fulfilled Homan's prophecy or design that sociology is being brought very close, if not identical, to the economic stance on the centrality of rational choices in economic behaviors. That is, given choices in the marketplace, an actor will choose a transaction to maximize his

---

[2] "The basic social processes that govern associations among men have their roots in primitive psychological processes, such as those underlying the feelings of attraction between individuals and their desires for various kinds of rewards. These psychological tendencies are primitive only in respect to our subject matter, that is, they are taken as given without further inquiry into the motivating forces that produce them, for our concern is with the social forces that emanate from them" (Blau 1964, p. 19).

[3] Reciprocity, in this case and in many other sociological works, implies balanced exchange or transactions of equal value (e.g., in price or money). This requirement for interaction goes beyond Weber's original conceptualization about social action, which only requires taking the other actor's interests into consideration. In that context, reciprocity does not require balanced exchange.

or her profit (e.g., more reward at less cost). Neo-classical economists have realized that certain assumptions of this profit-seeking theory are not likely to be met in reality (a perfect market, full information, and open competition), and have proceeded to specify conditions or institutions (bounded rationality, transaction costs) under which profit-seeking behavior may be moderated (see Williamson 1975; Coase 1984; North 1990). Many of the same arguments and conditions have been adopted by sociologists in analyzing organizational behaviors, power relationships, institutions, and social network and social exchange under the general rubrics of neo-institutionalism or economic sociology.

However, the significance of *relationships* in exchanges has not been ignored. From early on, anthropologists have paid attention to the relational aspect of exchanges and have argued strongly that many of these patterns are not based on economic or rational calculations. For example, Radcliffe-Brown (1952) described the exchanges among the Andaman Islanders as "a moral one – to bring about a friendly feeling between the two persons who participate" (p. 471). Malinowski (1922) drew sharp distinctions between economic exchange and social exchange (ceremonial exchange) in his analysis of Kula exchanges in the Trobriand Islands and suggested that "the real reward (of exchanges) lies in the prestige, power, and privileges which his position confers upon him" (p. 61). Levi-Strauss (1949) cited studies by Mauss, Firth, and other anthropologists in his argument that exchanges, including economic transactions, are "vehicles and instruments for realities of another order: influence, power, sympathy, status, emotion" and stated that "it is the exchange which counts and not the things exchanged" (Levi-Strauss 1969, p. 139). Gifts, for example, are exchanged between actors, but buying oneself a gift at Christmas time is meaningless (Ekeh 1974, p. 47).

Among the sociologists, Comte (1848) spoke of subordinating personal to social considerations, and Durkheim refuted Spencer's economic assumptions regarding the development of social groups. None of these scholars deny the implications of economic transactions in social exchanges, but they also emphasize the supraindividual (Levi-Strauss) and supraeconomic (Radcliffe-Brown 1952) nature of social exchanges and the significance of relationships. In each of these schemes, the relational orientation to social exchange is demonstrated in the commitment of specific actors to the exchanges on grounds other than the utility of specific resources transacted.

How are the two perspectives on exchanges to be reconciled? Several positions have been taken. One approach simply dismisses the significance of relationships in that any particular relationship is subjected to the decision-making choice of maximizing or optimizing profit. When a relationship generates a profit in transactions, it may be maintained;

when it does not, it is discarded. However, most neo-classical economists and their sociological allies take a moderate position, treating relations as the necessary "transaction cost" or "calculative trust" (Williamson 1985, 1993) in an imperfect market and under the condition of incomplete information. In this modified position, the relationship is recognized but is clearly subsumed under the transactional analysis.

Alternatively, those relationship-inclined scholars have argued that relationships are necessary and significant because not all behaviors and interactions are rational. This argument agrees that economic behavior follows the principle of rational choices, but it points out that not all behaviors are economic and thus rational. Social attractions and attachments are primitive survival instincts rather than the result of a calculation of gains and losses in alternatives. The problem here is that rational choices are seen as natural tendencies: rewards or reinforcements elicit actions and transactions, and the fittest survive. Consciousness or unconsciousness is irrelevant, as this principle applies to pigeons as well as to humans (Homans 1961, p. 80). Carrying this analysis further, it becomes problematic why some instincts are rational and others are not.

Still another identifiable argument concedes, sometimes more implicitly than explicitly, that rationality applies to social exchanges, but there are rational principles other than the individual profit-seeking motive. Because human beings take into account each other's interests in interactions and exchanges, relationships may be maintained to accommodate this rationality. There are many subarguments along this line of reasoning. Two seems quite pervasive in the literature. First, there is the argument that social approval, esteem, liking, attraction, and such are important motives for exchange. Notably in exchanges where the transactions are imbalanced, the reward for the shortchanged actor may be approval, esteem, liking, or attraction from the other actor. In this case, these symbolic rewards, rather than the material rewards (and its generalized medium, money) usually identified with economic exchanges, constitute meaningful rewards. However, for Homans, Blau, and Coleman, such rewards are different in kind but not in nature. Whether material or symbolic, as long as they represent value (or profit or interest), they are part of the rational calculation. Further, how such values have been developed is irrelevant to the theoretical development of social exchanges.

Another subargument is that human beings need trust (Luhmann 1979; Barber 1983; Misztal 1996). *Trust* may be defined as confidence or expectation that an alter will take ego's interests into account in exchanges. It represents faith that an event or action will or will not occur, and such faith is expected to be mutual in repeated exchanges. It is faith in morality, Misztal (1996) argues, that trust serves three functions: it promotes social stability (as a habitus), social cohesion (friendships), and collaborations. In other words, its motive is to maintain a group or community. Durkheim (1973) suggested that feelings of obligation and altruism as well as moral pressure, which restrains egoistic behavior, are the bases of solidarity. "Men cannot live together without acknowledging, and, consequently, making mutual sacrifices, without tying themselves to one another with strong, durable bonds" (Durkheim, 1964, p. 228). Durkheim strongly asserted the existence of a moral element in social life, which may entail the sacrifice of rewards, in quality and/or quality, on the part of the actors.

If solidarity and community are fundamental elements in human survival, why can they not be based on rational choices or economic behaviors? Simmel attempted one response, positing that exchange involves "a sacrifice in return for a gain" (Simmel 1971, p. 51) and that exchange is "one of the functions that creates an inner bond between people – a society, in place of a mere collection of individuals" (Simmel 1978, p. 175). He adds, "Without the general trust that people have in each other, society itself would disintegrate, for very few relationships are based entirely upon what is known with certainty about another person, and very few relationships would endure if trust were not as strong as, or stronger than, rational proof or personal observation" (Simmel 1978, pp. 178–179). The functioning of complex societies depends on a multitude of promises, contracts, and arrangements. Since "the single individual cannot trace and verify their roots at all," we must "take them on faith" (Simmel 1950, p. 313). *Faithfulness*, or *loyalty*, refers to the feeling of "preservation of the relationship to the other" (1950, p. 387). This need for rules of interaction and trust in complex modern society is clearly demonstrated in Parsons's proposal that trust is the basis for legitimating power to achieve collective goals and societal integration (Parsons 1963). Hechter's (1983) analysis of group solidarity also advances the rational basis for collectivity.

Luhmann (1988) further elaborates Parsons's media theory and his concept of symbolic generalization. Trust is seen as one of the generalized media of communication (others being love, money, and power), and as such reduces the complexity of the world faced by the individual actor by providing the capacity for "intersubjective transmission of acts of selection over shorter or longer chains" (Luhmann 1979, p. 49). But Misztal points out that "Luhmann is less forthcoming on the issue of how this function of trust helps to explain the actual formation of trust" (1996, p. 74).

The explanatory basis for trust, then, is the need in a complex society for individuals to rely on rules that are accepted by many people and that guide both interpersonal and impersonal exchanges – the institutions. Without such consensual rules and trust in them, societal functioning would cease. But Homans reminds us that "institutions, as explicit rules governing the behavior of many people, are obeyed because rewards other than the primary ones come to be gotten by obeying them, but that these other rewards cannot do the work alone. Sooner or later the primary rewards must be provided. Institutions do not keep on going forever of their own momentum" (1961, pp. 382–383). By *primary rewards*, of course, Homans is referring to basic individual needs for profits. Misztal agreed: "In Parsons' theory the significance of trust as a single explanatory device is clearly overstated. The notion of trust, used as a substitute for familiarity, conformity and symbolic legitimation, does not provide us with an effective instrument with which to analyze social reality" (1996, p. 72). According to Williamson (1985), unless cooperation also serves an egoistic motivation, the practices of cooperation will be unstable. This means that a social order based on trust not grounded in self-interest will be unpredictable and unstable; for this reason, trust is not always functional.

In summary, none of the arguments thus far that defend the significance of relationships in exchanges, once the transactional rationality is presented, seem satisfactory. What I will propose in the remainder of the chapter is another attempt to assert the significance of relationships in exchanges. The argument begins with the premise that rationality should be used as the basis for the theoretical development. Rationality is not a matter of conscious versus unconscious behavior. Nor does it rely on some norms or institutions; these come later. And it is not based on an expectation of ultimate transactional balance in the long run (e.g., repeated transactions will balance out gains and losses) (see Homans's refutation of these arguments for treating elementary social behaviors as rational: 1961, pp. 80–81). Here, simply, an exchange is seen as a process engaging two actors whose actions are based on calculations of gains and losses and on alternative choices in relationships and transactions. As long as such calculations and choices are made, the process is considered rational. Further, I assume that these calculations and choices are based on self-interest. This assumption does not rule out considerations of collective interest. What is assumed is that collective interest comes into the calculation only when it is embedded in self-interest; there is a self gain if the collective interest is served. What is not assumed is that collective interest, excluding self-interest, drives calculations and choices.

Transactional and Relational Rationalities

The critical element, instead, is the ultimate payoff: the kinds of rewards or resources that sustain or interrupt relationships and/or transactions. There are two ultimate (or primitive) rewards for human beings in a social structure: economic standing and social standing.[4] Economic standing is based on the accumulation and distribution of wealth (as indicated by commodities and their symbolic value representations, such as money), and social standing is based on the accumulation and distribution of reputation (as indicated by the extent of recognition in social networks and collectivities).[5] Each standing reflects the ranking of an individual relative to others in the structure over the command of the "capital" concerned. Wealth, therefore, is a functional calculus of the worth of commodities in terms of their value representation, money; reputation is a functional calculus of the worth of public awareness in social networks in terms of its value representation, recognition. Wealth is indicative of economic capital because the commodities and their value representation can be invested to generate certain returns. Likewise, reputation reflects social capital because the social networks and their value representation can be mobilized to generate certain returns. Through reputation, it becomes possible to mobilize the support of others for both instrumental and expressive actions. It is the capacity of resource mobilization through social ties, or social capital, that makes social relationships a powerful motivation for individual actors to engage in exchanges. Both economic and social standings enhance an individual's power and influence in the structure (over other members) and, thus, the individual's psychic well-being and physical survival as well.

Economic standing and social standing are complementary in that the former requires social legitimation and enforcement for its symbolic value (money), and the latter builds on the economic well-being of the group (or embedded resources in the network) in which the reputation is sustained. Without social enforcement, economic standing collapses; without collective wealth, social standing is meaningless. Yet, each standing can be seen as an independent motive in exchanges. Exchanges can be used to extract economic capital (resources through transactions) or social capital (resources through social relations).

Thus, transactional rationality drives the calculations of transactional gains and costs in exchanges, and relational rationality propels the calculations of relational gains and costs. Transactional rationality sees relationships as part of transactional gain–loss calculations, and relational rationality sees transactions as part of relational cost–benefit calcula-

---

[4] A third reward, political standing (or power), is also important, but probably is not as primitive as the other two rewards. Power, or the process of legitimation, reflects a process by which the other two primitive rewards are preserved or gained. The relationships among wealth, reputation, and power (legitimation) emerge in the discussions in the previous chapter and this chapter.

[5] The usual indicators of social standing include status (for position) and prestige (for occupant) (see Table 3.1 in Chapter 3). I adopt the more general term reputation to capture both, as overall esteem given to an actor by others.

tions. Relational rationality favors the maintenance and promotion of the relationship even when the transactions are less than optimal. Transactional rationality favors the optimal outcome of transactions even if it is necessary to terminate specific relations. While both rationalities are enacted by actors in most exchanges, for a given society at a particular time, institutions favor one rationality over the other, allowing moral judgment on the relative merits of one type of capital (economic or social) over the other. The remainder of this chapter will elaborate on these arguments.

Relational Rationality Elaborated

It seems intuitive, due to natural law and natural instinct, to understand the argument of transactional rationality – gain over cost in transactions and maintenance and accumulation of resources through transactions. Further, its calculation is helped enormously by the generalized medium of money (Simmel 1978). Gains and losses can be counted, and credits and debts documented, with ease. Accounting in relational rationality is not so easy or clear, even though Coleman (1990) notes that social credits (or credit slips) are central to the notion of social capital as well. In economic exchanges, not every episode is symmetric or balanced in the trade of goods. Imbalanced transactions incur economic credits and debts. However, it is strongly assumed that the balance of credits and debts will be achieved in the long run, but in a finite time frame, in repeated transactions.

In social exchanges where persistent relationships take on significance, episodic transactions are not necessarily symmetric or balanced. However, even in repeated transactions in a finite time frame, balanced transactions are not required. The critical element in maintaining relationships between partners is social credits (and social debts). In a persistent relationship where transactions are not symmetric even in the long run, the engaging actors are engaging in an ever greater creditor–debtor relationship – the tendency of one actor to give favors to another in imbalanced transactions. While the debtor gains, why would the creditor want to maintain the relationship and thus suffer transactionally? It is argued that the crediting actor gains social capital in maintaining the relationship. How? Presumably the creditor could call on (or threaten) the debtor to repay the debt. But so long as the creditor does not make such a demand, the debtor is perpetually indebted to the creditor. To be able to maintain the relationship with the creditor, the debtor is expected to take certain social actions to reduce the relational cost (or increase the utility of exchanges) for the creditor. That is, the debtor should propagate to others through his or her social ties his or her indebtedness to the creditor – a social recognition of credit–debt transactions, or social credit given to the creditor. *Propagation of indebtedness, or social recognition*, is a necessary action on the debtor's part for maintaining the relationship with the creditor. It leads to greater visibility of the creditor in the larger social network or community, and it increases general awareness (his or her reputation) as an actor who is willing to take a transactional loss in order to sustain the well-being of another actor in the community. The greater the social debt, the greater the need for the debtor to make an effort to disseminate (recognize) the indebtedness. From the creditor's point of view, imbalanced transactions promote the creditor–debtor relationship and the propensity to generate recognition.

Furthermore, two actors can maintain a relationship when both become creditors and debtors to each as imbalanced transactions over different kinds of commodities take place between them (giving different favors to each other). Each, then, is expected to propagate the favors rendered by the other in his or her social circles, thus promoting recognition of the other. Transactions are means to maintain and promote social relations, create social credits and social debts, and accumulate social recognition.

In a mass society, recognition can be accelerated with the use of public media as the means of transmission. Public recognition in a mass society makes recognition a public good, just as money is. Public recognition may take a variety of forms, including testimonies and banquets in one's honor, honorific titles, medals of honor, awards of distinction, certifications of service, and ceremonies of all types, none of which need involve a substantial economic payback. Thus, recognition can transcend particular social networks and become a mass-circulated asset, like money, in a social group.

Reputation, then, is defined as a function of (1) the creditor's ability to sustain unequal transactions (human and social capital), (2) the persisting credit–debt relationship, (3) the debtor's propensity (willingness and ability) to acknowledge the relationship through his or her social networks (recognition), and (4) the propensity (size) of the social networks (and generalized network – the mass network) to relay and spread recognition.[6] Reputation, then, is the aggregate asset of recognitions

---

[6] Another element, density of the network or strength of relations among actors, may also figure in the formulation of reputation. However, the association is not necessarily a linear one (either positive [the denser the network, the more likely recognition will spread] or negative [the sparser the network, the more likely it will spread]), as rumors do spread (Burt 1998b), sometimes quickly in less dense networks, as presumably more bridges become available. Because of the uncertainty in the association, I have left it out of the present formulation. Further research may identify the proper form of association, if any.

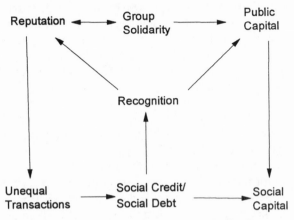

Figure 9.1 From social exchanges to capitalization.

received. It is a function of the extent to which one receives recognition in a social group. Collectively, a group's reputation is defined as the number of reputed actors in the group and the extent to which recognition is shared by the members known in other groups. Thus, the reputation of actors in social networks and a social group promotes the collective reputation of the social group.

Social credits, recognition, and reputation are all relationally and structurally based utilities. Without persistent social relations, these profits vanish. It is therefore rational for actors to engage in and commit to persistent relations that allow social credits and social debts to remain meaningful and to facilitate recognition. The greater the reputation of certain actors and the more actors enjoying a high reputation, the more the group's reputation increases. Identification with a more reputable group also enhances an actor's own reputation. Thus, there is an association between a group's reputation and the incentive for individual members to engage in persistent and maintained social exchanges and to identify with the group – group identification and group solidarity. Likewise, the groups' reputation and the reputation of an actor in the group propel the actor to continue engaging in exchanges in which he or she may remain a creditor. Reputation and group solidarity enhance the sharing of resources – the creation and sustaining of public capital. At the same time, reputation and group solidarity provide positive feedback and reinforcement of unequal transactions, social creditor–debtor relationships, and thus social capital for the actors.

Figure 9.1 depicts the hypothesized processes between microlevel exchanges and macrolevel reputation and group solidarity. For the sake of description, the process may begin with exchanges where transactions are seen as the means by which social creditor–debtor relationships emerge. Such creditor–debtor relationships then propel the spread of recognition in social networks, which eventually creates a generalized reputation that reinforces group solidarity and encourages public capital. With reputation and group solidarity, the social creditors and debtors gain social capital (embedded in social networks with strong ties and rich resources) and are further reinforced to engage in exchanges. Here the reciprocal and interactive processes between micro- and macrolevel linkages are seen as being facilitated by social networking – an essential element between exchanges and capitalization.

A group may promote solidarity and reputation by recruiting actors with a reputation established elsewhere in the society. By conferring recognition on specific actors, the group expects that these actors will identify with the group and be prepared to engage other members of the group in future exchanges. In this process, reputation and recognition are not consequences of microlevel exchanges, but antecedents to them. While the actors granted such recognition and reputation may not have been exchange partners with others in this particular group, they will become obligated to carry out such exchanges in the future, should they accept such recognition and added reputation. In this sense, microlevel exchanges and more macrolevel recognition and reputation are eventually reciprocal in causal relations.

A Summary

To summarize, some distinguishing characteristics of the two rationalities are presented in Table 9.1. The contrasts are necessarily sharp to highlight the comparison. In transactional rationality, typically implicated in the analysis of economic exchange, the purpose is to gain *economic capital (resources through transactions)* and the interest lies in the transactional aspect of the exchange – the extent to which resources are transacted, and sometimes mediated, by price and money. The utility of the exchange is to optimize transactional profit, and the rational choice is based on an analysis of alternative relationships producing varying transactional gains and costs. On this basis, the rules of exchange participation are two. First, if the relationship with a particular alter produces relative gain, then the decision is to continue the relationship for further transactions. If the relationship fails to produce relative gain, then there are two decision choices: (1) to find an alternate relationship that may produce relative gain or (2) to maintain the relationship but to suffer or to reduce the transactional cost. The decision between the two choices

Table 9.1. *Rationality of Economic Exchange and Social Exchange*

Element	Economic Exchange	Social Exchange
Exchange focus	Transactions	Relationships
Utility (optimization)	Relative gain to cost in transactions (transaction at a cost)	Relative gain to cost in relations (relationship at a cost)
Rational choices	Alternative relations Transactional cost and reduction	Alternative transactions Relational cost and reduction
Episodic payoff	Money (economic credit, economic debt)	Recognition (social credit, social debt)
Generalized payoff	Wealth (economic standing)	Reputation (social standing)
Explanatory logic	Law of nature Survival of the actor Optimization of gains	Law of humans Survival of the group Minimization of loss

is based on the relative weights given to the likely gain from a likely alternative relationship and to the likely transactional cost or its reduction in the maintenance of the current relationship. The critical analysis in economic exchanges focuses on symmetric transactions in episodic or repeated transactions.

Transactional rationality can be seen as a neo-Darwinian theory applied to exchanges – the survival of the fittest individuals. It is the instinct to find the partners who optimize resource gains through transactions with ego. The ability of ego to find relationships so that the transactional gain is relatively high or positive and the transactional cost is relatively low or nonexistent follows this instinct. Commitment to a particular alter-actor tends to be episodic and short-term, and the expectation is that the transactions are fair (more gain and less cost). Partnerships are incidental to the transactional requirements and may become binding through contractual rules so that the relationships reduce the transactional cost and justify their persistence. Therefore, transactional rationality follows the natural law and the rationality of natural choice. The actors who benefit more from repeated transactions not only enrich themselves, but collectively build a richer collectivity. Such is the argument for the invisible hand of transactional rationality.

Relational rationality, on the other hand, as implicated in social exchange, focuses on the relational aspect of the exchange – the extent to which a relationship is maintained and promoted, usually mediated by recognition (or the expectation that the other actor will spread it).

The motivation is to gain *reputation through recognition in networks and groups*, and the utility of an exchange is to optimize relational gain (maintenance of social relationships) – also an analysis of gain and cost. On this basis, there are also two exchange participation rules: One, if a specific transaction promotes a persistent relationship and the spread of recognition, then the transaction will be continued. Two, if the transaction fails to promote a persistent relationship, then two choices are considered: either (1) to find alternative transactions that will (e.g., to increase favors in transactions to entice and encourage recognition) or (2) to maintain the transaction and to suffer or reduce the relational cost (no gain or reduced gain in recognition). Again, the decision is a weighing process involving the relative likelihood of finding an alternative transaction and the relative relational cost.

Persistent relations promote the extension and dissemination of one's recognition through social connections. More persistent relations increase the likelihood of the spread of recognition. For recognition to keep spreading, the maintenance and promotion of persistent relationships are paramount. Social standing takes on meaning only when a network or group of individuals sharing and spreading the sentiment toward a particular actor persists. Thus, the larger the social connections, direct and indirect, the greater the effect of recognition and reputation. Individuals depend on the survival, persistence, and, indeed, ever-expanding nature of social circles to sustain and promote their social standing. Even those lower in social standing may gain transactionally if they remain participants in the social network and the group.

Transactional rationality is seen as invisible as it builds collective capital from individual capital, yet it depends on the generalized medium of money – a very visible form of capital requiring documentation in every transaction. Relational rationality also builds collective capital from individual capital; the more reputation its members possess, the greater the standing of the group. This relies on an even less invisible medium: recognition, or the spread of the sentiment toward an actor in a social group. It is this invisible hand that drives persistent social relations and group solidarity.

Transactional rationality can survive on an individual basis when partners in exchanges are interchangeable as long as they meet the requirements of transactional utility. Relational rationality depends on the survival of the group and the group's members. The more resources embedded in the social networks and the stronger the ties, the greater the collective benefit to the group and the relative benefit to each actor in the group.

Relational rationality is based on the principle of survival of the fittest group, a group with persisting relationships among its members. While animal instincts also show such relational rationality for family and clan members, it is only humans who show extensive and generalized relational rationality for solidarity of constructed groups beyond kin and clan criteria. Humans show an interest and ability to maintain persistent and profitable relationships at a reasonable transactional cost. Thus, relational rationality is a human law and is based on the rationality of human choice.

Further Analyses

The remainder of the chapter will be used to clarify some further issues. First, why is the term *reputation* preferred to other terms such as *social approval*, *social attraction*, and particularly *mutual recognition* or *social credits*, already available in the literature? Second, why is there a tendency in one community or society to focus on one type of rationality (transactional or relational) rather than another, and is it an indication of a historical tendency to have one rationality (transactional) superseding another (relational)? Third, what breaks down this exchange–collective solidarity linkage? Finally, are social capital and economic capital two polarized points on a single dimension, thus dictating a choice?

Reputation as Individual and Group Capital

So far, the argument for social standing such as reputation or social capital does not seem to differ from other similar arguments. Credits are seen as debts to be collected in later exchanges. Pizzorno (1991), for example, argues that mutual recognition promotes self-preservation. In order to preserve oneself, the price to be paid is the recognition that others will preserve, which presumably leads to others' recognition of one's right to preserve, a principle consistent with the argument here. However, one difficulty in using mutual recognition as the motive or justification for exchange is that mutuality implies reciprocal and symmetric actions and equity in ranking among actors. These actions and interactions lead to cohesive but homophilous memberships in a group – group solidarity without differentiation among members. What has been developed here is that recognition can be asymmetric in return for favors received in transactions and an episodic account of actions and reactions. Other terms, such as *social approval* and *social attraction*, also suffer from a similar problem. What is argued here is the need to take the next step: to recognize that it is possible to have unequal transactions in relationships and that these unequal transactions form the basis of differential social standing (reputation) among actors in a group.

Recognition offers legitimacy to the alter's (the creditor) claim to his or her resources. As recognition increases in episodes and spreads in the networks, we need a more generalized notion to capture the aggregation of episodes of such recognition accrued to an actor in a social group or community. *Reputation* is the choice proposed here, as it captures the notion that the asset can be possessed and differentiated by groups or individuals. A group can build, maintain, or lose a reputation. Likewise, within a group, individuals acquire, attain, or suffer different levels of reputation or ill repute. Thus, like wealth in economic exchanges, reputation is both an individual and a collective asset. Two other concepts seem to capture such an asset: *prestige* and *esteem*. However, prestige has been appropriated and is understood in the literature to grade positions in the hierarchical structure (e.g., occupational prestige). Esteem is widely used as either a social or a psychological process (e.g., self-esteem).

It should be noted that economists use reputation to account for the failure of economic explanations (e.g., market failures or imperfect information market). It is used as the latent variable accounting for investment in information or signaling (Klein and Leffler 1981), quality (Allen 1984), discipline (Diamond 1989), and commitment (Kreps and Wilson 1982). These other factors, then, are seen as being transmitted between transacting actors to reduce the moral hazard or transaction cost (Williamson 1985) or even to increase the price (Klein and Leffler 1981) and thus the payoff (see Zhou 1999 for a review of these accounts). Even though Grief (1989) mentions a coalition as a boundary within which reputation can be built and sustained, there is little concern or discussion among economists about the social or collective nature of reputation. Without an appreciation of its social nature, the term is reduced to an unobservable notion used to account for unexpected economic phenomena such as market failure.

In the present argument, reputation is understood as a network asset (see, e.g., Burt 1998b, for a similar yet different view). It is built on the processes of transactions and creditor–debtor relations and on the acts of recognition and dissemination in social and mass networks (see Figure 9.1). It reinforces the legitimacy of certain actors who claim their resources and positions and, at the same time, offers incentives for further social exchanges and unequal transactions among actors, enhancing their social capital. It also enhances the group or collective reputation, and thus solidarity and the building of public capital. I do not rule out other pathways leading to reputation; however, the present argument makes explicit a pathway to the construction and utility of reputation.

Institutionalization of Rationalities

If transactional rationality follows neo-Darwinism and natural law, it may be deduced that the natural selection process will eventually favors transactional rationality over relational rationality. Indeed, many examples and studies demonstrating the relational imperative of exchanges, especially from anthropological studies, draw on data and observations from ancient or primitive societies. It has been suggested that emphasis on interpersonal relationships reflects the nature of communities that are more homogeneous, less technologically developed, and less industrially developed, and where rituals, ascription, and emotion define exchanges. As a society develops technologically and industrially and becomes more diverse in skills, knowledge, and production, division of labor requires more rational allocation of resources, including the increasing importance of rationality for resource transactions in exchanges. It has further been argued that the relational significance of economic exchanges today represents residual effects from the past. As the selective process proceeds apace, relational significance will eventually be superseded and replaced by transactional significance. An analysis of exchange relations can be seen in a particular society, such as *guanxi* in the Chinese context (Lin forthcoming), or *blat* in the Russian context (Ledeneva 1998).

This view is paradoxical in that if transactional rationality is the law of nature, one would find that exchanges in the more primitive or archaic communities resemble natural instincts more closely. Indeed, Homans (1961) sees the development of more complex societies with increasing institutions as evidence of why more "primary" social behaviors (and exchanges) are becoming less visible. But these "subinstitutions" remain powerful, and unless they are satisfied by the new institutions and "good administration," they can come into conflict and disrupt them. Modern society and its multitude of institutions, then, is seen as the enemy of both transactional rationality and relational rationality.

Further, this thesis simply is not supported by facts. In studies of contemporary societies (such as China, Japan, northern Italy, and much of East Asia), even well-developed and economically competitive societies as the United States, Britain, Germany, and France, relationships remain an important factor even in economic transactions. The evidence shows that relationships in exchanges not only exist but thrive in diverse contemporary societies (Lin 1989).

If there is no logical ground or evidence to support a developmental view of relational rationality and transactional rationality, what accounts for the dominance of one rationality over the other? I propose that the

dominance of a rationality as an ideology reflects the stylized accounting of a society for its survival using its own historical experiences as
data. The theorized accounting becomes "truth" as it becomes embedded in its institutions (Lin forthcoming).

It is not hard to document that in some societies, survival and persistence are attributed to the development of wealth. Theories of wealth
and its development dictate institutionalization of transactional rationality as it characterizes the building of individual wealth and thus
collective wealth. Competition, an open market (and thus free choice of
relations in transactions), and reduction of transactional costs dictate
analytic assumptions and organizational principles. In other societies,
survival and persistence are attributed to the development of social solidarity. Theories of group sentiment dictate institutionalization of relational rationality, as it characterizes the building of collective solidarity,
and thus individual loyalty. Cooperation, networking, and thus maintaining *guanxi*, even at the cost of transactions, dictate analytic assumptions and organizational principles.

Once a rationality becomes the dominant ideology, institutions are
developed to implement, operationalize, and reinforce specific individual
and collective actions. Further, its explanatory scheme treats the other
rationality as either irrationality or noise or constraint.

The prevalence of institutional rules and the dominant ideology
ebb and flow in accordance with the rise or fall of historical experiences.
Since the nineteenth century, the Anglo-American experiences of
industrialization, technological innovations, and electoral democracy
have clearly led to its theorizing of accounting as the dominant
ideology. Wealth-building takes central stage in political strategies and
intellectual analysis. Social exchanges are markets for transactions.
Any relations that sacrifice transactional gain are attributed to an imperfect market due to lack of information, and social organizations and
social networks are necessary constraints due to such imperfections. Even
then, they inevitably incur transactional costs and should be analyzed
as such.

On the other hand, in many societies and communities, or, for
example, *guanxi* in the Chinese context, the willingness to maintain
social relations is seen as the expression and practice of the higher-order
law of morality, ethics, and obligations to other human beings. An actor's
social reputation and social standing are paramount. Reputation and
face are the core concepts in political strategies and intellectual enterprises, and transactions in exchanges are of secondary importance.
Sacrificing relationships for the sake of transactional gain is considered a lower-order rationality – as immoral, inhuman, unethical, or
animalistic.

Misrecognition and Ill Reputation

Breakdown among exchanges, relationships, recognition, and reputation can take place at every link in the process. It may begin at the exchange level, when a rendered favor in transactions is not recognized. When a creditor–debtor relationship is not recognized, the only basis for persistent exchanges is transactional utility, where relations and partners are accidental and secondary in choice considerations. When the transactional cost exceeds the benefit, the incentive to maintain the relationship no longer exists.

When a favor is recognized, the creditor can still disengage from the relationship if the network in which the recognition takes place is not resource-rich for the creditor. Recognition in a circle of baggers is not meaningful for a fashion designer or a scholar. Recognition in the wrong network or group may also be useless or even undesirable for a creditor. Acknowledging a scholar's advice in an article published in a third-tier journal will not enhance the reputation of the scholar, and in an article published in a mimeographed journal it may even damage the scholar's reputation. Further, if the recognition is not sufficient to reflect the extent of the favor given, disengagement may result. For example, acknowledging someone's help in a footnote when the helper did all the data collection and analysis would provide a disincentive for such help in the future.

Negative recognition may also occur if the debtor does not believe that the favor rendered meets the expectation. Spreading a bad word in the network can lead to negative recognition and a bad reputation (ill repute). In this case, the creditor can decide either to increase the favor in future transactions, reverse the direction of recognition, or avoid future transactions. The decision is a weighing process in which the relational gain (or recognition gain) is weighed against the added transactional cost or the cost of disengaging from the debtor and possibly from the network is weighed against having a tarnished reputation but remaining in a resource-rich group.

Similar considerations apply to a debtor or group perspective. When would a debtor be expelled from further exchanges? Is it the behavior of spreading a bad word while gaining transactional profit or playing the debtor game without ever considering granting favors? When would a group's solidarity begin to break down? If group solidarity is indeed based in part on the extent of reputation among its members and the extent of reputation of its leading "citizens," then is it the group size, or the relative number of debtors and creditors, or a function of both that would bring about the erosion of group solidarity?

In short, while this chapter focuses on the positive processes, there is a great deal to be developed regarding breakdowns in the social exchange processes. Such developments are equally important for a theory of social exchanges.

Complementarity and Choice Between Social and Economic Capital

The preceding stylized arguments suggest that both economic and social standing are meaningful criteria for survival and constitute fundamental bases for rational choices. Lest it sound as if it is being argued that the two types of rationality are polarized values on a continuum, and that the two types of rationality are mutually exclusive (an either-or proposition), let me hasten to add that there is no theoretical or empirical reason to propose that this should be the case. It is conceivable that relational and transactional exchanges are complementary and mutually reinforcing under certain conditions. In an ideal situation, a particular relationship may be profitable for both relational and transactional purposes. It may generate transactional gain for both actors, and both actors may engage in social propagation of the other party's contribution to their own gain, thus increasing each other's social capital. In this case, it is said that there is an *isomorphic utility function* for both the relationship and the transactions. An isomorphic utility function promotes exchanges between two actors, as the survival of each individual and the survival of the interacting group are both enhanced. In this idealized situation, the two types of rationality coexist, complement each other, and interact.

This does not hide the potential violence between the two rationalities. Transactional rationality recommends abandoning a particular relationship in favor of better transactions. Partners in exchanges are incidental; they exist so long as and only to the extent that such partnerships generate transactional gain. This principle clearly puts relational rationality in the second order of choice criterion. Thus, more often than not, a choice needs to be made between transactional rationality and relational rationality.[7] That is, optimal transactions do not match optimal relationships. According to the decision rules specified earlier, then, optimizing transactions would lead to a search for alternative relationships, and optimizing relationships would lead to imbalanced transactions. We may speculate that the choice between the two types of exchange is related to public capital – wealth and reputation – in the

---

[7] For primordial groups, the choice seems to favor relational rationality over transactional rationality (succession of children to properties; see Chapter 8).

larger group. Several alternative hypotheses may be posited. First, when one collective capital, say wealth, is low, it is expected that individuals favor the gaining of another collective capital, say, reputation. In this situation, two alternative and competing hypotheses are possible. In one formulation, the marginal utility principle would guide the explanation. What is expected, then, is that in a community with abundant wealth but lacking in reputational consensus (say, in a community with a large number of newcomers and immigrants but plenty of physical and economic resources), reputation is more valuable for individuals than wealth. Likewise, in a community with a good reputation but no wealth (say, a stable community with scarce physical or economic resources), individuals would tend to favor gaining wealth. However, in another formulation, the collective utility drives individual desires as well. When the collective asset is low on one form of capital, say wealth, but high on another, say reputation, the collective would favor standings based on the more abundant capital, reputation. Individuals would ascribe a higher value to reputation as well. Here I speculate that it is the collective utility principle that should operate.

Second, when both types of public capital are abundant, there is expected to be a strong correspondence and calculus between the two types of capital. That is, having more of one type of capital increases the desire for and likelihood of having more of the other type of capital. In a community where both wealth and reputation are abundant, either choice – striving for more wealth or for reputation – is rational. Gaining one type of capital would also increase the likelihood of gaining the other type of capital. Thus, in a stable community with abundant physical and economic resources, both wealth and reputation are important and complementary.

When a community lacks both wealth and reputation (an unstable population and a scarcity of physical and economic resources), it is expected that the community will be fragmented and contested in terms of the valuation assigned to wealth and reputation. Individuals are expected to strive for either wealth, reputation, or both, depending on the size of the social network in which they are embedded (the larger the network, the more likely reputational gains will be favored) and accessibility to physical and economic resources. The lack of collective consensus and patterns of exchanges make such a collectivity vulnerable to chaos or change. These conjectures should be investigated.

Nevertheless, beyond a level where bare survival is at stake or where capital has been accumulated by only a few members, desirable economic and social capital can be obtained in exchange relationships. An actor with high social status and a wealthy actor can borrow each other's capital in further promoting their own capital or building up the other type of capital. Accumulation of one type of capital also allows the actor to engage in exchanges promoting his or her other type of capital. If a banker donates money to the needy and the transaction is well publicized, it generates social credit and social recognition for the banker. Likewise, an esteemed physicist may lend her or his reputation in advertising a product and generate handsome monetary returns. Good capitalists understand that they must be both instinctive and human, and that it is good for them and for others as well.

It is also important to note that, in the final analysis, both transactional and relational rationalities are socially based. Without the legitimation and support of a social and political system and its constitutive members, the economic system, based on its symbolic and generalized medium, money, simply cannot exist. To say that relational rationality is subsumed under transactional rationality is instinctively attractive but humanly impossible.

10

Social Capital in Hierarchical Structures

In the previous two chapters, I initiated a conceptual formulation in which motivations of actions are shown to lead to certain types of interactions and the utility of social capital. I suggested that actions lead to the emergence of social structures with increasing complexity of positions, authority, rules, and agency (Chapter 8). The purpose of this chapter is to extend this line of conceptualization by examining access to and use of social capital in the context of a complex social structure – an organization. Here I begin by assuming stable and functioning hierarchies such as organizations and assess how actors, through their positions, may or may not access better social capital – resources embedded in other positions, especially hierarchically higher positions. Thus, the concern here is, first, to demonstrate structural constraints and, second, to show how actions to access social capital operate within these constraints.

Recall that the theory of social capital proposes that, in addition to the principal proposition that social capital generates returns, two factors affect access to social capital (Chapter 5). The strength-of-position proposition hypothesizes that a given position of origin in the hierarchical structure determines in part how well one may gain access to better social capital. It is a structural factor and is independent of individuals in the structure, although individuals may benefit as occupants of the positions. In contrast, the strength-of-(network)-locations proposition hypothesizes the potential payoff for individual action. Since normal interactions are dictated by the homophily principle, going beyond the routine set of frequent interactions and seeking out weaker ties or bridges represents action choices beyond most of the interactions and structural positions' normative expectations. *In relative terms, the strength of position should have greater effects on social capital than the strength of network locations.* This statement recognizes the significance of structural constraints everywhere in the social structure. The theoretical implications of these propositions will be further discussed later. In empirical systems, both factors are expected to operate, even though their relative effects may vary.

In the studies examining social capital in the status attainment process (Chapter 6), empirical evidence thus far strongly supports two of the three hypotheses: the social-capital hypothesis and the strength-of-positions hypothesis. Those with better origins tend to find sources of better social capital in job searches, and contacting a source of better resources or generally having better social capital increases the likelihood of finding a better job. These relations hold even after the usual status-attainment variables (e.g., education and first-job status) are taken into account.

However, evidence is equivocal on the strength-of-weak-ties hypothesis. A number of reasons have been offered for this; one could argue, for example, that strength of ties is not an adequate measure of the strength of network locations. More appropriate measures should reflect being part of a bridge or near a bridge, or being at or near structural holes, or being at locations with fewer structural constraints (Burt 1992, 1997). Or the strength of weak ties has been measured more as role identifications (relatives, friends, or acquaintances) or lack of intimacy (Marsden and Campbell 1984) rather than as network locations. Currently, there is a lack of empirical evidence confirming that these alternative measures would yield different results.

Another line of conceptual reasoning proposes that this result may be due to the interaction between the two exogenous variables: the strength of position and the strength of network locations (e.g., weaker ties) (see Chapters 5 and 6) for instrumental actions. Lin, Ensel, and Vaughn (1981) hypothesized a ceiling effect for weak ties. At the top of the hierarchy there is no advantage to using weak ties, since such ties are likely to lead to inferior positions and therefore inferior resources. The authors did not anticipate that weaker ties would be similarly ineffective toward the bottom of the structure. Marsden and Hurlbert (1988) also found that actors with the lowest origins did not derive greater benefit from contacts with weaker ties in gaining access to better resources than from contacts with stronger ties. Assuming that the interaction effects between the strength of position and the strength of ties occur only at both very high and very low positions of origin, it is interesting to speculate on why such interactions take place there. This is not so difficult to explain for positions near or at the top of the hierarchy. But it is more difficult to understand why positions near or at the bottom of the hierarchy do not derive more benefit from weak ties, since the theory suggests that the increased likelihood of reaching better social capital through such contacts should hold true for occupants of the lowest positions in a hierarchical social structure.

To pursue this line of reasoning, we need to consider structural parameters that dictate the interplay between strength of position and strength of network locations. What is needed is a formulation in which predictions can be made regarding the relative significance of structural constraints (as represented by strength of position) and individual actions (as represented by strength of network locations), given such structural characteristics. These considerations have led to the exploration of structural parameters and an assessment of their effects on the propositions. The remainder of this chapter delineates a set of structural parameters, variations of which provide the context for further specification of the two theoretical propositions.

Some terms require clarification here. I assume that a social structure consists of different levels, each of which can include a set of structurally equivalent positions. They are equivalent primarily on the basis of levels of similarly valued resources and authority and secondarily on the basis of similar lifestyles, attitudes, and other cultural and psychological factors. For our purposes here, the terms *levels* and *positions* are used interchangeably. Also, *social mobility*, as used here, refers to the voluntary aspect in an internal labor market. Involuntary social mobility, due to job dissatisfaction, lack of alternatives, or other "pushing" or forced factors, is excluded from consideration. As Granovetter (1986) pointed out, voluntary social mobility generally results in wage growth. Likewise, it is argued that voluntary social mobility accounts for the majority of rewards (greater authority, better wages and bonuses, and faster promotions) in hierarchies such as organizations.[1]

Structural Parameters and Their Effects

A hierarchy, I argue, can be described with variations and permutations of four general parameters: the number of levels in the hierarchy (the

---

[1] It is true that the beginning of a job search is often unplanned (see Granovetter 1974). Many job leads become available on casual occasions (e.g., parties) and through interactions with acquaintances. It is not necessarily the case that a job search begins with the purposive and active seeking out of contacts. However, this does not negate the basic premise that individuals are situated at different levels in the structure and therefore have access to casual settings involving persons who command certain types and amounts of resources and social capital. In fact, it has been empirically demonstrated (Campbell, Marsden, and Hurlbert 1986; Lin and Dumin 1986) that occupants of higher-level positions have greater access to more diverse and heterogeneous levels in the hierarchical structure than do occupants of lower-level positions and hence have greater command of social capital. Thus, it can be expected that casual settings for the higher-level positions are structurally richer in job information, as well as other types of information and influence. This structural advantage, deducible from the pyramidal assumption of the theory, has a distinct effect when the individual eventually launches a job search.

level differential), the distribution (absolute and relative number) of the occupants across the levels (the *size differential*), the distribution (absolute and relative amount) of valued resources across levels and among occupants (the *resource differential*), and the sum of all occupants and resources in the structure. The first and last parameters are computed for the entire structure; the second and third parameters can be computed for either the entire structure or portions of it.

In general, the social capital proposition, the primary proposition of the social capital theory, should hold regardless of the variations in these parameters. As long as the structure is hierarchical, access to and use of better social capital are expected to facilitate socioeconomic returns under any structural variations. However, the other two hypotheses require further specification relative to variations in the structural parameters. In the following sections, I will describe each parameter and assess the impact of its variation on the two propositions. For simplicity, the two propositions will be identified as the *positional effect* (the strength of the original position) and the *location effect* (the strength of network locations). Again, we must remain conscious of the dominant effect of structural constraints. Strength of position should have a relatively stronger effect than strength of locations everywhere in the structure, whereas each factor may vary in different parts of the structure.

Also, for generality, I will examine the relative effects of structure (the strength of positions) and networking (the strength of locations). For networking effects, I will employ the general location argument: that is, for instrumental actions, locations at or near a bridge – variously referred to as *structural holes*, *weaker ties*, or less *structurally constrained locations* – reflect the strength of better locations in their likelihood of accessing better social capital. While the descriptions often implicate organizations or firms, it is hoped that the propositions can be generalized to all hierarchical structures.

The Level Differential

First, the hierarchical structure can be specified by the number of levels within it. A *level* is defined as a set of social positions that have a similar command of resources and access to capital (including social capital) per occupant. In the occupational structure, for example, the crudest differentiation is based on occupational classifications consensually agreed upon in a given society. Each such classification, however, may be based on a combination of requirements, including the degree and presence of certain skills, training, experience, tenure, and location in an industry, as well as resources. A better differentiation would be one based on

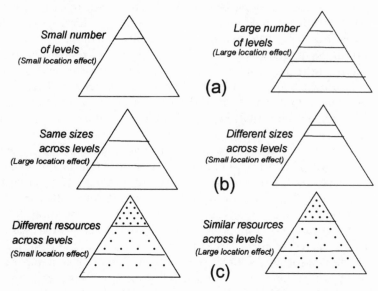

Figure 10.1 Three differentials and the relative significance of the location effect: (a) level differential; (b) size differential; (c) resources differential.

empirical examination of each occupational position's command of resources and access to social capital. The clustering of equivalent positions would then constitute a level in the structure.[2]

As illustrated in the top two figures (a) in Figure 10.1, we can describe the variation by identifying two theoretical extremes. At one extreme, the left figure, there are only two levels in the structure, and at the other, the right figure, there are many levels. The two-level system is expected to resemble a caste system in which one level has either all or most of the valued resources and the other has none or few. Thus, the positional effect should be stronger. In the multilevel system, the differentiation of levels reduces the relative inequality of valued resources across levels and therefore the positional effect. Thus, the expectation is that the number of levels will be negatively related to the positional effect.

The two-level structure minimizes interactions between levels, reducing the opportunity for finding and using bridges. In the multilevel struc-

---

[2] Breiger's work (1981) specifying a class hierarchy of occupations is based on the principles of internal and external heterogeneity of mobility. Thus, the classification system is deduced from mobility patterns rather than from resources and social capital. I suspect that there is a strong correspondence in the resulting empirical classifications based on the mobility and resource criteria. For theoretical and tautological reasons, an empirical derivation and demonstration of the resource-based hierarchies is necessary.

ture, however, bridging is maximized. This is not to deny that the networking effect should be present even in the two-level system whenever social ties across the two levels are formed. However, in this castelike arrangement, such ties are difficult to form and follow up on because there is little need for an upper-level occupant to respond to a relationship offered by a lower-level occupant, as all rewards (wealth, power, and reputation) can be found through social ties within the upper level. The expectation is that the number of levels in the structure will be positively related to the networking effect.

Thus, the number of levels in a structure has opposite consequences for structural constraint and individual action. On the one hand, in the two-level system, the structural constraint is strongest and provides little opportunity for effects of individual actions. On the other hand, differentiation of many levels in a structure lessens structural constraints and provides more opportunity for individual actions that gain valued resources. These effects are consistent with the general empirical observation that social mobility is related to the gradations or number of strata in an occupational structure or a labor market. Rather than explaining such a relationship solely in structural terms, these subhypotheses argue that it is both the loosening of structural constraints and the greater opportunity for action choices that account for greater social mobility across levels in a multilevel structure. However, these effects assume that either the number of occupants at each level is the same or variations in the number of occupants do not have any effect. In most hierarchical structures, this is not true.

The Size Differential

Variations in the relative number of occupants across levels are expected to influence positional and location effects. As in the preceding section, we can discuss this influence by examining two extreme situations, as illustrated in the two figures in the middle panel (b) of Figure 10.1. At one extreme (the left figure), every level has the same number of occupants, and at the other (the right figure), every level has a different number of occupants, the relative number decreasing from the bottom to the top of the structure. In this discussion, the number of levels is held constant. For convenience, we assume a sufficient number of levels so that both the positional and tie effects may occur.

In the equal-size structure, the opportunity for heterophilous interaction is maximal for all occupants. That is, each occupant has an equal opportunity to contact a person at a different level. In Blau's analysis of intergroup associations (Blau and Schwartz 1984; Blau 1985), he hypothesizes that in a two-group interaction situation, the intergroup association would be greater for the small group (i.e., the probability per person in Group A of associating with a person in Group B increases as the size of Group A relative to the size of Group B decreases). If it is assumed that in a hierarchical structure the relative sizes tend to decrease toward the top, then the derivation is that intergroup association initiated from a lower (and presumably larger) level (e.g., Group B) to a higher (and presumably smaller) level (e.g., Group A) decreases as the difference between the relative sizes of the two levels increases. However, as the difference in the relative sizes of the levels decreases, such upward association would be increased. Thus, it is argued that in the extreme case, in which all hierarchical levels have a similar number of occupants, there is maximal opportunity for heterophilous interactions across all levels and therefore equal opportunity for socioeconomic returns. In other words, an individual at each level has an equal chance to move up the ladder. This does not mean that everyone in the structure will have an equal opportunity to attain the same highest status. Depending on his or her initial position in the structure, each person will have an equal opportunity to interact with another person at a different level and move up the ladder.

As variations in the number of occupants across levels increase, they inhibit upward cross-level contacts. Intralevel interaction opportunities increase as the size differential increases at all levels, because most of the occupants of the larger levels tend to interact with others at the same level. Assuming that the relatively small levels are higher in the structure, the relative lack of interlevel actions initiated by the lower-level occupants reduces the potential probability effects of weak ties. Thus, the expectation is that the size differential is negatively related to the network location effect.

However, when a lower level is relatively smaller, this expectation does not hold. In such a structure, the chance is greater that lower-level occupants will have a relatively larger number of contacts with occupants at an upper level, which in turn promotes opportunity for mobility to that upper level. For example, in a structure where farm-related levels have relatively fewer occupants than do nonfarm blue-collar sectors, the tie effect should be relatively strong in the status-attainment process.

As for positional effects, variations in occupant numbers across levels have a positive effect. As the size differential increases, intralevel interactions increase among occupants in the larger, and presumably lower, level. These intralevel interactions reinforce the positional effect. The paradox is that as size differentials increase, they also increase the relative opportunity of contacts for these occupants in the smaller level with those in the larger level. In a pyramidal hierarchy (the higher the level, the fewer the occupants), the closer the level to the top, the broader the range of contacts across levels for its occupants; yet these occupants benefit not from heterophilous interactions for socioeconomic returns, but rather from their same-level contacts. In contrast, at or near the bottom of the structure, the opportunity for occupants who need heterophilous interactions for socioeconomic returns is structurally restricted by the large size of their level.

The Resource Differential

A third feature of the hierarchical structure is differential distribution of resources at various levels. Differentiation of levels can therefore be described in terms of distribution of resources as well as number of occupants. The resource differential can be calculated for the variation in resources across levels in a social structure or for a comparison between two levels. For the description of a social structure, as illustrated in the lower panel (c) in Figure 10.1, the resource differential may vary from minimal (when the resource differential is the same for every pair of contiguous levels) in the left figure to large (when it is different for every pair of contiguous levels) in the right figure. In the former case, the levels are said to be *equidistant* in resources. In the latter case, we assume that the differentials increase from the bottom to the top of the structure. That is, the higher up in the structure, the greater the resource differential between two contiguous levels, with the upper level having many more resources per capita than the lower level. Although this assumption is yet to be examined empirically, it is based on the theoretical argument that a marginal incentive or reward of a given amount of resources decreases toward the top of the hierarchical structure. Therefore, an increasing amount of resources is expected toward the top to maintain the same degree of incentive or reward.

It is expected that the equidistant structure increases the opportunity for the location effect. Heterophilous ties are equally likely to be initiated at each level. In the unequal-distance structure, however, it is harder for lower-level occupants to overcome the resource distance across levels, especially toward the top of the structure. Thus, the expectation is that the resource differential will be negatively related to the location effect.

For the positional effect, the opposite should be true. As the resource differential increases, so does the importance of the position of origin for socioeconomic returns. In a structure with a large resource differential, any upward mobility is difficult. But in such a system, when upward mobility does take place, the position of origin rather than the use of network locations should account for the movements. If the structure is equidistant, the positional effect should be relatively small.

If this hypothesis is valid, two consequences follow within any given empirical structure. First, since the hierarchical structure, by definition, rank-orders its levels by resources, it can be deduced that cross-level interactions are most frequent across contiguous levels and decrease for any two levels, depending on how far apart they are in the structure. Thus, we predict that social mobility (especially socioeconomic returns) should most likely occur across contiguous levels.

Furthermore, inhibition of cross-level interactions is contingent on the difference in the relative amount of per capita resources at the two levels; the interactions between contiguous levels may be attenuated or suppressed as the resource differential increases. In a structure where resource differentials increase toward the top, we predict that social mobility in that direction becomes increasingly difficult. At the very bottom, however, the resource differential between levels may be quite trivial, and thus the cross-level interactions will be substantial.

One interesting aspect of these variations is the implication they hold for any interaction related to socioeconomic returns. It is clear from the discussion so far that, toward the upper levels, there is much advantage in initiating (upward) cross-level interactions, since there is much more to gain because of the resource differentials. However, such initiatives are less likely to be reciprocated, since higher-level occupants have much less to gain from interacting with others at the lower levels. The result should be fewer cross-level interactions and generally a smaller effect from such interactions, since upper-level occupants are less likely to reciprocate actions initiated by lower-level occupants. When the interactions are successful, probably owing mostly to the positional effect, however, the payoff for the job seeker should be substantial. At the bottom, in contrast, cross-level interactions have little advantage or disadvantage since the resource differentials are small. Therefore, although it is expected that cross-level interactions will be frequent, such interactions will not generate significant benefit for the participants.

The Totality of Occupants and Resources

The final feature of the social structure concerns the absolute number of occupants and resources in the entire structure (e.g., industrial sector). *Critical mass* is used here to characterize the minimal requirements for a structure's absolute quantities of population and resources. These requirements vary, depending on the relative sizes of populations and resources in the external environment with which the structure interacts. Nevertheless, absolute numbers are important features of a structure. Associations within the structure are strongly affected by the constraints as well as the opportunities to gain resources in the external environment. Thus, analysis must be extended to the larger structure of which the initial focal structure is but a substructure. For example, in understanding social mobility in a particular labor market, we may wish to analyze the structural parameters of that segment. Analyses, however, must eventually be extended to considerations of other segments, so that relative mobility patterns may be assessed across segments. For the larger structure, similar parameters (the level differential, the location differential, and the resource differential) may be utilized to examine possible cross-segment mobility. No further elaboration and extension of these parts are necessary in this chapter.

Implications for Structure and Individuals

In summary, a consideration of the structural parameters has enabled us to specify conditions under which the positional effect and the tie effect vary. In ideal-typical terms, the positional effect should be maximal when the structure contains (1) a minimal number of levels, (2) a large occupant differential across levels, and (3) a large resource differential across levels. The network location effect should be maximal when the structure has (1) a large number of levels, (2) a small occupant differential across levels, and (3) a small resource differential across levels. Again, we must keep in mind that, even when the tie effect is strongest, the positional effect remains dominant.

The positional effect can be seen as an indicator of structural effects, and the location effect (especially the use of weaker ties) suggests the consequences of individual action. As explicated earlier, the normative mode of interactions is homophilous, involving participants with similar socioeconomic characteristics. In contrast, the use of weak ties tends to result in interactions involving participants with dissimilar socioeconomic characteristics. Heterophilous interactions are not totally without benefit for participants from higher status levels, since they may subsequently request or demand services from the lower-level participants. Nevertheless, the initiation and establishment of such interactions by lower-level persons represent action and effort. Viewed in this context, these principles have theoretical implications for the relative effects of structural constraints and individual choices. They also stimulate consideration of the dynamic balance between vertical (heterophilous) and horizontal (homophilous) interactions in a stable social structure. These implications will be briefly examined here.

Structural Constraints versus Social Capital

The theory describes structural conditions under which structural constraints and individual actions affect social mobility. Thus, it is relevant to the debate concerning structural versus action effects. In contemporary sociology, the structural view dominates. Much of the theoretical development and empirical work in the past three decades have supported and advanced the structural perspective. The theory presented here does not disagree with the view that structural effects are predominant. It also argues that the positional effect, for example, is relatively more important than the tie effect throughout the structure. However, the specification of structural parameters enables us to ask where and to what extent individual actions become possible and meaningful. The following discussion gives further attention to the relationship between this theory and selected prevailing structural theories.

Blau's theory of heterogeneity and inequality, along with Emerson and associates' dependence theory, exemplifies well the structural perspective. In a nutshell, Blau (1977, 1985; Blau and Schwartz, 1984) has argued that the distribution of a dimension (attribute) and the number of variables differing among groups in a population dictate the extent of association across groups. When the distribution of a dimension varies over a number of *nominal* or *graded* groups, such heterogeneity (for nominal groups) and inequality (for graded groups) promote intergroup association and can be examined over multiple dimensions (attributes). The extent of the congruence between the different heterogeneities and inequalities also affects intergroup association. When the differences in characteristics are closely related (consolidated), intergroup association should be low; when they are not closely related (cross-cutting), intergroup association should be high.

Although the present theory can be seen as an elaboration and extension of Blau's theory, there are several differences between the two. First, the present theory focuses on two types of social action: instrumental actions for gaining valued resources and expressive actions for maintaining valued resources. Though this chapter deals specifically with socioeconomic returns and mobility, and therefore instrumental actions, the distinction between instrumental and expressive actions plays a central role in the theoretical structure and has immediate consequences for patterns of interactions. Patterns of association differ for instrumental and expressive actions (Lin 1982). The expectation is that vertical (heterophilous) actions and interactions are effective for instrumental purposes, whereas horizontal (homophilous) actions and interactions are effective for expressive purposes. In Blau's formulation, there is a mixture of the two types of action, with the main emphasis perhaps on the latter. Intergroup marriage, for example, might be seen as primarily expressive, yet there are circumstances in which marriage takes on an instrumental aspect as well. The specification of the two types of action should clarify potentially conflicting empirical results. It can be argued that Blau's theory should be relatively more valid for the class of interactions intended for expressive purposes.

Second, the two theories' primary elements by which groups and positions are identified differ. Though both assume that these elements must be consensually arrived at, the basic criteria are different. For Blau, they are based on the attributes that people take into account in their social relations. For the theory presented here, they are based on resources. Whereas Blau convincingly argues that the use of attributes based on their influence on social relations at the microlevel does not necessarily affect consequent intergroup relations, the criterion of resources used in the present theory does not involve such a conceptual tautology. In later writings (e.g., 1985), Blau recognized the significance of resources in the identification of attributes. A modification of the definition of attributes in resource terms may resolve the difficulty.

A further consequence of the difference in criteria used to define groups or positions is that Blau's theory applies to both unranked and ranked groups, whereas the present theory assumes a hierarchical structure based on ranked positions. In the present theory, the determining factor of a social structure is the different amounts of valued resources various levels command. Therefore, the levels are hierarchically ordered.

This more restricted view of social structure offers an advantage in that it eliminates further controversy in ranking categorical variables. Categories of ethnicity and religion may be ranked in some social systems but not in others. For the present theory, the valued resources must be gradable, even if some of them represent social categories (e.g., race and gender). As long as they are consensually considered to be valued resources for a social system, they form the basis of the hierarchy in the structure. Even for expressive actions, as I have argued elsewhere (Lin 1982, 1986), such a hierarchical view of the structure helps to formulate predictions about patterns of action and interaction within or across levels. This specification may help elaborate differential patterns of intergroup associations. One may postulate, for example, that when categorical variables represent valued resources in a given social system, both the heterogeneity hypothesis and the inequality hypothesis may hold, whereas they diverge for other categorical variables.

Finally, Blau focuses on variation in the distribution of the number of individuals as the major source of structural variation. For both the heterogeneity and inequality principles, population distribution over the various categories or statuses affects intergroup associations. Although he has also identified the number of subgroups as having an impact, he assumes in the bulk of his work that the number of subgroups can be standardized for comparative analysis (1985, pp. 10–11). In other words, his theory tends to treat the number of subgroups as a constant.

The present theory specifically identifies the level differential and the size differential, along with the resource differential, as separate structural parameters. The effects of heterogeneity and inequality as proposed by Blau, therefore, can and should be further specified relative to the variations in both the number of levels (or groups) and the number of persons in them. For example, if a pyramidal structure is compared with an inverse-pyramidal structure, the inequality coefficient may be similar but the interlevel (group) associations may differ drastically. Empirically, an inverse-pyramidal structure may not exist, as discussed earlier, but most structures will have portions in which a lower level has fewer occupants than an adjacent higher level (e.g., agricultural vs. service sectors). For such a structure or substructure, the interlevel (intergroup) association is expected to be different from the usual one, in which the upper level has relatively fewer occupants. Likewise, while two structures have similar level and occupant differentials, their resource differentials may differ, and therefore their patterns of interlevel association may differ. For example, in a two-level caste system, where a small minority holds most of the resources, the association between the occupants of the two levels should be substantially different from that in another system in which the level and size differentials of the two levels are similar and there is little difference in their resources.

Having noted these differences, we can now describe Blau's association theory in greater detail. Chance encounters across levels or groups due to variations in a hierarchical structure can then be predicted according to the level differentials (the more levels or groups, the greater the number of such chance encounters), the size differentials (the more evenly distributed the occupants across levels or groups, the greater the number of such chance encounters), and the resource differentials (the smaller the difference in resources per capita across levels, the greater the number of chance encounters). The effects of the hierarchy (especially the resource differential), however, restrict these general principles of association. In the case of instrumental actions taken for the purpose of socioeconomic returns, reciprocity of association becomes problematic. For a person from a higher level to have a chance encounter with a person from a lower level may be structurally unavoidable (e.g., a banker and a cleaning lady), yet a more substantive and especially status-changing association (e.g., marriage) requires efforts to overcome the structural gap. It is for this type of association that the present theory attempts to clarify the potential effects of individual actions.

Similarly, the structural theory of Emerson and Cook can be explicated in view of the present theory. In their power-dependence theory, Emerson and Cook specify that structural parameters dictate exchange patterns and consequences, even though individuals engage in such exchanges to maximize their resources (Emerson 1962; Cook and Emerson 1978; Cook 1982; Cook, Emerson, Gillmore, and Yamagishi 1983; Emerson, Cook, Gillmore, and Yamagishi 1983). In their theoretical formulation of exchanges, structural dependence, or constraints (number of available exchange partners and distance to sources possessing resources), the type of exchange (e.g., negatively connected networks, in which only one pair of individuals can engage in transactions with one type of resource, and positively connected networks, in which new resources depend on combining two or more types of resources) and the resource salience (amount of resources available to each individual) result in further resource differentiation among individuals.

By specifying these parameters in a hierarchical structure, the present theory helps to predict in what types or parts of structures the rate of increasing dependence or resource differentiation will be faster or slower. If it is assumed that the resource differential increases toward the top of the structure, one would predict that power or resource differentiation increases faster for occupants positioned closer to the top of the structure. The size differential also predicts differences in the speed of differentiation. The greater the differential, the greater this differentiation, since the larger number of occupants at the lower levels will have fewer opportunities to interact with occupants at the higher levels. The level differential delineates resource distance and should help generalize to larger structures the experimental results of the Emerson–Cook studies, in which the number of positions/levels and occupants is necessarily limited.

Furthermore, the present theory fleshes out possible variations in actions taken by individuals in similarly structured positions. Cook and Emerson (1978) briefly examined such variations by demonstrating the effects of a stronger sense of equity and a stronger sense of commitment on resource differentials; they found some evidence that exercise of power or demand for resources was either curtailed (especially for women) or increased (especially for men). Such data hint at the possibility that individual actions vary beyond predictions based on their structural characteristics. The present theory, with its explicit specification of structural parameters that predict where such individual actions may be relatively large or small, may well refine and elaborate the strictly structural interpretation of the dependence theory to accommodate such empirical variations.

Individual Action versus Social Capital

As stated earlier, the individual perspective, rather than the psychological deductive viewpoint, has emerged in the American sociological literature. The effects of individual actions can be explored from two perspectives. The first focuses on the structural formations or changes due to such actions. For example, Coleman (1986a, 1986b, 1990) argues that social actors promoting their interests engage in social relations that, depending on the specific purposes of the actions involved, may result in a market system, an authority system, or a normative system. He describes the process by which each system evolves, emphasizing the emergence of norms and sanctions from the interacting actors with their respective interests. Rational or cognitive action is the assumed force in the forging of social relations and subsequent structures. In contrast, Collins (1981) sees emotion as the ultimate force behind interactions, in which individuals seek positive reinforcement and claim membership. Chains of such interaction rituals eventually form and provide cultural (conversational) and energy resources for repeated interactions, which develop into formal organizations and informal groups. These proposals focus on how individual actions can result in structural forms.

From the second perspective, individual actions are possible and meaningful under structural constraints. Burt's work (1982, 1992) explores structural actions, or actions taken by individuals who are at the same or neighboring positions to protect or promote their common resources and interests. He argues that individuals from different positions can coopt to alleviate structural constraints, and in the process can modify the structure of relationships.

Integration of these two perspectives and the present theory has interesting results. In Chapter 8, it was argued that social capital provides the critical link between individual interests and the emergence of structure. To have resources, one must form ties with others initially to protect and eventually to gain resources. Maintenance and protection of resources are seen here as driven by emotional or expressive forces, whereas resource gain requires mobilization of instrumental and cognitive motives and action. The resulting horizontal (homophilous) and vertical (heterophilous) interactions and relations constitute the elementary forms of social structure. Social structure allows access to and use of resources not necessarily in each individual's possession. Differential ability to manage and manipulate social capital helps dictate the emergence of hierarchical positions. Variations in the structural parameters are the evolutionary consequences of the emerging process and its interaction with external structures and resources.

Once structural parameters have become dominant forces, access to and use of social capital continue to motivate individual actions wherever and whenever possible in the hierarchical structure. The parameters (level differentials, size differentials, and resource differentials) assume different significance for different types and parts of the hierarchical structure. For example, the extent of collective actions by a given level's occupants, as well as the outcomes of such actions, are dictated by the relative number of occupants not only at the given level but also across levels. It would be interesting to postulate the structural conditions under which such collective actions will result in further consolidation of the given levels or elimination of variations in structural parameters. In the next section, one such analysis is offered as an illustration.

Mobility and Solidarity: Some Policy Implications

I have speculated (Lin 1982) that a stable social system requires a balance of opportunities for both homophilous and heterophilous exchanges. A system that does not provide sufficient opportunities for heterophilous exchanges reduces the opportunity for mobility and will experience fragmented populations with strong intralevel solidarity. This intralevel solidarity will promote the development of level (class) consciousness and potential class conflict. In contrast, a system that encourages a great degree of heterophilous exchange will experience much mobility and hence structural instability since solidarity will not prevail within population groups. The consequence may be a chaotic society in which transient interactions and lack of group solidarity threaten the integration of the system itself.

What this implies is that the structure must strive for adjustments in the number of levels, the distribution of occupants and resources among those levels, and the cumulation of occupants and resources. An increase in the differentiation of levels, perhaps inevitable in the industrialization process, must be accompanied by a redistribution of occupants and resources. That is, the size differential and the resource differential must be kept at reasonable ratios between levels. Significant size and resource differentials usually indicate a rigid structure.

As a crude illustration, let us assume that the American occupational structure is segmented by sex and race. We assume that occupational mobility follows sex and race specifications (e.g., a position vacated by a white male is filled by another white male). The 1999 distribution of occupants of the five major U.S. occupational categories (managerial and professional, technical, sales and administrative support, production/operations, and farm) by sex and race is shown in Table 10.1. For each race-by-sex combination, we may construct the occupant differential between two assumed contiguous occupation categories by dividing the occupant size of the "higher" category by that of the "lower" one. For example, for white males, the occupant differential between service occupations and production/operations occupations is .25 (5,694/23,084) and the occupant differential between administrative support occupa-

Table 10.1. *U.S. Employed Workers by Gender, Race, and Occupational Category (1999)*

Occupational Category	Employed Workers (thousands)			
	White Male	Black Male	White Female	Black Female
Managerial/professional	18,196	1,231	17,074	1,954
Administrative support	12,069	1,273	20,652	3,032
Service	5,694	1,216	8,333	2,204
Production/operations	23,084	3,244	4,345	836
Farm	2,847	164	767	16

Source: U.S. Department of Labor, *Employment and Earnings* (1999, p. 20).

Table 10.2. *Occupant Differentials by Gender, Race, and Occupational Category*

Occupational Category Pairs	Occupant Differential			
	White Male	Black Male	White Female	Black Female
Managerial: adm. support	1.51	.97	.83	.64
Adm. Support: Service	2.12	1.05	2.48	1.38
Service: Production	.25	.38	1.92	2.63
Production: Farm	8.11	19.83	5.67	52.00

Note: Differentials based on number of workers in Table 10.1, calculated by the ratio of the upper level to the lower level. The smaller number suggests a reduced opportunity for the lower-level occupants to move to the next higher level.

tions and service occupations is 2.12 (12,069/5,694). Assuming that the resource differentials are the same across these three occupational categories, the present theory would predict that structural constraints on mobility from production/operation occupations to service occupations are quite high: the positional effect would be strong and the tie effect weak. Structural constraints, however, should be quite low for mobility from service to administrative support occupations, where the positional effect is expected to be small and the tie effect large. These and other occupant differentials are presented in Table 10.2.

Now we can compare the patterns of mobility opportunities and the relative positive and tie effects for white and black males and females. As Table 10.2 shows, both black males and black females have greater structural constraints than their white counterparts for mobility to higher white-collar occupations (from service to administrative support, 1.05 and 1.38 for black males and females and 2.12 and 2.48 for their white counterparts; and from administrative support to managerial occupations, .97 and .64 for black males and females and 1.51 and .83 for their white counterparts). Thus, we would expect that for black males and females to move up in these white-collar occupations, they should expect relatively stronger position effects and weaker tie effects. Comparing males and females, we find that females do not suffer as much structural constraint in moving from service to administrative support jobs, but they do suffer greater structural constraint than their male counterparts in moving from administrative support to managerial occupations (1.51 and .97 for white and black males, respectively, and .83 and .64 for white and black females respectively). In attempting to move to the top tier of the occupational pyramid, then, females should expect relatively stronger position effects and weaker tie effects.

These are very crude data. We are not sure if, in fact, the American occupational structure is rigidly segmented by race and sex (in fact, we know that to some extent that this is a false assumption). The occupational categories here have been kept to a minimum (Breiger 1981, for example, proposed an eight-category classification for a hierarchical structure of American occupations). And the assumption that the resource differentials are constant across levels (occupational categories) is probably invalid. But given these assumptions, the theory informs us that, in such a structure, race and gender do make a difference in occupational mobility. Faced with greater structural constraints in moving up in white-collar occupations, blacks and females would experience difficulty in mobilizing social capital to overcome such structural deficiencies. Thus, the research agenda should shift to finding out how to make access to social capital more likely for structurally disadvantaged blacks and females.

This demonstration (within the limitations set by our assumptions) illustrates the utility of the social capital theory from both the structural and the individual perspectives. At the macrostructural level, the search for ways to overcome such constraints stimulates policy considerations. Is it possible to create vacancies to equalize the size differential? Is it possible to equalize the resource differential? Is it possible to combine these moves in some way? Or should the structure address the issue of reallocation of vacancies across sex and racial categories, thereby emphasizing the interfirm labor market rather than the internal labor market perspective (see such a position advocated in Granovetter 1986)? Unless the structure is capable of making such adjustments, chances are that mobility opportunities will remain structurally unequal and discontent will increase. In extreme cases, such immobility is cause for social revolution.

At the individual level, awareness of structural constraints and of flexibility within them may be reflected in the process of cognitive evaluation. To the extent that such evaluation is engaged in, the individual has the option of initiating action by seeking out heterophilous ties and better social capital. Because the nature, range, and quality of such ties vary at different levels in the hierarchy, the benefits of seeking them out also vary. There is also a risk of nonreciprocated action when the structural gap is too great, along with a loss of identification with other occupants of the initial level. Both may lead to a sense of alienation.

11

Institutions, Networks, and Capital Building

Societal Transformations

In Chapter 8, it was proposed that actions motivated by expressive and instrumental needs propel interactions with others beyond primordial groups so that social capital may be accessed. These purposive actions sustain two types of exchanges, as described in Chapter 9 – to gain and maintain two elementary payoffs: wealth and reputation. These two chapters describe the process from action to structure. Chapter 10 turns to the structure-to-action process by showing how hierarchical structures constrain actions accessing social capital. These are ideal types of linkage between action and structure; in reality, such processes are complicated by structures and processes mediating between actors and hierarchical structures. Unless we identify and describe how these middle-level structures and processes operate, we will be unable to understand how action and structure interact. Further, the two processes – from micro to macro and vice versa – should not be seen in isolation or each depicted as a one-way process. A comprehensive theory of social capital must capture the two-way process between action and structure, as mediated through certain middle-level structures and processes.

In this chapter, I argue that two such middle-level structures – institutions and networks – constitute the infrastructure of society. The framework conceives institutions and networks as the two main social forces guiding the interactions between actors and hierarchical structures and the flows of capital.

Many scholars have used network analysis to delineate this micro-to-macro process, including Coleman, White, Granovetter, Burt, Breiger, Wellman, Erickson, Marsden, Flap, and many others. For those engaged in social networks analysis, social resources or social capital constitute the core element of a sociological explanation. Purposive actions based on two motivational principles, minimization of loss and maximization of gain, lead to the formation of social networks (first the primary group and then secondary ties) for both sentimental and instrumental purposes.

Thus, social networks, as has been pointed out in this monograph, exist not only in hierarchical (e.g., economic) organizations (e.g., the social embeddedness of economic organizations; see Granovetter 1985) but also in the interrelations among individual actors (Granovetter 1973, 1974; Lin 1982; Burt 1992), so that transactions and exchanges take place not only within organizations and between organizations, but also among actors.

Institutional analysis proposes yet another meaningful tool to understand how organizations should be seen as tied to the larger environment (DiMaggio and Powell 1983, 1991; North 1990; Powell and DiMaggio 1991; Meyer and Scott 1992; Scott and Meyer 1994). The survival and persistence of an organization are seen as dependent not only on its efficiency or competitiveness in the marketplace, but also on its ability to adjust to and to comply with expected behaviors as dictated by larger social institutions in society. Subscribing to such social rules leads to isomorphic structuring and behaviors of multiple organizations, or institutional isomorphism (DiMaggio and Powell 1983), which cannot be explained by competitiveness or performance criteria alone.

The institutional and network perspectives are exciting because they clearly propose ways in which we can analyze how social forces, along with economic forces, describe interactions and transactions. They clarify, for example, why transaction costs are always positive and unevenly distributed. They also explain why motives and rationalizations for action by individuals as well as organizations extend beyond economic considerations. Without taking these forces into account, it is clear that we cannot begin to understand how or why individuals and organizations behave or even persist. The excitement, however, is tempered by the fact that gaps remain between concepts and the processes linking the concepts. Several examples illustrate this point.

A major assumption in institutional analysis is that institutions affect and even dictate behaviors of actors and organizations. What is not clear is how this process works. How do individuals learn the rules, and why should they subscribe to them? How are organizations matched with individual actors to improve their institutional resources and thus their chances for survival? In other words, what are the social mechanisms that credit and enforce the compliance of individual actors and organizations with institutional rituals and behaviors?

Another gap is in how institutions and networks are related. One obvious answer is that networks reinforce institutions as they add coherence to the structure (Zucker 1988). How then does one explain social movements, which usually involve an interconnected group of actors mobilizing capital to counteract prevailing institutions? Or, to be more specific, is it possible to specify how social capital is useful for instru-

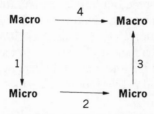

Figure 11.1 Four basic social processes. (Adapted from Coleman 1990, p. 8)

mental actions leading to gains in the prevailing institutions and organizations in some situations, and yet becomes an instrument for institutional transformation in other situations?

This chapter is a modest attempt to explore some of these issues and
questions. My approach is to propose a conceptual framework that identifies what I consider the key components in the two-way processes
depicted in Figure 11.1: namely, process 1 (macro-to-micro effects) and
process 3 (micro-to-macro effects). To do so in a single chapter, I have
made two choices. First, I will focus on the key points central to the proposed framework and sacrifice other points that are also significant but
that, for the time being, must be pushed to the background. For example,
this chapter has little to say about the state or technology, although both
are implicated in the descriptions of how various components interact. I
will have more to say about technology and social capital in Chapter 12.
Second, I will focus on the more general issues and sacrifice specifics. For
example, I will leave out descriptions of certain specific factors, such as
gender and ethnicity, which are universal in societies, and opt for gen-
eralities (using the term *prevailing institutions*).

Basically, I conceive institutions and networks as the infrastructure of
society – the vital social forces that link, hold, and consolidate actors
and organizations in society. They may not be the most efficient mechanisms, but they define the internal cohesion and external differentiation
for the actors and organizations. Of the two, institutions provide the
organizing principles for actions and interactions. They offer rhetoric
rationality and thus the map for organization and function. Most important, they uphold individual and collective identities. Networks, on the
other hand, enhance flexibility for reducing transaction costs beyond
what organizations can supply. They also provide mobile forces that fill
and link the gaps necessarily existing in society. Just as important, they
serve as possible vehicles for institutional transformation.

The remainder of the chapter describes how institutions and networks
work in tandem. Specifically, it will show how institutions organize and

interact with other major components of society (i.e., institutionalizing organizations, other social and economic organizations, and social networks) and facilitate the flow of capital among these components. The final section highlights the significance of social networks in institutional transformation.

The Institutional Field and Organization-Society Isomorphism

Institutions, seen as the organizing principles of interaction, can simply be defined as rules of the game (North 1990, p. 3) in a society and can be either formal or informal. These rules serve as the traffic guides in the flow and transactions of goods (both material and symbolic) among actors, including both individuals and organizations. Some rules are more important than others in that the actors are more consciously aware of them and feel the need to demonstrate more deliberately that the rules are followed in their actions and transactions. There are various explanations of how certain rules or institutions come into existence and assume dominant positions in a society. They may result from wars, revolutions, rebellions, colonization, occupation, disasters, acts of charismatic and authoritarian leaders, dominant class interests, or post facto rationality. To a large extent, they may be the result of historical path dependence (see David 1985 for the institutionalization of the QWERTY keyboard).[1] Institutions are cultural rather than scientific, because they do not require logical or empirical proofs or appreciate falsification. These rules create favored values for actions and interactions in the forms of morality, faith, ideology, decency, or capability (of healing and performing).

When organizations and individuals subject themselves to a similar set of institutions, they are said to be in an *institutional field* (Lin 1994b). Within an institutional field, actors (including individuals, networks, and organizations) recognize, demonstrate, and share rituals and behaviors, and subscribe to constraints and incentives as dictated by the social institutions. As such, they reduce transaction costs in measurement (computational abilities) and enforcement (North 1990) for actions and interactions among the actors.

An institutional field may define a society. However, the field may transcend a society's usual spatial boundary. For example, we can argue that

---

[1] There have been debates as to whether QWERTY actually performed less well than, say, the Dvorak system. However, even if they performed equally well, the fact that QWERTY historically emerged first represented a real advantage and was an important factor in its prevalence today.

ethnic Chinese communities in many urban ghettos around the world belong to the same institutional field as the proper Chinese society, defined within the boundary of the nation-state of China. Even though these communities and their members may speak different languages, live under the rules and laws of different states, and are subjected to different stratification and mobility constraints and opportunities, they obey the same fundamental rules extending and emanating from the structured relationships among family members (Lin 1989, 1995b). These rules guide their family lives, the celebration of certain holidays and festivities, ancestor worship, deferent treatment of elders, the upbringing of children with discipline and passion, the preference for tacit and informal agreements to formal or legal contracts in business transactions, the recognition of certain differential associations (given priority to family, clan, and village affiliations), and idiosyncratic rules of succession (transfer of authority by the rule of primogeniture and transfer of property by the rule of division among sons). Thus, institutional China is more encompassing than the state of China. Other institutional fields exist within a given a state. In the following discussion, the term *society* is used to refer to an institutional field.

In an institutional field, the extent to which organizations survive and persist depends on both their economic (technical) and social (institutional) performance. DiMaggio and Powell (1983, p. 148) used the notion of an organizational field to designate a "recognized area of institutional life: key suppliers, resources and product consumers, regulatory agencies, and other organizations that produce similar services or products" and hypothesized that organizations belonging to an organizational field become institutionally isomorphic in that their forms and practices becomes homogeneous because of increased sharing of interactions, information, and awareness of involvement in a common enterprise. An institutional field also involves the process of institutional definition and structuration (Giddens 1979), but it extends beyond specific types of organization (e.g., economic enterprises) or the requirement for interaction among all organizations. Organizations are said to belong to an institutional field when they are conscious of and abide by the rules of a specific set of institutions. By adjusting their internal structure and patterns of behavior, the organizations reduce transaction costs in interacting with other organizations dictated by the same institutions. The *organization-society institutional isomorphism* (Lin 1994b), therefore, is the prerequisite and imperative condition for organizational isomorphism. One assumption derivable from this imperative is that there is a positive correspondence between an organization's ability to perform institutional tasks and its hierarchical position in the society. Likewise, it can be assumed that most of the social networks constructed also attain

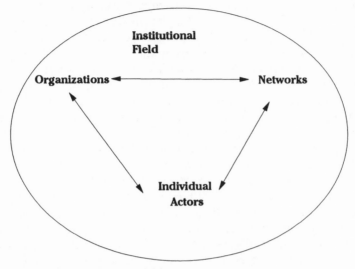

Figure 11.2 Institutional field.

isomorphism with the organizations. The *organization-network institutional isomorphism* is reflected in the overlapping rules of the game and the values assigned to certain resources (ideology) between networks (and informal organizations such as churches, chambers of commerce, veterans' groups, and bowling clubs). Figure 11.2 depicts a functioning institutional field where organizations, networks, and individuals are synchronized in terms of the rules of the game and the values of certain resources.

The Flow of Capital

Given the organization-network-society isomorphism imperative and the incentive for better positioning in the stratified system, organizations are expected to obtain and retain goods useful for transactions of both an institutional and a technical nature. One important type of such goods is workers capable of performing institutional and/or technical tasks. Correspondingly, the implication for individual actors seeking rewards or returns in society is clear: they need to demonstrate their possession of knowledge and skills, as well as their willingness and ability to be further trained and indoctrinated. The labor market therefore can be conceived as a marketplace where transactions of such goods between individual actors and organizations take place. Before the transaction of goods in the labor market is discussed further, it is important to explore the nature of the goods that flow into the institutional field.

The goods, as mentioned earlier, can be either material or symbolic. When certain goods are deliberately mobilized for a purposive action, they become capital. Capital is an investment of resources intended to generate returns. Thus, it is tailored by the actor to meet an organization's demand. In return, the actor may be rewarded with social (reputation), economic (wealth), or political (power) resources. For organizations as actors, such capital generates returns so that they can survive and thrive in the society or institutional field. For individual actors, it is capital that is transacted in the labor market.

Two types of capital dominate these transactions: *human capital* and *institutional capital* (Lin 1994b). Human capital reflects technical knowledge and skills. It is needed by organizations to compete successfully in the market. Institutional capital reflects sociocultural knowledge and skills about rules in the institutional field. Organizations need agents to exercise such knowledge and skills in performing as their representatives. Institutional capital contains elements of what is usually described as cultural capital (Bourdieu 1972/1977, 1980, 1983/1986) and social capital (Bourdieu 1983/1986; Coleman 1988, 1990; Flap and De Graaf 1988; Flap 1991). Cultural capital contains values, rules, and norms sanctioned by the dominant institutional field. Social capital reflects the extent of social connections, where embedded resources can be used to maintain or gain resources – including wealth, power, and reputation – valued in the institutional field. Individual actors who possess or can access cultural and social capital are potential laborers who can perform and fulfill an organization's obligations in the institutional field. Thus, organizations seek out such candidates in the labor market.

How does an individual actor demonstrate his or her human capital and institutional capital? Human capital, of course, can be demonstrated in examinations. Many organizations employ this method in assessing technical knowledge and skills. But examinations by themselves seldom capture the breadth and depth of human capital. More often, the assessment requires evidence of effort, commitment, and success in the process of acquiring such capital in the form of certification, credentials, or the evaluations of trusted assessors. Degrees, diplomas, certificates, and, equally important, testimonials have become important symbolic demonstrations of human capital.

Demonstration of institutional capital is much more complicated. Certain examinations or other methods of identification have been devised for this purpose. For example, in historical China, knowledge of Marxist–Leninist ideology, Mao Zedong's or Sun Yat-sen's thought, or

Confucianism appeared in examinations, and patrilineal ancestries, clan and regional affinities, or class/ideological credentials had to be accounted for. For the most part, this demonstration was reflected in certification, credentials, and testimonies. These symbolic identifications reflected the actor's acquisition of and affinity for prevailing institutions, and they might vary in different institutional fields. Even in contemporary China, these identifications may include Communist Party membership, clan and ethnic memberships, and affiliation with state-owned work units, but not membership in a church, temple, or social or professional association.[2] Complicating the situation is the fact that many societies use the same certification and testimonial procedures to demonstrate both institutional and human capital. We shall return to this issue shortly.

Now we turn to the issue of how resources are mobilized into capital and how capital is certified.

Institutionalizing Organizations and Social Networks: Crediting and Enforcing Agents

The process of acquiring both types of capital begins with intergenerational transfers of resources. Several processes are involved in the transfer. One process is socialization, wherein the family provides the setting in which training is conducted to develop actors (by way of imitation and cognitive training) with such valued resources. Another process is through the family's social networks. Parental networks provide opportunities to contact actors with valued resources. In still another process, parental resources afford an opportunity for actors to acquire additional resources on their own (e.g., through schooling).

Once differentially equipped with the transferred resources, the individual actor needs to mobilize such resources and turn them into capital, an investment for the purpose of matching with, and thus generating, returns from affiliation with an organization. Two avenues are available for turning resources into capital: processing by institutionalizing organizations or using resources embedded in social networks. An actor may go through a process of training, the result of which is certification clearly announcing the actor's acquisition of capital. Degrees, diplomas, and certificates are the usual signals. Another route is the use of social

---

[2] For an example of a taboo association and identification, read about the 1999 Falun Gong incidents in China (use Internet search engines such as Copernic 99 to find Falun Gong or Falun Dafa listings).

ties and connections for testimonies. Training is accomplished through an important component of society: institutionalizing organizations. While the following discussion focuses mainly on the process of mobilizing resources into institutional capital, a similar process for human capital also applies.

Institutionalizing organizations are one special type of organization whose purpose or mission is to train and indoctrinate actors with values and skills in performing rituals and behaviors associated with the prevailing institutions. They also differ from other organizations in that they process actors but do not employ or keep them.[3] Although some of them are specifically established to provide institutionalizing training, most of them also provide technical training in the form of schools, institutes, and colleges (e.g., cadre schools, military and police academies, seminaries, and scouting organizations). Thus, education through such organizations and the credentials thereby gained signify acquisition of both human capital and institutional capital.[4] The disentangling of the two types of capital embedded in educational credentials is a complicated task, but rough estimations are possible. For example, recent studies in China and Taiwan (Lin 1994a, b, 1995b) suggest that education can be decomposed as two-thirds representing human capital and one-third institutional capital.

Society and prevailing organizations also use institutionalizing organizations to enforce rules, rituals, and controlling behaviors. These organizations include prisons, mental hospitals, and labor and concentration camps. Actors in the institutional field are submitted to be processed if their behaviors are deemed deviant from those dictated in the prevailing institutions. Individual actors may be allowed to gain certification or credentials for institutional capital through these processes. Otherwise, they are in danger of being decertified or discredited, deemed inappropriate as players in the institutional field, and subjected to lower returns on their investment.

Social networks provide another avenue for turning resources into capital. Through social ties and networking, actors gain additional resources by accessing the resources of direct and indirect ties. Many networks are formed because of shared processes and experiences in institutionalization (e.g., alumni, occupational, and industrial associations). However, networks also form on the basis of other shared interests or experiences (e.g., bridge and bowling clubs, knitting and

---

[3] Institutionalizing organizations have regular staff primarily as trainers.

[4] Bourdieu (Bourdieu 1972/1977; Bourdieu and Passeron 1977) uses the term *cultural capital* to describe the process of indoctrinating students with dominant class values. What I am suggesting here is that cultural capital should be considered a subcategory of institutional capital in the context of organizations and markets.

exercise clubs, Elvis Presley and Michael Jackson fan clubs, or neighborhood groups). Through informal and often indirect ties, loose networks extend actors' reach beyond their immediate social circles.

These socially embedded resources may be turned into social capital when an actor activates and mobilizes a particular chain of ties for the purpose of pursuing purposive actions, such as finding a job. The mobilized resources are deemed useful because of the perceptions of the initiating and facilitating actors that they are institutionally valued. Thus, the testimonies provided by these ties on behalf of the initiating actor may further assure the target organization of his or her human capital. More importantly, these testimonies may offer assurance that the initiating actor possesses institutional knowledge and skills as well (trustworthiness, social skills, collegiality, loyalty, willingness to follow orders and carry out tasks, and other "appropriate" behaviors). Through the influence of these testimonies, an affiliation with an organization may be realized. This is an investment, because it results in eventual socioeconomic returns to the actor.

Further, while institutionalizing organizations and social networks process resources into capital, many organizations themselves also provide access to further technical and institutional skills, thus allowing selected workers to acquire additional capital. The concept of the *internal firm labor market* (Baron and Bielby 1980) describes investment in on-the-job training for human capital. Affiliation with a resource-rich organization itself signifies institutional capital, because it can generate further returns for the actor inside and outside the organization. Inside the organization, actors have the opportunity to learn and acquire additional institutional skills as the organization successfully engages in exchanges with other organizations in the institutional field. Experiences gained from participating in such exchanges are part of institutional skills training. Further institutional capital is gained as actors acquire authoritative positions within the organization, and are thus endowed with statuses and symbols associated with skills and knowledge of how to perform institutional tasks. Outside the organization, affiliation with a resource-rich organization signifies the actor's institutional skills, as well as his or her access to capital that is important for exchanges in the institutional field.

The preceding discussion describes how the infrastructure of society – namely, institutionalizing organizations and social networks – operates in tandem with other social and economic organizations, reinforcing and sustaining each other. In other words, it describing a stable and functioning institutional field. Figure 11.3 depicts a functioning institutional field.

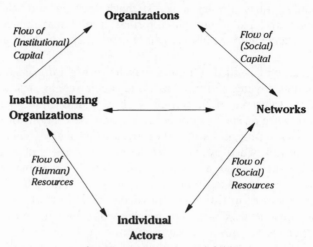

Figure 11.3 A functioning institutional field.

Networks as Vehicles for Institutional Transformation

However, embedded in these elements are the potential sources and processes for challenges to existing and prevailing institutions, as well as the emergence of alternative institutions. It is possible that organizations (Zucker 1988) or even individual actors (DiMaggio 1988: "institutional entrepreneurs") may trigger transformations. For example, organizations isomorphic with an alternative, external institutional field may be able to survive, persist, and eventually replace or be incorporated into existing prevailing institutions. Western religion, popular culture, and lifestyles are examples of alternative institutions to indigenous institutions in other societies, and they can transform indigenous institutions so long as participating actors' capital investment generates expected returns (e.g., social status), as the alternative institutional field holds an advantage in capital to indigenous institutions.

Charismatic leaders can also offer challenges to prevailing institutions. The personal charm and charisma of Mao Zedong in heralding the Great Cultural Revolution, mobilizing millions of youths, and up-ending existing institutions in 1960s China is a vivid example of the latter ("Rebellion is rational and revolution is not guilty!" was used to uproot existing organizations, cadres, and professionals who had invested capital in those institutions and organizations). However, actor-generated transformations are infrequent and rarely succeed.

The more interesting and powerful indigenous transformation process, I argue, begins with social networking. When a number of actors share alternative rules or values and begin to connect, the network may sustain their shared interests through solidarity and reciprocal reinforcement. For example, actors perceived as deprived or actually deprived of opportunities to acquire human or institutional capital may form networks and forge a collective identity. Whether such deprivation is based on gender, ethnic, religious, class, family origin, or other institutional criteria, networking is the first and essential step in developing collective consciousness. As the network expands and the number of participating actors increases, the pool of social capital increases. As shared resources grow, there is an increasing likelihood of a social movement, a process that can transform one or more prevailing institutions.

One straightforward way of generating institutional transformation by way of a social movement is to turn the movement directly into a rebellion or revolution. In extreme circumstances (e.g., mass starvation, external threat, or massive despair), a social movement can quickly generate overwhelming participation leading directly to the overthrow of prevailing institutions. The Russian Revolution in 1917 and the collapse of the former Soviet Union and the Communist states in Eastern Europe are examples. However, in most situations, the social movement involves a minority of actors and requires more elaborate processing in order to generate institutional transformation. Further, the usual goal is not to reject prevailing institutions, but rather to substitute an alternative institution for a prevailing one or to incorporate the alternative institution into the configuration of prevailing institutions.

A social movement can be sustained by turning the shared resources into capital and generating returns. That is, the movement must develop its own institutionalizing organizations in which alternative values and rituals are taught and new members are indoctrinated. Further, it must build or persuade organizations to recruit and retain the actors who have acquired such capital. Through these processes, the movement can then sustain itself and challenge existing institutions.

The mounting and sustaining of alternative programs in either existing or alternative institutionalizing organizations may generate and process alternative capital for actors. As the number of actors equipped with the alternative institutional capital increases, along with the growing pooled social capital through networking, the likelihood that other organizations may recognize the need to take the alternative institution into account in their actions increases. This recognition triggers the need to recruit and retain workers with the knowledge and skills to perform tasks dictated by the alternative institution. The alternative institutional capital will thus increasingly become a legitimate form of capital in the labor market, and the likelihood of the alternative institution's being absorbed into prevailing institutions is increased.

Figure 11.4 Processes of institutional transformation.

These two alternative routes of institutional transformation are depicted in Figure 11.4. In the following discussion, I will provide two examples of successful transformations using each of the two routes. The emergence of women's studies in American colleges illustrates how a successful transformation can occur when networking among interested actors infiltrates existing institutionalizing organizations, and the success of the Communist revolution in China demonstrates the successful (though much harder) building of alternative institutionalizing organizations.

Transforming from Within: Women's Studies in the United States

The growth of women's studies programs in the United States in the 1970s and 1980s is recognized as a stunning example of a new institution successfully infiltrating an existing institutionalizing organization (college) in a matter of years. The process can be traced back to the 1960s, when the civil rights movement ignited the women's liberation movement. A number of female faculty members such as Jessie Bernard, Alice Rossi, Gerda Lerner, Anne Firor Scott, and Sara Evans began to write about the perils of women in society and academia. Courses on women began to appear on several campuses in 1965 (the Free University of Seattle [Howe and Ahlum 1973]) and 1966 (at the New Orleans Free School, the University of Chicago, and Barnard College [Boxer 1982]). Yet, within a decade (by 1976), there were more than 200 programs in women's studies and some 10,000 courses being developed by 6,500 faculty members in 1,500 different institutions (Howe 1977). What accounted for this sensational success story of the decade in

American higher education? Several critical external factors created opportunities that made this new academic institution possible. The civil rights movement and the women's liberation movement found sympathy and synergy on American campuses, as antiwar and antidraft activities were generalized to questions and challenges to the status quo. At the same time, two-income families increased rapidly throughout the 1950s (Kessler-Harris 1982), and female students enrolled in college in growing numbers and proportions (e.g., in 1965, women earned 10 percent of all doctorates, and by 1979, 29 percent of all doctorates were conferred on women; see Stimpson 1986). Female faculty likewise continued to rise (e.g., by 1977, close to 32 percent of college faculty were women [Stimpson 1986, p. 31]). Thus, the pressure to change, as well as demographic changes in the higher education system itself, provided favorable structural opportunities for possible institutional transformation.

A closer examination of the actual process identifies four elements that made women's studies programs grow so rapidly. The most innovative element was the distribution and sharing of course syllabi, initiated by Sheila Tobias (first at Wesleyan and then at Cornell; see Chamberlain 1988, p. 134) in 1969. Following a conference on women in the winter of 1969, she collected the syllabi of seventeen women's courses and distributed the list at the annual meetings of professional associations in 1970 (*Feminist Studies I*, the collection, was initially printed and distributed from Cornell; Stimpson 1986, p. 4). The list was then distributed at the American Psychological Association's annual meeting in the fall of 1970 (Chamberlain 1988, p. 134) and was published by KNOW of Pittsburgh at about that time (Boxer 1982). The distribution was so successful and well received that *Feminist Studies* grew to ten volumes of syllabi and other course-related materials (Boxer 1982; Stimpson 1986). This distribution and sharing of course materials dramatically generated course development throughout American colleges. The ready-made student market (i.e., women students) responded enthusiastically. For example, a multidisciplinary course on "female personality" taught by Tobias and others at Cornell registered 400 students in the spring of 1970 (Tobias 1970). In the fall of the same year, coordinated courses about women began to appear on many campuses. The first officially integrated women's studies program was established at San Diego State University in September 1970.

The second networking element in this development was the use of professional meetings by female faculty and students to exchange information and reinforce the institutionalizing process. It was no surprise that the Modern Language Association (MLA) was the first association to provide this impetus, as women constituted a large proportion of its membership. In the spring of 1969, the MLA established a Commission on the Status and Education of Women, chaired by Florence Howe (Boxer 1982, p. 664), and charged it to study the status of female faculty in 5,000 English and modern language departments and to review the content of the curriculum in those departments. At the December 1970 MLA annual meeting, the Commission "offered to an audience of more than 1,000 women and men a forum that included a paper on the status of women faculty, another on the literary curriculum's male biases and female stereotypes, and two of the first lectures in feminist literary criticism to be heard" (Chamberlain 1988, p. 135). It also issued the first guide to women's studies under the title "Current Guide to Female Studies," listing over 110 courses. The second guide, published only a year later, listed 610 courses and fifteen organized women's studies programs, five of which granted degrees, with one at the Master's level (Howe 1977). Soon women's caucuses appeared in numerous other social science and humanity associations, whose annual meetings provided ready-made occasions for sessions, seminars, and exchanges. The association as the medium culminated in the founding of the National Women's Studies Association (NWSA) in 1977. The preamble to the constitution of the NWSA, drafted at the Founding Convention in San Francisco (January 13–17), stated that the organization was to "promote and sustain the educational strategy of a breakthrough in consciousness and knowledge" that would "transform" individuals, institutions, relationships, and, ultimately, the entire society (Boxer 1982, p. 661).

A third critical element in developing and institutionalizing women's studies in American colleges was the resources provided by a number of private foundations to support students, programs, and centers. In 1972 the Ford Foundation began a program to promote the advancement of women and help eliminate sex discrimination in all phases of education (Stimpson 1986). By 1979, more than $9 million had been granted to address these various issues. In 1980, the Foundation's board of trustees more than doubled previous Foundation allocations for women's programs. In 1972, the Foundation created the first national program of faculty and doctoral dissertation fellowships for research on women's roles. A series of grants established centers for research on women at leading colleges and universities throughout the country, including Stanford, the University of California (Berkeley), Wellesley, Brown, Duke, and the University of Arizona.

According to the Ford Foundation's own report, between 1972 and 1975, it gave out 130 postdoctoral fellowships and dissertation awards in women's studies. Fifty percent of the senior people it supported became prominent in women's studies, as did at least one-third of the people in the dissertation program. Between 1964 and 1979, Ford gave a total of $30 million to advocacy, research, and curriculum projects in women's studies (Stimpson 1986, p. 23). By 1986, the Ford Foundation had allocated $70 million since 1972 to support "a broad array of programming on behalf of women," including fellowship awards; grants to campus-based and independent centers for research; grants for "corollary" activities, especially publishing and national associations; and support for programs and centers mainstreaming minority women's studies (Guy-Sheftall 1995, pp. 5–6).

Other private foundations such as the Carnegie Foundation, the Rockefeller Foundation, the Rockefeller Brothers Foundation, the Andrew W. Mellon Foundation, the Helena Rubinstein Foundation, the Russell Sage Foundation, the Exxon Education Foundation, the Eli P. Lilly Foundation, and the Revlon Foundation quickly joined in support endeavors (Stimpson 1986, p. 23). This substantive support allowed the hiring and retention of many faculty associated with these programs and sustained the development of students dedicated to women's studies and ideology.

Finally, the networking approach adopted by many women's studies faculty and programs is also worth noting. The innovators made the conscious decision that rather than creating a discipline or department in isolation, they would adopt the model whereby the program would be run by a coordinator and faculty and students' committees (Merrit 1984). While the debate continues to the present, the prevailing organization remains this coordinator-committee structure. Most women's studies programs have opted for the gains of networking, collectivity, and multidiscipline/transdiscipline over possible resource losses and faculty tenure usually budgeted through college departments. Thus, faculty appointed in traditional departments and disciplines and students work together to develop courses and curricula across disciplinary lines.

The rapid development of women's studies in the late 1960s and early 1970s represents an institutional response to "an intellectual feast long denied" and "a classical instance of a movement without unified organization or direction," whose spread followed the geography of the new women's movement (Howe and Ahlum 1973; Boxer 1982). Yet it is clear that active initiation and networking among pioneers through informal exchanges of course syllabi and materials, their collective efforts through associations and meetings, and the adoption of the coordinator-committee structure coincided with the decision of private foundations to provide resources generating critical masses of faculty and students. All of this contributed to a massive participation and penetration of existing institutionalizing organizations (the colleges in the changing world of the 1960s and early 1970s), demonstrating how a rapid transformation from within prevailing institutionalizing organizations can occur.[5]

In summary, the process of women's studies program development shows that networking among actors with a shared ideology and dedication took advantage of both external and internal opportunities for the prevailing organizations to mobilize and institutionalize potential labor (women students) quickly. Once such cumulated labor (capital) gained a sufficient number and capital, there was little resistance both within the institutionalizing organizations and within society at large. We should also note that this example refutes the great-man theory of institutional transformation. Despite some notable innovators in the movement (Tobias, Howe, and others), it was clear that the movement, through the networking of many actors, would move forward and keep gaining momentum without charismatic or intellectual stars.

Examples of such successful institutional transformation from within are few and infrequent, because few emerging institutions are accorded so many favorable external and internal conditions (i.e., the changing pattern of female participation in the workforce, the breakdown of the status quo, the increasing presence of actors [female students] in the institutionalizing organizations sharing and demanding identity-supporting ideology and knowledge, and the readily receptive sources of resources [the private foundations]). Furthermore, some emerging or alternative institutions may demand more than integration or mainstreaming within the framework of existing institutions; they may demand substitution and subversion. When an alternative institution directly challenges and intends to subvert prevailing institutions, institutionalization may take a direct route and process. The following section offers a successful example of this type: the Communist revolution in China.

Constructing Alternative Institutionalization: The Communist Revolution in China

When the Communist Party was first organized in the 1920s, it was clear that it was attempting to use both transforming strategies: infiltrating existing institutionalizing organizations when opportunities arose and/or

[5] Women's studies programs are not without their problems and controversies. Since the very early days, debates have raged over significant issues such as (a) "structurelessness" of networking both within and across campuses and its potential control by elites (Freeman 1972–1973); (b) the ideological split between the "socialist feminists" and "cultural feminists" ("Marxists" and "Matriarchs"), or feminist activities versus academicians, or practice versus theory (Boxer 1982); (c) the necessity or possible dominance of the construction of a feminist theory (Boxer 1982); and (d) the neglect of women of color and lesbians (Guy-Sheftall 1995).

establishing alternative institutionalizing organizations when such opportunities were not available. In the end, it was the alternative institutionalizing organizations that helped transform the scale of the movement. It may be informative to describe in a brief historical account here how such strategies were implemented.

An account of the revolutionary institutional transformation of the Communist educational system inevitably starts with Mao Zedong's personal efforts to establish alternative educational institutions. These "official" historical constructions should be understood in the context of modern school reform in early-twentieth-century China, which preceded the formal establishment of the Chinese Communist Party (CCP) in 1920 and the advent of Mao. Nevertheless, it was true that the Russian Revolution generated much intellectual interest in China, and after May 4, 1919, when students took to the streets in Beijing, Shanghai, and other cities in protest against possible territorial concessions to the Japanese, intellectuals and educators took on added important roles in educational reforms and innovations. Many Chinese intellectuals, including Marxists, led the way and set the stage before Mao's interest and participation in innovative educational institutions. Li Dazhao and Cai Yuanpei, two leading intellectuals in the 1910s, for example, advocated "dignity of labor" (Pepper 1996, pp. 96–97).

These progressive movements were echoed in the provinces as well. In the province of Hunan, for example, in 1916, the normal school at Changsha inaugurated a "labor association" designed to accustom students and teachers to manual labor. Among other things, they performed janitorial duties and practiced farming on campus (Shanghai Jiaoyu Chubanshe 1983, pp. 66–69). A workers' night school had also been set up in 1916, but interest soon flagged among teachers and staff, so students took over the project. Student activist Mao Zedong was director of the night school for about a year during 1917–1918 (Shanghai Jiaoyu Chubanshe 1983, pp. 62–63; Pepper 1996, p. 96). Soon after he finished his formal education at the First Hunan Provincial Normal School in Changsha, Mao was appointed as the acting principal of the elementary school attached to the normal school in 1920 by Yi Peiji, director of the school system and the highest education official in the provincial government (Pepper 1996, p. 96).[6] Mao thus became directly involved in educational reform within the context of existing innovative school systems.

[6] Yi was a leading progressive education in the province, and Mao's appointment was one of many that he made to inaugurate his reform-minded administration at First Normal. Yi took over as the headmaster at First Normal in September 1920. He hired progressive teachers, these teachers moved onto campus, and girls were enrolled in 1921 (Pepper 1996, p. 97).

In 1920, when small Communist cells were being formed in cities around the country, Mao took the lead in organizing one for Changsha as well, and at about the same time, he took up his duties at the elementary school. Representatives from all of these groups gathered in Shanghai in July 1921, the official founding date of the CCP. Mao returned to Changsha as secretary of the CCP for Hunan Province. By this time, he had become a critic of the system itself and saw education reform as only a place to begin to teach Marxism (Pepper 1996, p. 99).

Also in 1920, Bertrand Russell visited Changsha, suggesting that socialism and even communism could be achieved without war, violent revolution, or limitations on personal freedom. The use of education was to change the consciousness of the propertied classes. Mao wrote in letters to friends that Russell's view was good in theory but would not work in practice, as education required money, people, and facilities. But all these resources, most importantly the schools and the press, were already capitalist-controlled. In addition, capitalists controlled all the other societal institutions necessary for perpetuating their existence. Hence, the nonpropertied class, despite its numerical superiority, would be helpless to turn education to its own ends. The only solution was for the Communists to "seize political power" (two letters to Ts'ai Ho-shen [Cai Hesen] dated November 1920 and January 1921; trans. in Schram 1963, pp. 214–216).

In August 1921 Mao left the elementary school and, with a few friends, founded the Self-Study University, with the aim of combining the form of the old academy with the content of modern learning, and creating an institution appropriate to "human nature and convenient for study." It would strive to become an institution of "truly popular learning" (Pepper 1996, pp. 98–99). It was clear that Mao understood the importance of alternative institutionalization. The Self-Study University opened in the autumn of 1921, with a strong Marxist orientation. The university sponsored a series of public lectures on Marxist theory in 1922, and by its second year was openly recruiting and training CCP workers. The Self-Study University is regarded as the first training institution for revolutionary cadres in China (Cleverley 1985, p. 89), although it passed quickly into history when it was closed down by the military governor in late 1923 on the grounds that it was promoting unorthodox ideas and threatening public order.[7]

---

[7] Mao was not the only radical education reformist. Liang Shuming declared that the new education was of no use to anyone. He was enthusiastic about Tao Xingzhi's experimental normal school project and turned similarly to rural reconstruction. These projects were most extensively implemented in Zouping (Tsou-p'ing) County, Shangdong, between 1931 and 1937. Liang founded the Shangdong Rural Reconstruction Institute, which trained his new-style rural administrators and managers. James Yen conducted

The strategy of infiltrating existing institutionalizing organizations was also much in evidence during a period when the Nationalist Party (KMT) and the CCP joined forces during the late 1920s. In 1927 the KMT formed a coalition with the CCP with the aim of defeating the northern warlords and forming a national government. CCP cadres joined KMT officials in several training ventures, the most urgent of which was the preparation of the new army at the Whampoa Military Academy. From July 1924 to September 1926, the KMT Propaganda Department organized with the Peasant Movement Training Institution, which was established to train rural organizers for the First United Front. The Communists Peng Pai, Lu Yiyuan, Ruan Xiaoxian, Tend Zitang, and Mao Zedong all served as directors, and many Communists served as lecturer-teachers (Han 1987, pp. 52–53). In 1926 Mao led a field study group from the Peasant Institute to Haifeng to observe the rural activities of Peng Pai, a student who had returned from Japan and the CCP peasant mobilization leader. The Hai Lu Feng Soviet had its own school system, which included a Party school, as well as Communist Youth Corps and Pioneers organizations (Cleverley 1985, p. 92). In the seminal paper "Investigations of the Peasant Movement in Hunan," published in 1927, Mao confessed to a switch of allegiance from support for modern schools in the countryside to rural schools acceptable to peasants (Cleverley 1985, pp. 93–94).

At both Whampoa and the Peasant Movement Institution, Communists including Mao actively recruited and indoctrinated students into the Marxist ideology and the CCP. In each case, an institutionalizing organization established by the KMT for training its own cadres was infiltrated effectively by the Communists for their own purposes. By 1929, the KMT realized how effectively the CCP was able to infiltrate the institutionalizing organizations as well as other government and military units, and it conducted a "Party purification" campaign to expel the Communists and eliminate their influence on the KMT.

Having failed to continue their infiltrating strategy, the Communists had no option but to begin establishing their own institutionalizing organizations. The first attempt by the CCP to introduce a socialist education began in the Jiangxi Soviet and lasted from 1929 to 1934. As it evolved, the Jiangxi school system was based on Lenin elementary

large-scale education reforms in Ding County, Hebie, in the mid-1920s (Pepper 1996, pp. 103–105). The KMT attempted rural reconstruction, with an education component, in Jiangxi in the early 1930s. George Sheperd, with the participation and help of many missionaries and Christian universities in China, also experimented with educational reform in Lichuan County, Jiangxi (Pepper 1996, pp. 123–124). All these educational reforms were short-lived, as Japan soon invaded many of China's coastal provinces in the 1930s.

schools, a middle school in each township, and a Lenin Normal School in Ruijin for teacher training. In these schools, classes were open to adults, school textbooks had socialist content, technical facilities were promised, and full use was made of the resources of the Youth Vanguard, the Children's Corps, and the labor unions in social education (Cleverley 1985, pp. 95–96). As the Communists engaged in a desperate battle against the KMT's repeated attempts to encircle and eliminate the Communist stronghold in Jiangxi, the Jiangxi schools operated at a low level of efficiency. Student attendance was irregular, school buildings and facilities were inadequate and often commandeered for war purposes, and desks were taken away as props for air raid shelters (Cleverly 1985, p. 97).

Finally, in the autumn of 1934, about 75,000 to 100,000 Communists broke out of the KMT blockade in Jiangxi, embarking on the exodus later known as the Long March. A year and 6,000 miles later, a small number (no more than 20,000) arrived in the northwest (Pepper 1996, pp. 127–128). Yan'an became the capital of the Shaanxi-Gansu-Ningxia (Shaan-Gan-Ning) Border Region in early 1937. One important task for Mao and his comrades was to create a school system in which Communist political and military cadres could be trained and produced quickly. Xu Teli, a former teacher of Mao from Hunan, initially headed the border region's education office. He was succeeded as head of the department by Zhou Yang, another cultural luminary from Shanghai (Pepper 1996, p. 130). Gaining breathing room as the KMT fought battles against the invading Japanese and reached a compromise with the CCP in establishing a united front against the Japanese, Mao and others urgently organized many higher-level institutions for CCP members and "united front" youths to fill and expand depleted positions for political and military cadres and managers.

The CCP schools included the Central Research Institute, which trained "theoretical" cadres; the Central Party School, which trained senior and middle-ranking cadres at both the tertiary and secondary academic levels; and the Military Academy, which trained senior and middle-ranking military cadres. The best-known united front school was the Chinese People's Anti-Japanese Resistance Military and Political University (Zhongguo renmin kangri zhunshi zhengzhi daxue), or Kangda.[8]

According to the "Educational Method at K'angta" (Mobilization Society of Wuhan 1939, pp. 81–97; Seybolt 1973, pp. 333–348), Kangda

---

[8] Other schools open to both cadres and noncadres included the Lu Xun Academy of Art and Literature, the Natural Science Academy, the Chinese Medical University, and the National Minorities Institute (Pepper 1996, pp. 150–151).

was "a school for the anti-Japanese United Front, and [did] not belong to any party or faction. Enrollment [was] not closed to members of any anti-Japanese party, nor to any classes of society, and at the same no one [was] excluded on the basis of race, religion, creed, sex, or occupation. In terms of its mission and objectives, K'angta [was] a school devoted to filling the needs of the national war of resistance by creating elementary- and intermediate-level military and political cadres for the anti-Japanese war" (Mobilization Society of Wuhan 1939, p. 81). It was based on "K'angta's own educational policy: politically (a National United Front against Japan), militarily (offensive warfare), and spiritually (a revolutionary tradition)" (p. 81).

Yan'an University (Yanda), which was created in 1941, merged most of the united front institutes, with the overriding aim of applying mass-line principles and practical applications. It was reorganized as a comprehensive university in 1944. Mao's address at the opening ceremony in May indicated that it was mainly a university for the study of politics, economics, and culture, and students had to learn how to put those subjects to work in the service of the border region. It was clearly a descendant, in spirit at least, of Mao's old Self-Study University (Pepper 1996, p. 152).

Training in the management of border education took place at Yan'an University, where a specialized two-year curriculum covered the general situation of education and culture in the Border Region; elementary and middle school education; social education; the investigation of teaching materials; and educational thought in present-day China (Pepper 1996, p. 103). Students also took courses in Chinese revolutionary history, Border Region reconstruction, revolutionary philosophy, and current affairs.

These schools implemented the so-called ten exemplary socialist education principles: correct objectives, firm leadership, good school spirit, political education, integration of theory and practice, simplified content, shortened schooling, lively teaching, revolutionary-minded teachers, and self-reliance (Cleverly 1985, p. 103). In reality, courses were generally six months long, with students specializing in either politics or military strategy (Cleverly 1985, p. 102) and sometimes being moved on quickly to assignments in the field even before they graduated (Pepper 1996, p. 151).

In actuality, these institutionalizing organizations were charged with several missions. First, they produced educated youth who served in production, labor, and military forces for the Border Region, namely, the CCP-controlled region. Second, they promoted the united front of anti-Japanese forces. On the surface, this could be interpreted as the CCP's willingness to work with the KMT in resisting the Japanese. But in substance, it extended welcoming arms to all who were willing to work with the CCP, even if they were formerly or presently associated with the KMT or self-proclaimed no-party members. This tactic effectively eroded solidarity within the KMT and weakened the potential alliance between the no-party members and the KMT.

Third, the CCP insisted that all educational units be under the direct control of the CCP in ideology and administration. The ideology, as proclaimed by Mao Zedong, was "the cultural ideology of communism led by the CCP" and the "culture of new democracy." In other words, "the mass culture of anti-imperialism and anti-feudalism" was the "theoretical foundation, on which the proletarians, through the CCP, lead the cultural and educational work" (Mao Zedong 1940, 1942, 1949; Qu 1985, pp. 1–9). In administration, each school was designated under the jurisdiction of a party organ. In 1941, in the "Decisions Regarding Yan'an Cadre Schools," it was made explicit that every school would be under the jurisdiction of a central CCP unit; for example, Yanda was under the jurisdiction of the CCP Cultural Commission. The Propaganda Bureau was responsible for joining each school in the planning, investigation, and supervision of uniform curricula, teachers, teaching materials, and budgets (Qu 1985, p. 7).

Under the banners of anti-Japanese and united fronts, the CCP actively recruited youth throughout China to its schools. Between May and August 1938, 2,288 educated youths signed up (Qu 1985, pp. 17–18). While the early 1940s were the hardest years in the Border Region and the education process was haphazard, these schools trained hundreds of thousands of revolutionary cadres. Kangda alone graduated about 200,000 political and military personnel from its various campuses between 1937 and 1946. By the time World War II ended in 1945, the Communists had not only replenished lost cadres but, much more significantly, had established their own institutionalizing organizations, effectively producing hundreds of thousands of diehard cadres who provided the backbone in organizing armies, peasants, intellectuals, and the urban poor. The institutionalizing organizations at Yanan and throughout the Border Region must share the credit for the defeat of the KMT in a matter of four years.[9]

---

[9] In contrast, a social movement without the opportunity or structure to institutionalize members may evaporate. The 1989 Tiananmen incident in Beijing is a good example of a social movement that failed (Lin 1992b). While the movement drew millions to Tiananmen Square at its peak, it never had the opportunity to indoctrinate followers. Some participants realized the need and proposed to establish a Democracy University, but the movement was forcefully put down on June 4.

Summary

We may summarize the framework and outline of a theory proposing institutions and networks as the infrastructure through which capital building results in societal maintenance and transformation. The theory begins with several definitions. An institutional field is one in which individual and organizational actors are consciously aware of the rules dictated by a set of institutions and abide by them or enact them accordingly in their actions and interactions. Organization-society institutional isomorphism is the extent to which organizations in an institutional field act and transact in accordance with the rules dictated by prevailing institutions. Likewise, organization-network institutional isomorphism promotes and reinforces prevailing institutions. An institutionalizing organization is one that processes individual actors for the purpose of acquiring and indoctrinating them with the knowledge and skills to perform rituals and behaviors consistent with the rules dictated by prevailing institutions.

The theory employs several assumptions (explaining mechanisms) as well: (1) striving for organization-society isomorphism is the general tendency of all organizations in the institutional field; (2) the rank (or status) of an organization reflects the extent of its isomorphism with prevailing institutions; and (3) one indication of organization-society institutional isomorphism is the extent to which an organization recruits and retains actors with institutional capital.

From these definitions and assumptions, a number of propositions may be constructed, categorized into two social functions: social integration and social change. For social integration, the following hypotheses have been formulated:

> Hypothesis 1 (for transfer of personal resources): there is an intergenerational transfer of personal (institutional and human) resources. That is, the greater the parental personal and social (institutional and human) resources, the greater the children's personal resources.
>
> Hypothesis 2 (for accumulation of social resources): personal resources are positively associated with the heterogeneity and richness (reaching to the top) of resources in one's social ties and social network.
>
> Hypothesis 3 (for conversion of resources into capital): personal resources (both human and institutional) and social resources are positively associated with the likelihood of being included in processing by institutionalizing organizations.

Certification of institutionalization reflects human and institutional capital.

Hypothesis 4 (for the flow of capital in the labor market): institutional capital (including social capital), along with human capital, is positively related to recruitment and retention by a higher-ranking organization.

For social change, the following hypotheses have been formulated:

Hypothesis 5 (networking for alternative institutions): a network that is homogeneous relative to an alternative institutional value makes a positive contribution to group solidarity and identity (as reflected in pooling and sharing of resources).

Hypothesis 6 (constructing alternative programs in institutionalizing organizations): the size of the pooled resources of a social network catering to an alternative institution is positively related to the efforts made and the likelihood of success in establishing alternative programs in institutionalizing organizations.

Hypothesis 7 (for accepting alternative institutional capital by organizations): the extent of alternative programs and their processed actors is positively related to the recruitment and retention by higher-ranking organizations of actors with the alternative institutional capital.

Hypothesis 8 (for institutional transformation): the extent of alternative institutional capital processed by institutionalizing organizations and organizations is positively related to the integration of the alternative institution into prevailing institutions (or the substitution by the alternative institution for a prevailing institution).

Concluding Remarks

In this chapter, institutions and networks are conceived as the two basic components of society; they provide the basic rules for the flow of capital in society. The framework and its components allow us to integrate a number of existing and potential theories/hypotheses. For example, the human capital theory and the institutional capital theory are reflected in the processes linking actors through institutionalizing organizations to organizations. Social capital theories are captured in the processes linking actors through social networks to organizations. Social movements (e.g., the resource mobilization theory) can be described in the processes linking actors through social networks to institutionalizing organizations and organizations and to institutions themselves.

The ultimate contribution of this conceptual scheme may lie in its ability to highlight how the two major social forces, institutions and networks, provide the basis for actions and transactions in economic and other markets. These forces help explain why a society remains stable even when transaction costs are always positive and uneven. Organizations and individual actors can coordinate and transact because they share same rules in an institutional field, through the mediation and processes of institutionalizing organizations and social networks. The same scheme suggests the dynamics by which institutional transformation may occur. Once the principles of how institutions and networks create, sustain, and change the rules of actions and transactions are set, it is then logical to bring the contributions of the state and technology into the analysis and examine how interest and agency complement or contend in these processes. In the next chapter, I will examine the intimate relationship between technology and social capital.

12

Cybernetworks and the Global Village

The Rise of Social Capital

One recent controversy in the study of social capital has been an issue raised by Putnam (1993, 1995a, 1995b): whether social capital has been on the decline in the United States for the past three or four decades. Putnam argues that there should be a positive association between social capital and political participation, and he measures social capital in terms of participation rates in social associations or secondary/tertiary associations such as PTAs, Red Cross associations, unions, church-affiliated groups, sports groups, and bowling leagues. Political participation is indicated by voting, writing to Congress, participating in rallies and political meetings, and so on. Putnam has observed that both participation rates have declined in the United States over the past thirty years or so. This has led him to conclude that social capital or civic engagement has been on the decline, and this decline might be responsible for a decline in democratic and political participation. Further, he suggests that the culprit may be the rise of television viewing. As television has gained popularity, the younger generations of Americans are no longer interested in participating in civil associations. Indeed, he suggests, even when they go bowling, they may bowl as individuals rather than as groups or leagues.

Putnam's thesis and research have been challenged from a variety of theoretical and methodological perspectives. These challenges fault Putnam's work primarily on two grounds. First, he committed errors in measuring social capital. For example, it has been pointed out that he erred in the analyses of the General Social Survey data (Greeley 1997a); he should have used "amount of time dedicated to voluntary work" (Greeley 1997b, 1997c; Newton 1997) rather than mere membership in certain organizations; he excluded certain types of associations (especially organizations emerging in contemporary America [Schudson 1996; Greeley 1997a, 1997b, 1997c; Minkoff 1997; Newton 1997]); and membership in an association is not the same as civic-mindedness or civic energy (Schudson 1996). Second, assuming that his measurements of social capital were acceptable, Putnam blamed the wrong culprit; other factors have been more critical than television viewing (Schudson 1996; Skocpol 1996).[1]

Whether social capital is rising or declining largely depends on how it is defined and measured (Greeley 1997b; Portes 1998; Lin 1999a). In addition, its significance lies in the consequences selected for analysis. When it is measured using multiple concepts such as memberships, norms, and trust, there is a danger of confusing a causal proposition (e.g., networks promote trust or vice versa) with multiple indicators of the same thing (networks, trust, and norms all measure social capital). When it is applied to a collectivity as well as to individuals, there is also a danger of the ecological fallacy (e.g., conclusions drawn from one level are assumed to be valid for another).

Following the theory proposed in this volume, I argue that social capital should be measured as embedded resources in social networks. This definition ensures consistency in the measurement and in theory as originally conceived (Bourdieu, Coleman, Lin). It also demands and allows macrophenomena to be examined for the processes and mechanisms by which social capital, thus defined and measured, is invested and mobilized to achieve certain goals at the community or societal level. From this perspective, then, the debate on whether social capital has been declining or rising in the United States or any society remains to be demonstrated and verified, as none of the studies carried out so far clearly employ the notion that social capital is reflected in the investment and mobilization of embedded resources in social networks. Membership in associations or social trust may or may not be adequate surrogate measures of social capital; their linkage or association with social capital must be clearly demonstrated before any meaningful debate can proceed.

By focusing the definition and measurement of social capital on embedded resources in networks, I will argue in this chapter that there is clear evidence that social capital has been on the ascent in the past decade – in the form of networks in cyberspace (Lin 1999a). Further, this ascent has consequences beyond community or national boundaries. The

---

[1] There is substantial literature blaming Putnam for using the wrong dependent variable (e.g., importance of good government: Skocpol 1996; the importance of political organizations: Valelly 1996; the importance of national community: Brinkley 1996; the importance of inequality in political participation: Verba, Schlozman, and Brady 1995, 1997; the importance of national elites: Heying 1997; the importance of political institutions: Berman 1997; the importance of institutional incentives: Kenworthy 1997; the importance of culture: Wood 1997). This literature does not address issues directly related to social capital.

hypotheses advanced here are two: (1) social capital in the form of cyber-networks is clearly on the rise in many parts of the world, and (2) the rise of cybernetworks transcends national or local community boundaries; therefore, its consequences (both positive and negative) must be assessed in the global context. I begin with a broad survey of the emergence of cybernetworks and the time- and space-transcending social capital they offer.

The Internet and Cybernetworks: Emerging Social Capital

Cybernetworks are defined as the social networks in cyberspace, and specifically on the Internet.[2] These networks are constructed by individuals and groups of individuals – through e-mail, chat rooms, news groups, and clubs (Jones 1997b; Smith and Kollock 1999) – as well as by informal and formal (e.g., economic, political, religious, media) organizations for the purpose of exchanges, including resource transactions and relations reinforcement. Cybernetworks have become a major avenue of communication globally since the early 1990s; an overview of their extent and scope is informative here.

Since late the 1970s and early 1980s, personal computers (PCs) have penetrated workplaces and homes around the globe. Their presence and pervasiveness have overtaken many other communication commodities in North America, Europe, and East Asian countries. In 1997, U.S. consumers bought more computers than automobiles, according to Steven Landefeld, director of the Bureau of Economic Analysis (*USA Today*, March 17, 1999). Worldwide PC sales has overtaken television sales in 2000, according to Paul Otellini of the Intel Architecture Business Group (Intel Developer Forum, February 25, 1999). In fact, PC sales already outnumbered sales of TV sets in 1998 in Australia, Canada, Denmark, and Korea. In 1999, 50 percent of U.S. households had computers, and 33 percent were online (Metcalfe 1999).

E-commerce has become big business (Irving 1995, 1998, 1999). In 1998, online shopping orders totaled $13 billion (with an average order amount of $55), and it was projected to reach $30 to $40 billion in 1999 (the Boston Consulting Group, as quoted in *PC Magazine*, March 9, 1999, p. 9). The greatest growth is expected in travel (88 percent in 1999 over 1998), PC hardware (46 percent), books (75 percent), groceries (137 percent), music (108 percent), and videos (109 percent) (Jupiter Communication, as quoted in *PC Magazine*, March 9, 1999, p. 10). It

[2] A portion of this section is taken from Lin (1999a).

has been estimated that 24 million U.S. adults plan to buy gifts online in 1999, or almost quadruple the 7.8 million who said they bought gifts online in 1998; online holiday shopping alone in 1999 could exceed $13 billion (International Communications Research, as quoted in *PC Week*, March 1, 1999, p. 6). During 1999, Internet commerce, which is growing thirty times faster than most world economies, will reach $68 billion (Metcalfe 1999, quoting International Data Corp.). By the year 2002, the projection is that online shopping will account for $32 billion in convenience items such as books and flowers, $56 billion in researched purchases like travel and computers, and $19 billion in replenishment goods such as groceries (Forrester Research Inc., as quoted in *PC Week*, January 4, 1999, p. 25). Another projection suggests that 40 percent of Web users will be online buyers by 2002, resulting in $400 billion in e-commerce transactions (International Data Corporation, as quoted in ZDNet Radar, Jesse Berst, "Technology of Tomorrow," January 6, 1999). In the first half of 1998, one out of every five retail stock trades occurred online. There are now an estimated 4.3 million people shopping for stocks and funds online, and online trading is expected to reach 31 percent of the total U.S. investment market by 2003 (Wilson 1999, quoting Piper Jaffray, *PC Computing*, March 1999, p. 14).

On March 16, 1999, the U.S. Commerce Department scrapped a sixty-year-old industry classification system that had little relevance to an information-based economy (*USA Today*, March 17, 1999, p. A1). For example, computers had not even been an industry category; they were grouped with adding machines. A new system was installed that better reflected the new categories created by the information revolution. The system is also designed to be similar to those in Mexico and Canada as trade with those countries continues to grow (*USA Today*, March 17, 1999, p. A1). Further, the Commerce Department will begin publishing figures that show the impact of online shopping on retail activity, a key indicator of the nation's economic health. Until now, the Commerce Department has lumped online shopping figures together with catalogue sales in its overall retail sales numbers. New figures that break out Internet sales as a separate entity will be available by the middle of 2000 for 1998 and 1999 (*Info World*, February 15, 1999, p. 71).

Use of the Internet for communications and networking has been more recent but even more phenomenal in growth than PCs themselves. Since the invention of the hypertext technique by Tim Berners-Lee in the 1980s at CERN (the European Particle Physics Laboratory in Geneva, Switzerland) and the introduction of the World Wide Web to the Internet in the summer of 1991, Internet growth in the past decade has been nothing short of revolutionary. In 1995, 14.1 million of 32 million U.S. households had modems, and by January 1999, 37.7 million of 50 million U.S.

households had modems (*USA Today*, March 17, 1999, p. 9D). World-wide, there were 68.7 million Web users in 1997 and 97.3 million in 1998, and the projection is that the number of Web users will exceed 300 million by 2001 (World Trade Organization estimate, March 12, 1998). Two-thirds of the people who will be online by 2002 were not online in early 1999 (Metcalfe 1999, quoting International Data Corp.).

More than 45 million PC users in the United States accessed the Internet regularly in early 1998, a 43 percent increase in the first quarter of 1998 versus the first quarter of 1997. Nearly 49 percent of all U.S. households had at least one PC (*ZD Market Intelligence*, January, 1999). In 1999, for the first time, most users – 51 percent – lived outside the United States (Metcalfe 1999, quoting International Data Corp.). The number of Internet users in China surged to 1.5 million in 1998 from 600,000 in 1997 (Xinhua News Agency, January 15, 1999). There were reportedly 4 million Internet users in China in 1999. U.S. Internet guru Nicholas Negroponte predicted in January 1999 that the number of Internet users in China would balloon to 10 million by the year 2000 (Reuters, January 15, 1999).

Female participation on the Internet has also increased dramatically. In January 1996, only 18 percent of Net users aged eighteen or above were female; by January 1999, fully 50 percent of the users were female (*USA Today*, March 17, 1999, p. 9D). By the end of the year, it was expected that women will become the majority of users on the Internet (Metcalfe 1999, quoting International Data Corp.). In 1997, more e-mail was sent than letters via the post office for the first time.

PC experts have announced, to no one's surprise, that the Internet is changing everything. Michael J. Miller, editor-in-chief of *PC Magazine*, wrote in February 1999 that the Internet changes "the ways we communicate, get information, entertain ourselves, and run our businesses" (*PC Magazine*, February 2, 1999, p. 4). In January 1999, Paul Somerson stated the same thing in *PC Computing*. It is practically impossible to get a credible estimate of how many discussion groups, forums, and clubs of multiple types have been formed and are continually being formed. What is the implication of cyberspace and cybernetwork growth for the studies of social networks and social capital? The short answer is: incredible.

In view of the dramatic growth of cybernetworks, a fundamental question can be raised: do cybernetworks carry social capital? If so, there is strong evidence either that the recent argument that social capital has been on the decline is false or that the decline has been arrested. I suggest that indeed we are witnessing *a revolutionary rise of social capital*, as represented by cybernetworks. In fact, we are witnessing a new era in which social capital will soon supersede personal capital in significance and effect.

Cybernetworks provide social capital in the sense that they carry resources that go beyond mere information purposes. E-commerce is a case in point. Many sites offer free information, but they carry advertisements presumably enticing the user to purchase certain merchandise or services. They also provide incentives to motivate users to take actions. The Internet has also provided avenues for exchanges and possible formation of collectivities (Fernback 1997; Jones 1997b; Watson 1997) These "virtual" connections allow users to connect with others with few time or space constraints. Access to information in conjunction with interactive facilities makes cybernetworks not only rich in social capital, but also an important investment for participants' purposive actions in both the production and consumption markets.

Just as pertinent is the debate on whether globalization of cybernetworks represents a reproduction of the world system where the core states or actors continue to dominate and indeed "colonize" peripheral states/ actors by incorporating the latter into global economic systems dominated by the former (Brecher and Costello 1998; Browne and Fishwick 1998; Sassen and Appiah 1998). This argument is supported by evidence that international organizations, international corporations, and international economic forms, such as commodity chains, are dominated by the values, culture, and authority of dominant states' corporations or by these states themselves. There is much concern about the increasing inequality of access to cyberspace around the world. As the rich countries and actors gain greater access to capital in cyberspace, the poor countries and actors are largely shut out from the cybercommunity.

Yet, cybernetworks suggest, at least for those who gain access to cyberspace, the possibility of a bottom-up globalization process whereby entrepreneurship and group formations become viable without the dominance of any particular class of actors (Wellman 1998). Do cybernetworks suggest a neo-globalization process? While not denying that the dominant states and actors remain actively interested in controlling the development of cyberspace, I argue that cybernetworks represent a new era of democratic and entrepreneur networks and relations in which resources flow and are shared by a large number of participants with new rules and practices, many of which are devoid of colonial intent or capability.

With the increasing availability of inexpensive devices and ever-increasing Web capabilities that transcend space and time, we are facing a new era of social networks in the form of global villages. Globalization of cybernetworks is a double-edged sword. More sharply than ever, it demarcates the haves and the have-nots in terms of accessing capital embedded in cyberspace. Access to computers, other devices, and the Internet remains distributed unequally because of social (e.g., lack of education and facility in the language), economic (e.g., ability to acquire computers and gain access to the communications infrastructure), and political (e.g., authoritarian control over access) constraints. Yet, within the cybernetworks, it is no longer necessary or possible to reproduce the core-peripheral world system, in which the core actors establish links and networks to peripheral actors for their continuing domination of information, resources, and surplus values. Instead, information is freer and more available to more individuals than ever before in human history. It is also clear that constraints and control over access are waning fast as computer and communication costs decrease and technology leapfrogs the traditional authoritarian control of access.

There is strong evidence that an increasing number of individuals are engaged in this new form of social networks and relations, and there is little doubt that a significant part of the activities involve the creation and use of social capital. Access to free sources of information, data, and other actors has created growing networks and social capital at an unprecedented pace. Networks are expansive and yet at the same time intimate. Networking transcends time (connecting whenever one can and wants to) and space (accessing sites around the globe directly or indirectly if direct access is denied). Rules and practices are being formulated as such networks are constructed. Institutions – borrowed from past practices, deliberately deviating from past practices, or consensually developed by participants – are being created as such networks (e.g., villages) are being built.

There is little doubt that the hypothesis that social capital is declining can be refuted if one goes beyond the traditional interpersonal networks and analyzes the cybernetworks that emerged in the 1990s. We are witnessing the beginning of a new era in which social capital is far outpacing personal capital in significance and effect. We need to compile basic data and information on the extent to which individuals are spending time and effort engaging others over cybernetworks, compared to the use of time and effort for interpersonal communications, other leisure activities (TV watching, travel, eating out, movie- and theatergoing), attending civic and local meetings, and so on. We also need to estimate the amount of useful information gathered through cybernetworks compared to traditional media.

In the next section, I will offer a case study, concerning the recent Falun Gong movement in China, as an example of how cybernetworks provide social capital in a social movement and sustain collective action even within an extremely constrained institutional field. This example shows how cybernetworks facilitate the use of social capital over space and time, and demonstrates effectiveness in generating and sustaining a social movement in a global context. Whether the movement itself has any merit is of no interest here.

Falun Gong: A Case Study of Social Capital and Social Movement

Falun Gong (Cultivation of the Wheel of the Law), also known as Falu Dafa (the Great Law of the Wheel), is a Chinese meditation and exercise technique proposed by Li Hongzhi (Li 1993). Li contends that it evolved out of Buddhism and captures the truth of the universe through both Buddhism and Taoism, the two highest-level religions in the world. According to Li, the principle of the universe is contained in a turning Wheel that, upon cultivation, can be contained in the lower abdomen of the cultivator. The Law can be expressed in three principles: Zhen (truth or truthfulness), Shan (compassion, kindness, or benevolence), and Ren (tolerance or forbearance). Practicing these principles helps the individual acquire the Wheel and keep it turning. The Wheel may turn in either direction. When it is turning clockwise, it brings the principles of the universe into the body as energy; when it is turning counterclockwise, it projects the principles outward to share the energy with others. Not everyone, in fact seldom anyone, acquires such energy at its powerful maximum, but most people can learn to keep the Wheel turning. As cultivation advances, more wheels can be built in the body from the root Wheel at the lower abdomen.[3]

---

[3] Li was born in 1951, in a city in Jinlin Province, in northeastern China. According to Li, he was born on May 13, 1951 (Li 1994, p. 333), but the government has claimed that he changed the original date of birth on his official registration card from July 7, 1952 (www.peopledaily.com.cn/item/flg/news/072306.html) to May 13 in order to have it coincide, by the lunar calendar, with the birth day of Sakyamuni, or Siddhartha Gautama, the founder of Buddhism, on April 8). Li has contended that the original record was incorrect, and he has no interest in becoming a modern-day Sakyamuni. From 1970 to 1978, he worked at an army stud farm and played the trumpet in a forest police unit in Jilin, and worked as an attendant at a hotel run by the police unit. In 1982, after leaving the army, he worked at the security department of the Changchun Cereals Company (*People's Daily*, July 22, 1999). In 1991 he quit that job and became involved in the practice and instruction of *qigong* (cultivation of inner energy, a general and popular term for many forms of Chinese exercise to enhance inner energy).

According to the biography attached to one of the books he wrote (Li 1994), he started learning the Law from a master between the ages of four and twelve. He learned the principles of Zhen, Shan, and Ren and achieved the highest level of cultivation when he was eight, at which time he allegedly could become invisible, pull rusted nails from frozen pipes without effort, float off the ground, and penetrate through walls. He then met another master at the age of twelve and learned martial arts. In 1972, he met a third master who taught him to cultivate his mind for two years. The next master was a woman

The Falun Gong Organization

Li started propagating Falun Gong in 1992 in his native region of Changchung, Jinling, and then moved to Beijing and other cities throughout China. He charged no fees and claimed that all his income from workshops was donated to furthering the Falun Gong. Falun Gong spread quickly, and Li's workshops and lectures drew huge audiences. He found the Falun Dafa Research Society in Beijing, and his lectures were compiled into volumes.[4] Over the next two years, an informal yet rigid structure emerged (Li 1996, pp. 132–133). The Society served as the highest national coordinating office under his direct command. In various provinces, regions, and cities, general teaching/assisting centers (*fudao zhong zhan*) were established. According to the Chinese government report, there were thirty-nine of them by July 1999 (*People's Daily*, July 30, 1999), each led by a coordinator appointed by Li and the Society (Li 1996, p. 135). These centers, in turn, coordinated teaching stations (1,900, according to the government report) scattered throughout cities and townships and, under these stations, cultivation or exercise spots or sites (28,000, according to the government report). In most cases, the coordinator had to participate in workshops conducted by Li himself, and no one else was allowed to conduct workshops (Li 1996, p. 144). At each exercise site (*niengong dian*), there were tutors (*fudaoyuan*) and practitioners. Practitioners gathered at each site regularly to cultivate, or perform exercises and study Li's writings and lectures (from audio- and videotapes) (Li 1996, pp. 144–145, 148). Centers, stations, and sites could cooperate (p. 150) and lean on (*guakau*, or affiliated with) local work units (1996, p. 152).[5] However, their leaders could not also par-

---

who taught him the principles of Buddhism. In this fashion, he continued encountering new Buddhist or Taoist masters as he elevated himself to higher levels. He then began teaching others. After observing and studying various forms of *qigong*, he decided in 1984 to popularize his teachings by writing and editing his lectures. During this process, amazingly, all fourteen of his masters returned to help and instruct him. The Wheel of Law method, Falun Gong, was finalized in 1989. He spent the next two years observing how his disciples followed these instructions and elevated themselves to high levels. However, according to official reports (*People's Daily*, July 22, 1999), Li did not begin learning *qigong* until 1988. He studied with two masters of *qigong*, mixing in some movements from Thai dance that he had learned while visiting Thailand.

In 1992, he "was ordered to go out of the mountain" (Li 1993, p. 112; 1994, p. 341) and started general training and lecturing throughout China.

[4] As of April 1999, The Falun Dafa Web site listed fourteen volumes, which are mostly compilations of Li's lectures (falundafa.ca/works/eng/mgjf/mgjf4.html).

[5] For example, a site could "borrow" the yard of a work unit. Centers could be listed as affiliated with various work units for administrative reporting purposes, because voluntary or civic groups or associations, even professional associations, do not carry official administrative status and must "lean on" (be officially affiliated with) a work unit to gain recognition by the government.

ticipate in other forms of cultivation (e.g., qigong, or energy cultivation) or other groups and associations, and the stations and points could not participate in other associations' activities, except in exhibitions and "athletic event" demonstrations.

Thus, despite his persistent claim that Falun Gong or Dafa had no organization, Li had created a hierarchical organization with powerful and efficient top-to-bottom control. This organization, built on social networks and under the direction of a single leader and ideology, created its own institutions and institutionalizing organizations (see Chapter 11) through which new members were recruited, trained, and placed in an ever-expanding labor market.

Li left China in 1995 and the Society, under his direct guidance, continued to play the role of national coordination (Li 1996, pp. 169–170). However, he stressed that cultivation was more important than organization (p. 175), and leaders and practitioners were urged to learn his writings and lectures through thorough memorization (pp. 105, 138, 169). Since Li was the only one who could conduct workshops, the leaders and practitioners could only read, repeat, and discuss his "scriptures" (*jinwen*, or quotations from his books and lectures) together at each exercise site or on their own. Leaders were forbidden to freely interpret and extend his teachings (p. 171). Thus, Li remained the only authority in the hierarchical organization.

Li employed the same strategies in deploying and extending his organization globally. He began lecturing in the United States in 1996. In November 1996, the first international "experience sharing" meeting of Falun Gong was held in China, attended by practitioners from fourteen countries and regions. In 1998, the first North American "experience sharing" meeting was held in New York. Other meetings were held in Canada, Germany, Singapore, and Switzerland. Falun Gong has grown like wildfire throughout China, especially in cities since 1992, and has spread to North America, Australia, Asia, and Europe. By early 1999, Li claimed to have over 100 million practitioners worldwide. Some scholars have estimated the number of practitioners in China to range between 20 to 60 million; the Chinese government puts the number at around 2 million (Reuters, July 25, 1999).

The Suppression and the Protest Movement

As Falun Gong grew, it caught the attention of the Chinese media and government, first fascinating them with its claims of incredible feats of curing and supernatural powers and then alarming them by its hierarchical organization; enthusiastic, cohesive, disciplined practitioners; and enormous popularity. In June 1996 one of the largest newspapers in

China, *Guangming Daily*, started criticizing Falun Gong, drawing strong responses from the practitioners. The responses further alarmed the government. In the same year, the government banned five Falun Gong books. In 1997, the Ministry of Security investigated Falun Gong for possible illegal religious activities but did not draw any conclusions. In July 1998, the Ministry designated Falun Gong as a devious religious sect and conducted investigations. The Ministry of Civil Affairs also conducted investigations. Practitioners responded vigorously by staging sit-ins at various official sites and buildings. Cultivation continued to flourish at many exercise sites, and Li's writings and lectures were readily available in print, and on audio- and videotape. In fact, there was a growing industry in China and abroad in the production of Falun Gong–related publications and materials, without the awareness or approval of Li or his Research Society.

The final confrontation began with the publication of an article by He Zhuo-xiu, a scientist and a member of the Chinese Academy of Sciences, in *Science and Technology Review for Youth (Qing Shao Nian Ke Ji Bao Nan)*, a monthly publication issued by the Tianjin Normal University. In the article (issue 4, 1999), He challenged the claimed scientific basis of Falun Gong and warned that it might be harmful for youth to practice. This article drew immediate responses from Falun Gong followers in Tianjin, who visited the publishing office and demanded a retraction of the article and a public apology. Starting on April 20, the Falun Gong practitioners began a sit-in demonstration. The gathering drew 3,000 on April 22 and 6,300 on April 23 (*People's Daily*, July 23, 1999). Without satisfactory responses from the publisher, the Tianjin cultivators decided to appeal to the national government and CCP leaders in Beijing.

Practitioners began to converge on Zhongnanhai, the compound in central Beijing housing the core government and CCP leaders and their families, on the evening of April 24. On April 25, more than 10,000 Falun Gong practitioners from several provinces and cities[6] gathered at Zhongnanhai.[7] They held silent sit-ins outside the compound, demanded a meeting with Party leaders, submitted an appeal, and sought official approval of their activities. Two representatives met Lo Gan, secretary of the Political and Legal Commission of the Central Committee, as well as Zhu Rongji, who joined in the conversation, but no commitments

---

[6] According to the official report (*People's Daily*, August 4, 1999), demonstrators came from Hebei, Liaoning, Beijing, Tianjin, Shangdong, Helongjiang, Anhui, and other locations.

[7] The official estimate put the number of protesters at over 10,000. Other eyewitness reports estimated between 20,000 and 30,000 protesters. It was difficult to separate some bystanders from participants, and the police eventually blocked off the area except for through traffic, preventing other practitioners from joining in.

were received. At the urging of the police, they eventually scattered after 9 P.M.

This incident sent a shock wave through the CCP leadership, for it was probably the first time since the Party gained control of the country in 1949 that the Party and the government failed to receive any information beforehand that an unauthorized gathering of any reasonable size would take place. Furthermore, such a gathering took place at Zhongnanhai, the nerve center of control. The Party not only saw this as a failure of intelligence but also sensed a strong threat to its authority and immediately swung into action. Jiang Zemin apparently issued a directive that evening for immediate investigations. A thorough review of the intelligence apparatus followed, and a nationwide investigation of Falun Gong proceeded with haste and determination. Realizing that Falun Gong practitioners had penetrated many Party and government bureaucracies, offices, and institutes; that the number of Falun Gong cultivators was considerable (some scholars estimate it to be up to 60 million in China – the same size as the CCP membership, even though the Falun Gong and Li claim to have over 100 million cultivators, most of whom reside in China); and that the Falun Gong was well organized, thoroughly disciplined, and quick to mobilize, the Communist leadership considered it a serious threat to the core political ideology, to the Party organization, and to the absolute command of the Party in all spheres of life (Central Committee Circular 19, July 19, 1999). Efficiently coordinated organization, extensive participation, and collective cohesion convinced the CCP leadership that Falun Gong constituted a serious threat to the Party's ideological and organizational hold over the country. Also stunning was the large number of Falun Gong practitioners in the Party's most sensitive offices and work units.

The Party outlawed Falun Gong on July 19 and immediately began arresting coordinators and important trainers throughout China, searching and ransacking their homes, confiscating and destroying books and related materials, and conducting a major reeducation campaign to eradicate Falun Gong involvement in the Party and the government. The campaign had three phases: elevating learning, or a reindoctrination in Marxist ideology; educational transformation, or persuading those involved in Falun Gong to recognize and admit wrongdoings (involvement in the Falun Gong); and organizational treatment, or ridding work units and areas of all elements of Falun Gong. All Party apparatuses, including investigative and disciplinary units, propaganda, the united front, Communist youth, and united women's groups were to be mobilized to unveil Li's and Falun Gong's activities and intents, and were to control all situations so as to accomplish "early discovery, early reporting, early control, and an early solution" in "defending social and political stability" (Central Committee Circular, July 19, 1999). For the next month, sustained, all-out efforts were made to eliminate Falun Gong in China.[8]

Cybernetworks and Falun Gong

What is fascinating from our perspective is that these events provide a vivid and powerful demonstration, for the first time in history, of how cybernetworks were implicated in a major social movement and countermovement. Moreover, it is most interesting, but probably not surprising, that this happened in a society under the rigid and powerful political command of a single political party and ideology: China.

As soon as Li left China in 1995, an Internet system was created by Falun Gong (falundafa.ca; falundafa.org; falundafa.com) through which direct communication and interactions were established between Li, who now resided in the United States, and his followers throughout the world, including China. The Web site, called Minhui (roughly, "clear understanding"), was supplemented by an e-mail system. These systems sustained the efficiency of the organization at all levels (from the Research Society and general teaching centers all the way down to many exercise sites and individual practitioners). There were more than forty linked sites in many countries, including the United States, Canada, Australia, Sweden, Germany, Russia, Singapore, and Taiwan. It is not known how many PCs in China were linked to these sites, but no doubt the connections were massive. Several pieces of evidence support this assertion. Li's site was originally identified as the Overseas Coordinating Office of the Falun Dafa Research Society. By 1997, exchanges over the networks were so rampant that the Unit had to issue a statement to rein in control. This statement, issued on June 15, 1997, warned that cybernetworks had been used to include other religious ideologies or *qigong* (cultivation of inner energy, a common exercise in China) content; to insert materials not approved by Li and the Research Society, including personal interpretations and the marketing of products; and to include materials illegally. The statement reminded all users that any materials, conversation records, or correspondence not contained in Li's public lectures or publications could not be included on the Internet, and materials to be sent through the Internet had to be checked by teaching centers' coordinators in various countries and regions. It asked all users to report violations of these rules, via e-mail, to the Overseas Coordinating Office (www.falundafa.org/fldfbb/gg970615.htm).

---

[8] The Party claimed that it was all right to practice Falun Gong as a *qigong* exercise. But in reality, all public Falun Gong practices were dispersed and not allowed.

On August 5, 1997, the Overseas Unit's site (www.falundafa.org) was formally merged with the site of the China Falun Dafa Research Society, and it issued an Internet statement to overseas practitioners advocating the holding of various meetings, in various languages, to increase the voice of Dafa in media around the world; the selection and inclusions of Caucasian practitioners as trainers and facilitators of Caucasian practitioners' participation; the spread of Li's publications through translation and the Internet; and an organization of visiting groups to China to learn and practice Dafa (www.falundafa.org/fldfbb/tz970805.htm). On August 8, 1998, the Research Society issued an Internet message to Falun research associations and teaching centers in all countries, indicating that the cybernetworks for Falun Gong had achieved, or almost achieved, total and comprehensive linkage with all teaching centers around the world, including those in China. In this notice (www.falundafa.org/fldfbb/setup c.htm), the Society expressed satisfaction at the use of the Internet to spread the true words of Li (his published and publicly stated works only), as well as the activities of associations and teaching centers around the world. However, due to the enormous increase in personal e-mail addresses, the Society had discovered the dissemination of information not related to Dafa or related to religions, unverified statements by Li, and even misinformation in the name of the various associations or the Research Society. Thus, it announced the establishment of a Bulletin Board that would carry Li's instructions and the Research Society's announcements, the content of which could be copied and forwarded. Other individualized content would be modified or eliminated from all sites. All "irrelevant" sites would be notified and corrected through the Bulletin Board (www.falundafa.ca/fldfbb).

Thus, by the summer of 1998, the Research Society and Li had established a comprehensive cybernetwork linking all or most teaching centers, as well as many individual practitioners, and exercised control over the flow of content. The extent to which this cybernetwork played a critical role in the mobilization of practitioners from many provinces and cities to converge on Beijing and Zhongnanhai on April 25, 1999, remained unknown. The fact that the CCP and government intelligence apparatus, which penetrates deeply into every corner of Chinese society, had no prior knowledge about the movements of thousands of practitioners, many of whom took trains and buses, suggests that the cybernetworks with direct linkages and access to information from the Research Society (now run in the United States), and among the teaching centers, exercise sites, and individual Internet users, might have played a key role in dissemination of information about the upcoming sit-down demonstrations.

This suspicion was confirmed in part by Li himself. On May 2, 1999, in interviews with Chinese and foreign media in Australia, Li was asked how he kept in touch with the 1 billion practitioners around the world. He replied: "Not any direct channels, because as you found out that here was a conference and so I found out too. Why should I say that we all know what is happening anywhere? Everyone knows about the Internet; this thing is very convenient throughout the world. Wherever there is a meeting, it appears in the Internet and many regions around the world learn soon and I learn too. I really do not have any exchanges with them, not even telephone calls" (www.falundafa.org/fldfbb/tomedia/ tochinesemedia.html). When reporters asked Li how the practitioners knew to go to Zhongnanhai on April 25, if they were not organized, as Li claimed, he replied: "You all know about the Internet; they found out on the Internet. Also, the practitioners in different regions were friends and relayed this information to others" (www.falundafa.org/fldfbb/tomedia/ toenglishmedia.html). To deny having any organization might be true in the legal sense (the Falun Dafa Research Society had not registered with the Ministry of Civil Affairs), but certainly there was every evidence that the Society, teaching centers, and exercise sites formed a hierarchical structure through which information flow and authority were commanded. Thus, we could not consider Li's reply as valid. But the fact remained that the cybernetworks were well placed by then to be used by the organization to disseminate any information it wanted, and Li's statement did not deny that the networks were involved in the mobilization process.

After the April 25 incident and the strong and shocking responses from the Party and the government, the use of the Internet between the Minhui Site and individual users was intensive and extensive. To facilitate the flow of information, the Minhui Site constructed a file, called News and Reports, to carry information from China through the Internet. For the month of June 1999, this file (www.falundafa.org/china) contained 156 messages (all but 14 messages were specifically dated), and at least half of them were identified as originating from inside China. The locations identified included Beijing, Tianjin, Shanghai, Shangdong, Nanchang, Weifang, Qingdao (Shangdong), Hebei, BenXi, Linyi (Shangdong), Shenyang, Dalian, Qiqihar, Shijiazhuang, Guangzhou, Qinghungdao, Daqing, Fuzhou, Tonghua, Zhengzhou, Jaingsu, Hangzhou, Fujian, Taiyuan, Weihai, Jiangshu Qidong, Wuhan, Harbin, Hubei (Xishui), Changsha, and others.

The extensive use of the Internet was again confirmed when the government shut down several Internet sites in China that provided free or paid e-mail services. For example, 263.net shut down more than 1,000,000 of its free e-mail addresses on July 22 for several days, and when it came back on, the service was greatly curtailed and monitored.

In the meantime, the Internet was used widely by the Party and the government to attack Li and Falun Gong. Extensive essays were written and transmitted over Web sites (e.g., *People's Daily*, Xinhua Press, and many other Web-site links to the Chinese government and the media) to discredit Li (e.g., about his falsified birth date, his tax evasion, the lowly jobs he held, the brevity of his *qigong* education, and his possible connections with the Central Intelligence Agency). Other reports provided personal and eyewitness accounts of individuals being victimized by Falun Gong. Articles reported confessions and renunciations of Falun Gong practitioners, especially among Party members and cadres. Finally on July 29, 1999, a new Web site (www.ppflg.china.com.cn) was created by *People's Daily* dedicated to "unveiling Falun Gong, for the Health and Life of the People." It contained columns including "reporting and commenting, surveying and analyzing, comments from the people, tragic stories, selected letters, relevant websites, and messages from visitors."

There were also reports that many of the Falun Gong Web sites experienced hacking (AP, July 31, 1999) and at least one attempt that appeared to originate from the Chinese national police bureau in Beijing. Bob McWee, a Falun Gong practitioner and manager of a Web site, falunusa.net, uncovered the Internet address from which hacking was attempted on his machine, along with two telephone numbers in Beijing. When the Associated Press called the numbers, the person who answered the phone identified them as belonging to the Public Security Ministry. A telephone operator at the Ministry said they belonged to the Internet Monitoring Bureau.

It is clear that for the first time in history, a movement and a countermovement occurred in cyberspace, apparently with dramatic effect.

Discussion

The Falun Gong incident serves as a vivid contemporary illustration of how social networks and capital provide the mechanisms and processes by which an alternative ideology, challenging prevailing ideology and institutions (see Chapter 11), can be institutionalized. The Falun Gong incident was considered the most serious challenge to the CCP since the Tiananman Square incident in 1989 (Lin 1992b). However, there are significant differences between the two social movements. Falun Gong involved much broader participation, drawing practitioners from all age groups, all social and occupational strata, and both urban and rural populations (though probably disproportionately from cities and townships), as well as enjoying a well-organized and strongly hierarchical structure of command, and having the advantage of the Internet as well as cell phones (the Tiananmen Square participants could only use the newly available fax machines effectively). While the Tiananman Square incident died down quickly after June 4, 1989, Falun Gong had the benefit of a cybernetwork that remained in operation after July 20, 1999, and in communication with some users inside China.

Falun Gong provided no political ideology in the traditional sense, but it did offer an alternative ideology to the prevailing ideology. The events of 1999 illustrate that social networks built on a singular alternative ideology can mobilize individuals into a cohesive collectivity. From this collectivity have emerged alternative institutionalizing organizations in the form of teaching centers and exercise sites where "cultivation" involves not only exercises and meditations, but, more importantly, reading and studying the ideology – Li's teachings. These effective organizations provided the training ground for new recruits, indoctrinated them with the ideology, and absorbed them into the social networks. With the aid of the cybernetworks, these social networks have created revolutionary and powerful means to mobilize capital, social and others, making viable massive social movements even in a most constrained and repressive institutional field. The leaders of the prevailing ideology and institutions correctly recognized these challenges and considered them a serious political struggle. In the Central Committee's circular banning Falun Dafa, the first point made was that Party members "must recognize the political nature and serious damage of the Falun Gong organization." A subsequent essay recognized the Falun Gong organization's serious challenge to the CCP's guiding principles (Qiu Shi, 1999).

Li and his followers steadfastly denied that there was any organization (*zuzhi*), on the ground that they had no physical location, no visible hierarchy, and no visible leaders. But it was clear that Li had put together a most efficient organization, with sophisticated means of communication such as a cybernetwork, to recruit, train, retain, and mobilize followers and create collective social capital. It is doubtful that Li intended to challenge the sovereignty of the Communist Party in China, but the alternative ideology and institutions he created could have eroded the Party by winning over its members and penetrating its organizations, thus chipping away at its institutional capital and human capital to the extent that its effectiveness and capability for absolute one-party and one-ideology rule would have been seriously if not irretrievably damaged.

Research Agenda

The growth of cyberspace and the emergence of social, economic, and political networks in cyberspace signal a new era in the construction and development of social capital. No longer is social capital constrained by time or space; cybernetworks open up the possibility of global reaches in social capital. Social ties can now transcend geopolitical boundaries, and exchanges can occur as fast and as willingly as the actors care to participate. These new developments provide new opportunities as well as challenges for accessing social capital, and thus alert us to reconsider theories and hypotheses on social capital that have so far been built largely on observations and analyses of localized, time-constrained social connections. Systematic research efforts must be made to understand and assess this new form of social capital. Here I offer several contradictions and challenges worthy of research attention.

1. How can we extend notions and theories of localized social capital to global social capital and to social capital captured in cybernetworks? For example, what is a civil society in the global village? How can we extend our analysis of the contribution of social capital to national assets such as democratic society or political participation or to community assets such as trust and cohesion? What are the equivalent global assets? Do we need to develop new notions, or can we apply the theories and methods we have developed to understand a global civic society or a global engagement? Even if we can make such extensions, which I doubt we can without modifications, how do we compare localized versus global social capital and their consequences? Are the traditional localized embedded resources losing their utility (e.g., local cohesion can no longer rely solely on localized social capital) or will they retain their returns for the local community? If these localized networks remain meaningful, what do cybernetworks mean in this context? How can national participation be seen as a component of this larger global context or village (Ananda Mitra 1997 in Jones 1997a)?[9] Do cybernetworks represent added social capital or do they replace localized social capital? Does being a citizen of a community or a nation takes precedence over being a resident of a global village, or vice versa, and under what conditions? In cases of conflicting interests or loyalties for an actor in her or his access to localized and global social capital, how does the actor choose between the privileges and responsibilities of each?

2. In one sense, cybernetworks provide an equalizing opportunity in the access to social capital. Given the easy, low-cost access to cybernetworks that is being provided to more and more people around the world, the abundance and flow of information, the multiplicity of alternative channels as sources and partners, and the increasing need for and gratification of almost instantaneous exchanges, power differentials will

---

[9] I use the term *village* to suggest that rules, practices, and institutions for cybernetworks are still largely in flux and are being developed.

inevitably suffer degradation. Multiple routes may mean less dependence on certain nodes and less power to these nodes. Will such alternative routes reduce the significance of network locations or bridges? Does this mean, then, that there will be an equalizing or democratization process in cybernetworks? Likewise, authority will become harder to exercise. As the Falun Gong case demonstrates, social capital is now carried across time and space, and traditional authorities can no longer control and command resources, as before. Alternative and counterprevailing ideologies will not be so easily stamped out or suppressed.

This process has already appeared in the economic sector. For example, emerging companies like Dell and Gateway entered the Internet early, and by reducing transaction costs involving intermediaries and stockpiling of inventories, they sold computers faster and at a lower price. This has offered them a significant competitive advantage over traditional companies such as IBM, Compaq, and Hewlett Packard, which rely on third parties for sales and services. These companies will have to either switch or lose business and competition as they face the enormous task of maintaining the traditional way of doing business and adapting to new avenues to interact directly with buyers. In stock trading, electronic trading companies such as Charles Schwab, E-Trade, and Datek similarly allow individuals to trade at a lower cost and a faster transaction rate, forcing companies such as Merrill Lynch to adapt to the new rules, again at the risk of losing relations with their local and regional dealers. The pressure on traditional firms and industries is enormous. Travel agencies, car dealers, insurance companies, banks, and stockbrokers all face the challenge of either changing fast in adopting cybernetworks to do business or facing death (Taylor and Jerome 1999). Such is the force of cybernetworks for equalizing power.

Yet, will power disappear? Hardly (Reid 1999). Resourceful actors in cyberspace will accrue more resources, make alliances, acquire or merge with other resourceful actors, and block off alternative routes with proprietary hardware and software to establish themselves as the essential bridges or structural holes in the cybernetworks. New rules and practices are being developed for firms to deal and take advantage of the information economy (Breslow 1997; Kelly 1998; Shapiro and Varian 1999). Microsoft is doing it by cornering operating systems and major applications. America Online is attempting to do it by blocking off access to its users from outside. Telephone companies, cable companies, and satellite firms are all competing or combining to gain a competitive edge over the Internet. Elite universities and research institutions have established their own supercomputing and Internet systems. Government and other agencies and firms will acquire extensive information on individuals and make such information available to actors and agents who have the power, authority, or wealth to pay for or gain access to such information. The federal Advisory Commission on Electronic Commerce, convened in June 1999, was to devise recommendations on e-commerce taxation policies. In April 2000, it recommended to Congress that the moratorium on the Internet tax be continued for six years.

At the same time, access to cyberspace itself has enlarged the gulf between the haves and the have-nots. The Internet, for example, may have equalizing effects for citizens of North America, Europe, Australia, New Zealand, and East Asia, allowing them to acquire social capital. Yet, it may also have further differentiated these societies and their citizens from the rest of the world, especially Africa. According to the 1999 International Data Corporation/World Times Information Society Index (*PC* magazine June 8, 1999, p. 10), which tracked fifty-five countries that accounted for 97 percent of the global gross national product (GNP) and 99 percent of information technology expenditures, the information gap between rich and poor countries has continued to widen.[10] About 150 countries representing 40 percent of the world's population were not included in the Index; they accounted for 3 percent of the world GNP and less than 0.5 percent of all information technology expenditures. Without computers, linguistic facilities, and electricity and telephones, many citizens around the world have been excluded from accessing, participating in, and exchanging within cybernetworks.

The digital divide in social capital may also be further differentiating people along socioeconomic class, ethnic, religious, and residential lines. In the United States, the top-ranked information economy in the world, inequality in access to computers and the Internet is substantial. In the 1999 report *Falling Through the Net: Defining the Digital Divide*, the U.S. Department of Commerce (Irving 1999) showed significant gaps in households with and without e-mail across income, urban-rural, race/origin, education, and marital status categories. These gaps increased from 1994 to 1999. As can be seen in Figure 12.1, in 1999, 40 to 45 percent of U.S. households with incomes of more than $75,000 had access to e-mail, compared to only 4 to 6 percent of those with incomes of $14,999 or less. Figure 12.2 shows that over one-fifth (21.5 percent) of white households had access to e-mail, whereas less than 8 percent of black and Hispanic households did. Education (Figure 12.3) told the same story: Over two-fifths (38.3 percent) of the households with persons holding bachelor's or higher degrees had access to e-mail, whereas less than 4 percent of those with some high school or less did.

---

[10] The top ten countries in information technology expenditure were, in order, the United States, Sweden, Finland, Singapore, Norway, Denmark, the Netherlands, Australia, Japan, and Canada.

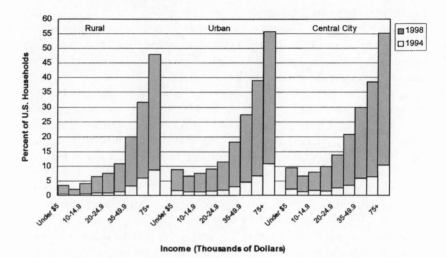

Household Income	Rural		Urban		Central City	
	1994	1998	1994	1998	1994	1998
Under $5,000	0.5	3.0	1.8	7.0	2.1	7.5
5,000-9,999	0.0	2.1	1.2	5.6	1.4	5.3
10,000-14,999	0.5	3.7	1.4	6.2	1.8	6.3
15,000-19,999	0.9	5.6	1.5	7.7	1.6	8.4
20,000-24,999	0.8	6.7	2.0	9.5	2.6	11.3
25,000-34,999	1.3	9.5	3.0	15.3	3.5	17.3
35,000-49,999	3.4	16.4	4.5	22.7	5.8	23.8
50,000-74,999	6.0	25.7	6.7	32.2	6.5	32.1
75,000+	8.7	39.3	10.8	44.8	10.3	45.0

Figure 12.1 Percentage of U.S. households with e-mail by income and by rural, urban, and central city areas. (From National Telecommunications and Information Administration [NTIA] and U.S. Census Bureau, U.S. Department of Commerce, using November 1994 and December 1998 Current Population Surveys)

Regional divides (Figure 12.4) likewise showed inequality: residents in urban and central cities had much greater access to e-mail than rural households (except in the Northeast). Married couples (with no children or with children less than eighteen years old) were much more likely to have access to e-mail than other types of households (Figure 12.5).

The gaps between the rich and the poor, the urban and the rural, the educated and the uneducated, and the dominant ethnic/racial/religious groups versus others have undoubtedly become worse between developed and less developed countries. For example, in the United States, almost half of all Internet users are females, whereas in China, females

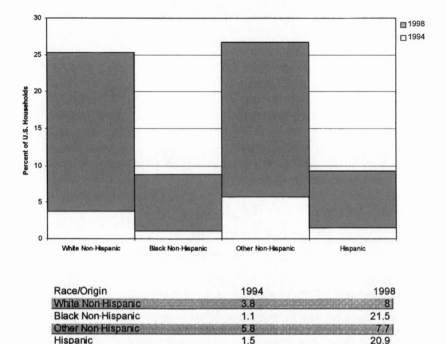

Race/Origin	1994	1998
White Non-Hispanic	3.8	8
Black Non-Hispanic	1.1	21.5
Other Non-Hispanic	5.8	7.7
Hispanic	1.5	20.9
		7.8

Figure 12.2 Percentage of U.S. households with e-mail by race/origin, 1994 and 1998. (From National Telecommunications and Information Administration [NTIA] and U.S. Census Bureau, U.S. Department of Commerce, using November 1994 and December 1998 Current Population Surveys)

accounted for only 15 percent of Internet use in a recent survey (CNNIC 1999). About 60 percent of Chinese users were college educated (versus 38 percent of U.S. users).

Thus, ethnic and gender differences in Internet use (Poster 1998; Sassen 1998, Chaps. 5 and 9) and the level of the country's technological development increase inequality (Castells 1998, Chap. 2), and are compounded by societal development. In other words, because technological capabilities and all forms of capital differ across nations, inequality in social capital is growing fast and further in cybernetworks. Social class differences in accessing social capital in cybernetworks may be diminishing in advantaged societies, yet they may be increasing in disadvantaged societies. Take language as an example: computers, the Internet, and communication around the globe are dominated by the English language, ranging from the development of codes to routine user

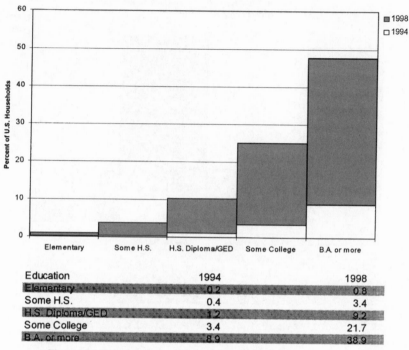

Education	1994	1998
Elementary	0.2	0.8
Some H.S.	0.4	3.4
H.S. Diploma/GED	1.2	9.2
Some College	3.4	21.7
B.A. or more	8.9	38.9

Figure 12.3 Percentage of U.S. households with e-mail by education, 1994 and 1998. (From National Telecommunications and Information Administration [NTIA] and U.S. Census Bureau, U.S. Department of Commerce, using November 1994 and December 1998 Current Population Surveys)

commands. English-language countries, already advantaged through earlier industrial developments in the nineteenth and twentieth centuries, have continued to gain an advantage through the growing capabilities of computers and the Internet. It is true that other countries, due to their large populations (e.g., China), may develop their own linguistic cyber-communities, but the language gap will continue to increase the inequality of social capital in cybernetworks. Analysis of inequality of social capital inevitably relies on the comparison of subunits such as nations, regions, or communities. In this sense, traditional communities and national boundaries will remain meaningful so long as gaps in social capital remain significant along these lines.

This divide involves more than the availability of technologies. As computers decrease in cost and satellite services begin to provide wide coverage around the world, the more demanding resources or the absence of capabilities to access cyberspace and cybernetworks such as

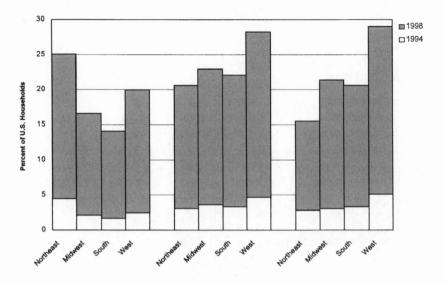

Region	Rural		Urban		Central City	
	1994	1998	1994	1998	1994	1998
Northeast	4.5	20.6	3.1	17.5	2.8	12.7
Midwest	2.1	14.4	3.6	19.4	3.1	18.3
South	1.7	12.4	3.3	18.8	3.3	17.3
West	2.5	17.4	4.7	23.5	5.1	23.9

Figure 12.4 Percentage of U.S. households with e-mail by relation, by rural, urban, and central city areas, 1994 and 1998. (From National Telecommunications and Information Administration [NTIA] and U.S. Census Bureau, U.S. Department of Commerce, using November 1994 and December 1998 Current Population Surveys)

education, linguistic facilities, and sociopolitical constraints will require far greater efforts and difficult changes.

3. The mixing of material and idea goods as social capital in cyber-networks is unprecedented. Information may be free, but the cost is exposure to imposed idea/material messages, especially commercial messages. While this cost is traditional, as it has been in printed media for centuries and in television for decades, the integration of economic and marketing messages in cybernetworks is much more thorough. There is no clear demarcation between senders and receivers of such mixed messages; all exchanges are potential (voluntary or involuntary) carriers of such messages. Although currently they are primarily commercial/material in nature, they may extend to political, religious, and other

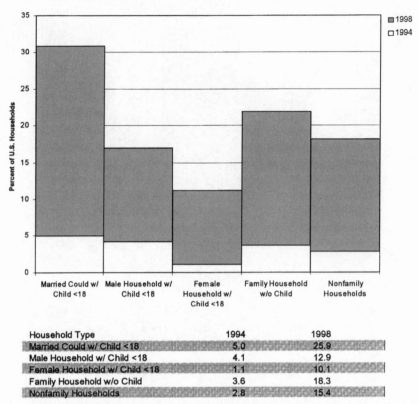

Household Type	1994	1998
Married Could w/ Child <18	5.0	25.9
Male Household w/ Child <18	4.1	12.9
Female Household w/ Child <18	1.1	10.1
Family Household w/o Child	3.6	18.3
Nonfamily Households	2.8	15.4

Figure 12.5 Percentage of U.S. households with e-mail by household type, 1994 and 1998. (From National Telecommunications and Information Administration [NTIA] and U.S. Census Bureau, U.S. Department of Commerce, using November 1994 and December 1998 Current Population Surveys)

content/idea arenas. Thus, free information in cybernetworks may become increasingly "expensive." Can technology to block out such unwanted messages keep up with the technology and political leverage to plant them?

4. Free access to and networking in cyberspace have blurred the boundary of social capital – the privilege of privacy (personal resources) and freedom to access information (social resources). Cyberspace has attained unprecedented freedom to transmit information. Privacy issues loom large, as the ability to seek and find information about others expands at a shocking rate (Burkhalter 1999; Donath 1999). For example, there is unprecedented access to pornography on the Internet

compared to traditional print and visual media. Transmission of hate messages (Zickmund 1997; Thomas 1999) and crime (Castells 1998, Chapter 3), as well as love or romance, has led to opportunities as well as tragedies (see Jeter 1999 for an account of an Internet romance ending in death).

Still more serious is the clash between freedom of information and privacy. The issue is no longer that of preventing children from gaining access to certain information; it concerns anyone's right to gain access to information about anyone else. In the United States, for example, it is possible, at no cost or minimal cost, to gain access to digitized information about other people's bank accounts, mortgage accounts, stock accounts, prison records, driving licenses and violations, substance abuse records, and much more information associated with the Social Security number. One person's freedom to gain information may be the invasion of someone else's privacy. Does social capital have a boundary, and if so, who sets the boundary? Unlike traditional social networks, where interpersonal relationships constrain the flow and content of shared resources, cybernetworks reduce such relationships and constraints to a minimum.

Freedom to provide information on the cybernetworks has also caused unprecedented sociolegal problems. When is something considered pornography by the community standard as the notion of community blurs? When is hate information sufficiently damaging to a group of individuals to be banned? When is violence advocated sufficiently to be considered as motivating or urging actions? Courts are involved, for example, in ruling on whether and to what extent information about certain social taboos can be propagated over the Internet (MacKinnon 1997; Morrow 1999). What legal actions are possible or necessary for planting false information for gains in the stock market (Jarvis 1999)?

When such messages are transmitted across community and national boundaries, who has the legal authority to regulate them? If legal entities such as national governments engage in cyberwars (e.g., hacking other governments' data or sending hate or revolutionary messages), are international organizations capable of mediating and regulating them? There will be tremendous debates and implementation issues on the balance between social control and the newfound freedom over the cybernetworks.[11]

In the economic and commercial sector, some national and international actions are being taken to address issues of property rights and

[11] According to the Georgetown Internet Privacy Policy Study conducted in 1999, 94 percent of the top 100 Web sites and 66 percent of all sampled Web sites surveyed had privacy policies. However, which policies are implemented and the consequences of these policies remain to be studied.

regulations (e.g., taxation). On July 1, 1997, the Clinton administration issued *A Framework for Global Electronic Commerce*, presenting the U.S. government's strategy to facilitate the growth of e-commerce. Subsequently, Congress enacted legislation that accomplished four of the president's objectives: (1) the *Internet Tax Freedom Act* placed a three-year moratorium on new and discriminatory taxes on Internet commerce; (2) the *Digital Millennium Copyright Act* ratified and implemented the World Intellectual Property Organization (WIPO) Copyright Treaty and the WIPO Performances and Phonograms Treaty, protecting copyrighted material online; (3) the *Government Paperwork Elimination Act* encouraged prompt implementation of e-filing and record-keeping systems by the federal government; and (4) the *Children's Online Privacy Protection Act* protected the privacy of young children online. In May 1998, the World Trade Organization (WTO) reached an agreement by which members would continue the practice of not imposing customs duties on e-commerce transmissions. The Organization for Economic Cooperation and Development (OECD) and industry groups issued a declaration in October 1998 supporting the tax principles outlined in Clinton's strategy and opposing discriminatory taxation imposed on Internet and e-commerce. But at the moment, the growth of cybernetworks is substantially outpacing such national and international efforts to regulate them.

5. Actions seem to gain the upper hand in interactions with structures in cybernetworks (McLaughlin, Osborne, and Ellison 1997; Smith 1999; Wellman and Gulia 1999). Individuals, groups, and organizations can create institutions and capital by forming chat rooms, clubs, and groups without many structural constraints. Rules and practices are being created and implemented as these "villages" evolve (Agre 1998). What are the motives for extending networks in cyberspace, and what are the intended goals and payoffs (Kollock 1999)? Is wealth superseded by reputation, power, or sentiment as the expected return in such villages? Are there definitions and declarations of membership, control of boundaries, and rules of exchange and commitment in sharing resources?

Capital in the form of credentials is being created and conferred, and markets for the capital are being created. In higher education, for example, tens of thousands of courses were available online in 1999 (telecampus.edu), and the estimate was that the number of people taking at least one college course over the Internet would triple by the year 2002 to about 2.2 million in the United States alone (*PC World*, July 1999, p. 39). Virtual degrees were rapidly being granted online (e.g., virtual universities such as Jones International University, accredited by the North Central Association of Colleges and Schools, 1999, www.jonesinternational.edu and virtual masters in business administration offered by Duke University, among others).

Social movements challenging existing institutions have benefited from the opportunity afforded by cybernetworks to mobilize social capital. The Falun Gong incident created a new ball game in challenging existing ideologies and institutions. Will cybernetworks improve the opportunities for peaceful transitions and transformations, or will they accelerate dramatic changes in social institutions (Gurak 1999; Uncapher 1999)? Will they supplement or replace face-to-face exchanges for social capital? Will they help the disadvantaged in mounting collective actions (Schmitz 1997; Mele 1999)?

Inevitably there will be tensions, conflicts, violence, competition, and coordination issues among the villages in cyberspace. When and how do villages claim self-defense or self-interest and invade other villages for resources? How do villages become imperial or colonial powers? How do villages defend themselves and form coalitions? Will a "United Nations" emerge in cyberspace, and under what rules and practices? Would such a global body be dominated by the core villages?

Concluding Remarks

The thesis that social capital is on the decline in the United States and elsewhere is obviously premature and, in fact, false. The rise of the Internet and cybernetworks signals a revolutionary growth of social capital. This form of communication has begun to show a "correcting" trend if we take seriously Putnam's hypothesis that TV viewing is the culprit accounting for the decline of social capital in the more traditional form of participation in social associations and groups. A Nielsen survey conducted in July 1999 shows that since it began monitoring in August 1998, home use of the Internet and online services has continued to cut into TV viewing. Wired homes watched an average of 13 percent less TV (about one hour daily) than others – equivalent to thirty-two hours per month. The number of wired homes rose from 22 million in 1997 to 35 million in 1999, an increase rate of 60 percent in less than two years. Gary Gabelhouse of Fairfield Research in Lincoln, Nebraska, reported (*USA Today*, July 20, 1999) that TV viewing was down from four and a half hours daily in 1995 to about two hours in June 1999, when the survey of 1,000 U.S. adults was conducted. He stated, "People are shifting away from passive TV-style entertainment." His data further showed that researching and communicating on the Internet, rather than being entertained, took up 70 percent of the average sixty-four minutes a day of online time. The term *couch potato* may still characterize certain age groups, but the fact that TV viewing time is down significantly on weekdays, after school and work (4:30–6 P.M.) – 17 percent less TV watching than other groups, and even during prime time (8–11 P.M.) (wired homes' TV use was 6 percent less than that of others) – indicates that a new wired generation that clearly prefers to seek information and interactions through cybernetworks is quickly emerging.

This revolution, based on "the triumph of capitalism, the English language, and technology" (Bloomberg 1999, p. 11), has indeed transformed individuals, groups, and the world with shocking speed and in shocking ways (Miller 1999; Zuckerman 1999). Yet, at the same time, it has brought about a further unequal distribution of capital among societies and individuals. The paradox is that while the revolution widens the divide between those who gain access to more and richer capital and others who are being shut out of such opportunities and benefits, those in the cybernetworks have seen an equalization of opportunities and benefits as wide-open competition and channels reduce power, and thus capital differentials, among groups and individuals.

With the increasing development of technology and the continuing presence of commercial interests, cybernetworks fuse socio-economic-technological elements in social relations and social capital. This new feature poses new questions regarding access to and use of social capital. As technology has already made it possible to create virtual reality (e.g., audiovisual, three-dimensional, touch-sensitive) and transcend time (using wireless and inexpensive equipment, for example), such that love, passion, hatred, and murder are being "real-ized" and personalized (e.g., Internet romances and murders have occurred: *Washington Post*, March 6, 1999, p. A2; decency and free speech are clashing: *Time*, February 15, 1999, p. 52; personal data and histories are becoming increasingly public: *USA Today*, January 18, 1999, p. 3B; Yugoslav sites used e-mail to engage in cyberwar during the Kosovo conflict: *Wall Street Journal*, April 8, 1999), will cybernetworks break the dominance of elite classes and differential utility in social capital? Yet, technology requires resources and skills. While the globalization process is underway, cybernetworks may tend to exclude many underdeveloped societies and disadvantaged members of many societies. Will these developments further unequalize the distribution of social capital? And under what conditions? Will these developments further segregate the world into the haves and the have-nots? Analyses must evaluate these questions relative to different aspects of social capital (information, influence, social credentials, and reinforcement) and different outcomes (instrumental and expressive).

I suspect that the entire spectrum of the development and utility of all forms of capital can be examined on cybernetworks, which fundamentally are relations and embedded resources – a form of social capital. We need data on cybernetworks as global villages – the formation and development of social groups and social organizations (the villages), especially (1) how each group and territory is defined or undefined (closure versus openness); (2) how membership is claimed, defined, or acknowledged (i.e., residents and citizens); (3) what the membership is composed of (e.g., demographics: individuals, households, and clusters; age, gender, ethnicity, linguistics, socioeconomic assets); and (4) how resources are distributed within a village and across villages: class and inequality among villages. In short, then, much work is urgently needed to understand how cybernetworks build and segment social capital. The topics just mentioned will provide data that will allow scholars to understand new institutions and cultures as they emerge, as well as the interactions between human and social capital. Most importantly, I suggest, they will provide clues as to whether and how social capital may be outpacing personal capital in significance and effect, and how civil society, instead of dying, may be expanding and becoming global.

Part III

Epilogue

13

The Future of the Theory

The present volume does not allow full treatment of all aspects of a social capital theory. The immediate future of such a theory depends on continuing refinement of both the theory itself and measurements of the concepts involved. As mentioned in the Preface, I chose to focus on the instrumental aspect of social capital and thus shortchanged its expressive aspect, not that my own research efforts have ignored the latter (Lin, Simeone, Ensel, and Kuo 1979; Lin, Dean, and Ensel 1986; Lin and Ensel 1989; Lin and Lai 1995; Lin and Peek 1999). There is a substantial and thriving literature on the effects on mental health and the well-being of social support, social networks, and social resources. To do justice to the expressive aspect of social capital would require perhaps another monograph of comparable size. I also abbreviated the coverage of social capital as a collective asset, because my evaluation convinced me that its theoretical and research viability can be extrapolated from the formulations as outlined in this monograph rather than being treated as a separate and independent entity (see Chapters 2, 8, and 12). However, it is appropriate to use this last chapter to present, no matter how briefly, some thoughts on issues of theoretical integrations incorporating these aspects as well.

Modeling Social Capital

A comprehensive social capital model needs to investigate (1) investment in social capital, (2) access to and mobilization of social capital, and (3) returns on social capital. While the discussions throughout this monograph have clarified social capital's definition, elements, and measurements, it is necessary to discuss briefly the types of outcomes that can be considered expected returns. I propose two major types of outcomes: (1) returns on instrumental action and (2) returns on expressive action (Lin

1986, 1990, 1992a). Instrumental action is taken to obtain resources not possessed by the actor, whereas expressive action is taken to maintain resources already possessed by the actor.

For instrumental action, we may identify three possible returns: economic, political, and social. Each return can be seen as added capital. Economic return is straightforward and is in terms of wealth, including earnings, assets, and so on. Political return is similarly straightforward, as it is represented by hierarchical positions in a collective. Social gain needs some clarification. It has been argued that reputation is an indication of social gain (Chapter 9). Reputation can be defined as the extent of favorable/unfavorable opinions about an individual in a collective. As delineated in Chapter 9, a critical issue in social exchange where social capital is transacted is that the transaction may be asymmetric: a favor is given by alter to ego. Ego's action is facilitated, but what is the gain for alter, the giver of the favor? Unlike economic exchange, where reciprocal and symmetric transactions are expected in the short or long term, social exchange may not entail such an expectation. What is expected is that ego and alter both acknowledge the asymmetric transactions that create the former's social debt to the latter, who accrues social credit. Social debt must be publicly acknowledged for ego to maintain his or her relationship with alter. Public recognition in the network spreads the reputation of alter. The greater the debt, the larger the network, and the stronger the need for ego and alter to maintain the relationship; the greater the propensity to spread the word in the network, the greater the reputation gained by alter. In this process, alter is gratified by the reputation, which, along with material resources (such as wealth) and hierarchical positions (such as power), constitutes one of the three returns fundamental in instrumental actions.

For expressive action, social capital is a means to consolidate resources and defend against possible resource losses (Lin 1986, 1990). The principle is to access and mobilize others who share interests and control of similar resources so that embedded resources can be pooled and shared in order to preserve and protect existing resources. In this process, alters are willing to share their resources with ego because the preservation of ego and its resources enhances and reinforce the legitimacy of alters' claim to like resources. Three types of return may be specified: physical health, mental health, and life satisfaction. Physical health involves maintenance of physical functional competence and freedom from diseases and injuries. Mental health reflects the ability to withstand stresses and to maintain cognitive and emotional balance. The homophily principle informs us that persons with similar characteristics, attitudes, and lifestyles tend to congregate in similar residential, social, and work environments that promote interactions and associations. Similarly, the frequency and intensity of interactions increase similar attitudes and lifestyles.

Thus formulated, the theory permits certain predictions regarding the process of maintaining mental health; namely, that access and use of strong and homophilous ties promote mental health. Maintenance of a health status, regardless of its definition and origin (which can be either instrumental, i.e., losing a job or expressive, i.e., having arguments with a spouse), requires sharing and confiding among intimates who can understand and appreciate the problems involved. Likewise, it is expected that strong and homophilous ties promote sharing of resources, which in turn enhances life satisfaction, as indicated by optimism and satisfaction with various life domains such as family, marriage, work, and community and neighborhood environments.

Returns to instrumental actions and expressive actions often reinforce each other. Physical health offers the capacity to endure a heavy work load and responsibility to attain economic, political, and social statuses. Likewise, economic, political, or social statuses often offer resources to maintain physical health (exercises, diet, and health maintenance). Mental health and life satisfaction are likewise expected to have reciprocal effects with economic, political, and social gains. However, factors leading to instrumental and expressive returns are expected to show differential patterns. As mentioned earlier, it may well be that open networks and relations are more likely to enable access to and use of bridges to reach resources lacking in one's social circle and to enhance one's chances of gaining resources/instrumental returns. On the other hand, a denser network with more intimate and reciprocal relations among members may increase the likelihood of mobilizing others with shared interests and resources to defend and protect existing resources/expressive returns. Further, exogenous factors, such as community and institutional arrangements and prescriptive versus competitive incentives, may contribute differentially to the density and openness of networks and relations and to the success of instrumental or expressive actions.

With the core elements of social capital, types of returns, and differential patterns of causal effects identified, it is possible to conceive an analytic model (Lin 1999a). As can be seen in Figure 13.1, the model contains three blocks of variables in causal sequences. One block represents preconditions and precursors of social capital: the factors in the social structure and each individual's position in the social structure, both of which facilitate or constrain the investment of social capital. Another block represents social capital elements, and a third block represents possible returns for social capital.

The process leading from the first block to the second block describes the formation of inequality of social capital: structural elements and

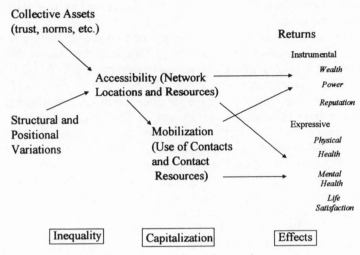

Figure 13.1 Modeling a theory of social capital.

positional elements in the structure affect opportunities to construct and maintain social capital. This delineates patterns of differential distributions for social resources that are embedded, accessed, or mobilized (capital deficit [Chapter 7]). It should further demonstrate that there are social forces that determine such differential distributions. Thus, it is incumbent on a theory of social capital to delineate the patterns and determinants of the three ingredients of social capital or the *inequality of social capital* as collective assets, accessible social resources, and mobilized social resources. Two types of causation forces are of special interest to scholars in this analysis: structural and positional variations. A structure may be characterized by many variations, such as diversity in culture and ideology, level of industrialization and technology, level of education, extent of physical and natural resources, economic productivity, and so on. Within a structure, individuals may be described as occupying different positions in social, cultural, political, and economic strata. These variations may be hypothesized to affect differential investment (i.e., the norm differentially encourages or discourages certain members from investing in social capital) and opportunities (i.e., certain positions offer better or worse chances of acquiring social capital).

Within the second block, there is a process linking two elements of social capital: access to social capital and use of social capital. The process linking the two elements is the process of social capital mobilization. That is, given the unequal distributions of social capital, how would an individual be enabled or disabled to mobilize such capital for specific actions? This is where the model, while recognizing structural contributions to social capital as captured in the inequality process, also emphasizes possible choice action in mobilization.

Third, the theory needs to demonstrate that the three ingredients are connected. Thus, it needs to propose a causal sequence in which embedded resources constrain and enable individual choices and actions. The general expectation is that the better the accessible embedded resources, the more likely they can and will be mobilized in purposive actions by an individual.

Finally, the process linking the second block (social capital) and the third block (outcomes) represents the process whereby social capital produces returns or yields. Here the theory should demonstrate how social capital is capital or how it generates return or gain. That is, it should propose how one or more of the elements of social capital directly or indirectly impact an individual's economic, political, and social capital (resources) or her or his physical, mental, and life well-being. The more intriguing questions are (1) why certain individuals have better or worse cognitive maps to the locations of better embedded resources; (2) why, given adequate perceptions, some actors are more or less willing to mobilize optimal ties and resources; (3) why certain intermediary agents are more or less willing to make appropriate efforts on their behalf; and (4) why certain organizations are more or less receptive to being influenced by social capital.

Macro- and Microimplications

These conceptualizations – as individual components and processes discussed in this monograph – are not new; they merely synthesize accumulated knowledge and findings. Research (as reviewed in Lin 1999b) has verified the proposition that social capital enhances an individual's attained statuses, such as occupational status, authority, and placement in certain industries. Through these attained positions, social capital enhances economic earnings as well. These relationships hold up after family background and education are taken into account. Burt (1997, 1998) and others (Podolny and Baron 1997) have shown that advances and economic rewards are also enhanced in organizations for individuals at strategic locations in informal networks. Those closer to structural holes or bridges (and thus less structurally constrained) seem to gain better returns, presumably because such locations give these individuals better opportunities to access certain capital in the organization.

Research is progressing on how organizations use social capital in recruiting and retaining individuals. Fernandez and associates

(Fernandez and Weinberg 1997) have shown that referrals increase applications, lead to better-qualified candidate recruitment, and reduce costs
in the screening process. Putnam's studies (1993, 1995a, 1995b) indicate
the same in terms of participation in civic associations (e.g., churches,
PTAs, the Red Cross) and social groups (bowling leagues). Coleman
(1990) provides examples of diffusion of information and mobilization
through social circles among radical Korean students (i.e., a network as
capital), a mother moving from Detroit to Jerusalem in order to have
her child walk to a playground or school safely (a norm as capital), and
diamond traders in New York utilizing informal ties and informal agreements (network and trust as capital). Portes (1998) also specifies "consummatory" and instrumental consequences of social capital (see Portes
and Sensenbrenner 1993 for the consummatory consequences – solidarity and reciprocal support – of social capital for immigrant groups). The
primary focus here is on the development, maintenance, or decline of
collective assets.

At the mesonetwork level, the focus shifts to how individuals have differential access to resources embedded in the collective. The question
posed is why certain individuals in a given collective have better access
to embedded resources than others. The nature of social networks and
social ties becomes the focus of analysis. Granovetter (1973, 1974, 1982,
1985, 1995) proposes that bridges, as usually reflected in weaker ties,
provide better access to information. Burt (1992, 1997, 1998) sees that
strategic locations in the networks (structural holes or constraints) imply
better or worse access to information, influence, or control. Lin (1982,
1990, 1994a, 1995a, 1999a) has suggested that hierarchical positions
as well as network locations facilitate or hinder access to embedded
resources. Embedded resources are indicated by the wealth, status, and
power of social ties.

At the microaction level, social capital is reflected in the actual linkage
between the use of embedded resources in instrumental actions. For
example, there is substantial literature on how informal sources and their
resources (contact resources) are mobilized in job searches and their
effects on attained socioeconomic statuses (Lin, Ensel, and Vaughn 1981;
De Graaf and Flap 1988; Marsden and Hurlbert 1988).

Research in the area of returns on expressive actions has also been
extensive. Much is known about the indirect effects of networks on
mental health and life satisfaction (Berkman and Syme 1979; Wellman
1981; Kadushin 1983; Berkman 1984; Hall and Wellman 1985; Lin
1986; House, Umberson, and Landis 1988; Lin, Ye, and Ensel 1999).
That is, network locations enhance the likelihood of accessing social
support, which in turn improves one's physical or mental well-being.
Another arena for potential theoretical and research work concerns the

synergy and tension between instrumental and expressive actions for the well-being of individuals as well as society. The fact that success in society, either for expressive or instrumental purposes, relies significantly on who you know and who you "use" modifies both the functional explanation of social mobility and the structural determinism of individual behavior. While structural characteristics impose a range of possible behaviors, including communication access, individuals have certain degrees of freedom in the manipulation of the social structure for their own benefits. The degree of such freedom is determined both by the individual's position in the structure and by his or her own strategic choices.

On a still broader level, this theory reminds us that both instrumental and expressive behaviors have structural significance. Expressive behaviors, which have received much research attention in the past, point to the types of social interactions that promote horizontal linkages among individuals with similar characteristics and lifestyles. Such behaviors reinforce the solidarity and stability of social groups. However, instrumental behaviors dictate equally significant social interactions providing vertical linkages. Such behaviors allow greater social mobility and greater sharing of resources in society.

There is intrinsic complementarity as well as tension between the two types of behavior. Excessive instrumental actions risk the loss of group identity and solidarity as one attempts to move from one position to another. On the other hand, excessive expressive behaviors promote the stagnation of social segmentation and nurture the development of class consciousness and class conflict. The relative frequency and intensity of instrumental and expressive interactions in a society, I believe, holds the key in determining the dynamics of stability and change. I postulate that the persistence of a given social structure depends on the relative amounts of expressive and instrumental interaction actually taking place among its members. The optimal points of such interactions for both persistence and change should be the focus of future theoretical and empirical explorations.

References

Abell, Peter. 1992. "Is Rational Choice Theory a Rational Choice of Theory?" Pp. 183–206 in *Rational Choice Theory: Advocacy and Critique*, edited by J. S. Coleman and T. J. Fararo. Newbury Park, CA: Sage.

Agre, Philip E. 1998. "Designing Genres for New Media: Social, Economic, and Political Contexts." Pp. 69–99 in *Cybersociety 2.0: Revisiting Computer-Mediated Communication and Community*, edited by S. G. Jones. Thousand Oaks, CA: Sage.

Alchian, Armen. 1965. "Some Economics of Property Rights." *Il Politico* 30(4):816–829.

Alchian, Armen and Harold Demsetz. 1973. "The Property Right Paradigm." *Journal of Economic History* 33:16–27.

Allen, Franklin. 1984. "Reputation and Product Quality." *Rand Journal of Economics* 15:311–327.

Angelusz, Robert and Robert Tardos. 1991. "The Strength and Weakness of "Weak Ties." Pp. 7–23 in *Values, Networks and Cultural Reproduction in Hungary*, edited by P. Somlai. Budapest: Coordinating Council of Programs.

Barber, Bernard. 1983. *The Logic and Limits of Trust*. New Brunswick, NJ: Rutgers University Press.

Barbieri, Paolo. 1996. "Household, Social Capital and Labour Market Attainment." Presented at the ECSR Workshop, August 26–27, Max Planck Institute for Human Development and Education, Berlin.

Baron, James N. and William T. Bielby. 1980. "Bringing the Firm Back In: Stratification, Segmentation, and the Organization of Work." *American Sociological Review* 45 (October):737–765.

Becker, Gary S. 1964/1993. *Human Capital*. Chicago: University of Chicago Press.

Beggs, John J. and Jeanne S. Hurlbert. 1997. "The Social Context of Men's and Women's Job Search Ties: Voluntary Organization Memberships, Social Resources, and Job Search Outcomes." *Sociological Perspectives* 40(4):601–622.

Ben-Porath, Yoram. 1980. "The F-Connection: Families, Friends, and Firms and the Organization of Exchange." *Population and Development Review* 6:1–29.

251

252   *References*

Berkman, Lisa F. 1984. "Assessing the Physical Health Effects of Social Networks and Social Support." *Annual Review of Public Health* 5:413–432.

Berkman, Lisa F. and S. Leonard Syme. 1979. "Social Networks, Host Resistance, and Mortality: A Nine-Year Follow-up Study of Alameda County Residents." *American Journal of Epidemiology* 109:186–204.

Berkman, Sheir. 1997. "Civil Society and Political Institutions." *American Behavioral Scientist* (March–April) 40(5):562–574.

Bian, Yanjie. 1994. *Work and Inequality in Urban China.* Albany: State University of New York Press.

——— 1997. "Bringing Strong Ties Back In: Indirect Connection, Bridges, and Job Search in China." *American Sociological Review* 62(3, June):366–385.

Bian, Yanjie and Soon Ang. 1997. "Guanxi Networks and Job Mobility in China and Singapore." *Social Forces* 75:981–1006.

Bielby, William T. and James N. Baron. 1986. "Men and Women at Work: Sex Segregation and Statistical Discrimination." *American Journal of Sociology* 91:759–799.

Blau, Peter M. 1964. *Exchange and Power in Social Life.* New York: Wiley.

——— 1977. *Inequality and Heterogeneity.* New York: Free Press.

——— 1985. "Contrasting Theoretical Perspectives," Department of Sociology, Columbia University.

Blau, Peter M. and Otis Dudley Duncan. 1967. *The American Occupational Structure.* New York: Wiley.

Blau, Peter M. and Joseph E. Schwartz. 1984. *Crosscutting Social Circles.* Orlando, FL: Academic Press.

Bloomberg, Michael R. 1999. "Ties That Bind." *Bloomberg,* June:11.

Bose, Christine and Peter H. Rossi. 1983. "Gender and Jobs: Prestige Standings of Occupations as Affected by Gender." *American Sociological Review* 48:316–330.

Bourdieu, Pierre. 1972/1977. *Outline of a Theory of Practice.* Cambridge: Cambridge University Press.

——— 1980. "Le Capital Social: Notes Provisoires." *Actes de la Recherche en Sciences Sociales* 3:2–3.

——— 1983/1986. "The Forms of Capital." Pp. 241–258 in *Handbook of Theory and Research for the Sociology of Education,* edited by J. G. Richardson. Westport, CT: Greenwood Press.

——— 1990. *The Logic of Practice.* Cambridge: Polity.

Bourdieu, Pierre and Jean-Claude Passeron. 1977. *Reproduction in Education, Society, Culture.* Beverly Hills, CA: Sage.

Boxer, Marilyn J. 1982. "For and About Women: The Theory and Practice of Women's Studies in the United States." *Sings: Journal of Women in Culture and Society* 7(3):661–695.

Boxman, E. A. W. 1992. "Contacts and Careers." Ph.D. diss., University of Utrecht, the Netherlands.

Boxman, E. A. W., P. M. De Graaf, and Henk D. Flap. 1991. "The Impact of Social and Human Capital on the Income Attainment of Dutch Managers." *Social Networks* 13:51–73.

Boxman, E. A. W. and Hendrik Derk Flap. 1990. "Social Capital and Occupational Chances." Presented at the the International Sociological Association XII World Congress of Sociology, July, Madrid.

Brecher, Jeremy and Tim Costello. 1998. *Global Village or Global Pillage*. Boston: South End Press.

Breiger, Ronald L. 1981. "The Social Class Structure of Occupational Mobility." *American Journal of Sociology* 87(3):578–611.

Breslow, Harris. 1997. "Civil Society, Political Economy, and the Internet." Pp. 236–257 in *Virtue Culture*, edited by S. G. Jones. London: Sage.

Brewer, Anthony. 1984. *A Guide to Marx's Capital*. Cambridge: Cambridge University Press.

Bridges, William P. and Wayne J. Villemez. 1986. "Informal Hiring and Income in the Labor Market." *American Sociological Review* 51:574–582.

Brinkley, Alan. 1996. "Liberty, Community, and the National Idea." *The American Prospect* 29:53–59.

Browne, Ray Broadus and Marshall William Fishwick, eds. 1998. *The Global Village: Dead or Alive*. Bowling Green, OH: Bowling Green State University Popular Press.

Burkhalter, Byron. 1999. "Reading Race Online: Discovering Racial Identity in Usenet Discussions." Pp. 60–75 in *Communities in Cyberspace*, edited by M. A. Smith and Peter Pollock. London: Routledge.

Burt, Ronald S. 1982. *Toward a Structural Theory of Action*. Orlando, FL: Academic Press.

　1992. *Structural Holes: The Social Structure of Competition*. Cambridge, MA: Harvard University Press.

　1997. "The Contingent Value of Social Capital." *Administrative Science Quarterly* 42:339–365.

　1998a. "The Gender of Social Capital." *Rationality and Society* 10(1):5–46.

　1998b. "Trust Reputation, and Third Parties." Unpublished paper. Chicago: University of Chicago.

Campbell, Karen E. and Barrett A. Lee. 1991. "Name Generators in Surveys of Personal Networks." *Social Networks* 13:203–221.

Campbell, Karen E., Peter V. Marsden, and Jeanne S. Hurlbert. 1986. "Social Resources and Socioeconomic Status." *Social Networks* 8(1):97–116.

Castells, Manuel. 1998. *End of Millennium*. Malden, MA: Blackwell.

Chamberlain, Mariam K., ed. 1988. *Women in Academe: Progress and Prospects*. New York: Russell Sage Foundation.

China Internet Network Information Center (CNNIC). 1999. "The Development of the Internet in China: A Statistical Report" (translated by the China Matrix).

Cleverley, John. 1985. *The Schooling of China: Tradition and Modernity in Chinese Education*. Sydney: George Allen & Unwin.

Coase, Ronald H. 1984. "The New Institutional Economics." *Journal of Institutional and Theoretical Economics* 140:229–231.

Coleman, James S. 1986a. *Individual Interests and Collective Action*. Cambridge: Cambridge University Press.

1986b. "Social Theory, Social Research: A Theory of Action." *American Journal of Sociology* 91:1309–1335.

1988. "Social Capital in the Creation of Human Capital." *American Journal of Sociology* 94:S95–S121.

1990. *Foundations of Social Theory.* Cambridge, MA: Harvard University Press.

Collins, Randall. 1981. "On the Microfoundations of Macrosociology." *American Journal of Sociology* 86:984–1014.

Comte, Auguste. 1848. *General View of Positivism.* Stanford, CA: Academic Reprintes.

Cook, Karen S. 1982. "Network Structure from an Exchagne Perspective." Pp. 177–199 in *Social Structure and Network Analysis*, edited by P. V. Marsden and N. Lin. Beverly Hills, CA: Sage.

Cook, Karen S. and Richard M. Emerson. 1978. "Power, Equity and Commitment in Exchange Networks." *American Sociological Review* 43:721–739.

Cook, Karen S., Richard M. Emerson, Mary R. Gillmore, and Toshio Yamagishi. 1983. "The Distribution of Power in Exchange Networks: Theory and Experimental Results." *American Journal of Sociology* 89(2):275–305.

Dahrendorf, Ralf. 1959. *Class and Class Conflict in Industrial Society.* Stanford, CA: Stanford University Press.

David, Paul. 1985. "Clio and the Economics of QWERTY." *American Economic Review* 75:332–337.

De Graaf, Nan Dirk, and Hendrik Derk Flap. 1988. "With a Little Help from My Friends." *Social Forces* 67(2):452–472.

Diamond, Douglas W. 1989. "Reputation Acquisition in Debt Markets." *Journal of Political Economy* 97:828–862.

DiMaggio, Paul J. 1988. "Interest and Agency in Institutional Theory." Pp. 3–22 in *Institutional Patterns and Organizations: Culture and Environment*, edited by L. G. Zucker. Cambridge, MA: Ballinger.

DiMaggio, Paul. J. and Walter W. Powell. 1983. "The Iron Cage Revisited: Institutional Isomorphism and Collective Rationality in Organizational Fields." *American Sociological Review* 48 (April):147–160.

1991. "Introduction." Pp. 1–38 in *The New Institutionalism in Organizational Analysis*, edited by Walter W. Powell and Paul J. DiMaggio. Chicago: University of Chicago Press.

Donath, Judith S. 1999. "Identity and Deception in the Virtual Community." Pp. 29–59 in *Communities in Cyberspace*, edited by M. A. Smith. London: Routledge.

Durkheim, Emile (trans. G. Simpson). 1964. *The Division of Labour in Society.* New York: Free Press.

1973. *Moral Education: A Study in the Theory and Application of the Sociology of Education.* New York: Free Press.

Ekeh, Peter P. 1974. *Social Exchange Theory: The Two Traditions.* Cambridge, MA: Harvard University Press.

Elias, Norbert. 1939/1978. *History of Manners.* New York: Pantheon.

Emerson, Richard M. 1962. "Power-Dependence Relations." *American Sociological Review* 27:31–40.

Emerson, Richard M., Karen S. Cook, Mary R. Gillmore, and Toshio Yamagishi. 1983. "Valid Predictions from Invalid Comparisons: Response to Heckathorn." *Social Forces* 61:1232–1247.

England, Paula. 1992a. *Comparable Worth: Theories and Evidence*. New York: Aldine de Gruyter.

———. 1992b. "From Status Attainment to Segregation and Devaluation." *Contemporary Sociology* 21:643–647.

England, Paula, George Farkas, Barbara Kilbourne, and Thomas Dou. 1988. "Explaining Occupational Sex Segregation and Wages: Findings from a Model with Fixed Effects." *American Sociological Review* 53:544–558.

Ensel, Walter M. 1979. "Sex, Social Ties, and Status Attainment." Albany: State University of New York at Albany.

Erickson, Bonnie H. 1995. "Networks, Success, and Class Structure: A Total View." Presented at the Sunbelt Social Networks Conference, February, Charleston, SC.

———. 1996. "Culture, Class and Connections." *American Journal of Sociology* 102(1, July):217–251.

———. 1998. "Social Capital and Its Profits, Local and Global." Presented at the Sunbelt XVIII and 5th European International Conference on Social Networks, Sitges, Spain, May 27–31.

Fei, Xiaotong. 1947/1992. *From the Soil*. Berkeley: University of California Press.

Fernandez, Roberto M. and Nancy Weinberg. 1997. "Sifting and Sorting: Personal Contacts and Hiring in a Retail Bank." *American Sociological Review* 62 (December):883–902.

Fernback, Jan. 1997. "The Individual within the Collective: Virtual Ideology and the Realization of Collective Principles." Pp. 36–54 in *Virtual Culture*, edited by Steven G. Jones. London: Sage.

Fisher, Irving. 1906. *The Nature of Capital and Income*. New York: Macmillan.

Flap, Henk D. 1991. "Social Capital in the Reproduction of Inequality." *Comparative Sociology of Family, Health and Education* 20:6179–6202.

———. 1994. "No Man Is an Island: The Research Program of a Social Capital Theory." Presented at the World Congress of Sociology, Bielefeld, Germany, July.

———. 1996. "Creation and Returns of Social Capital." Presented at the the European Consortium for Political Research on Social Capital and Democracy, October 3–6, Milan.

Flap, Henk D. and Ed Boxman. 1996. "Getting Started. The Influence of Social Capital on the Start of the Occupational Career," University of Utrecht, the Netherlands.

———. 1998. "Getting a Job as a Manager," University of Utrecht, the Netherlands.

Flap, Henk D. and Nan Dirk De Graaf. 1986. "Social Capital and Attained Occupational Status." *Netherlands Journal of Sociology* 22:145–161.

Forse, Michel. 1997. "Capital Social et Emploi." *L'Année Sociologique* 47(1):143–181.

Freeman, Jo. 1972–1973. "The Tyranny of Structurelessness." *Berkeley Journal of Sociology* 17:151–164.

Giddens, Authory. 1979. *Central Problems in Social Theory: Action, Structure, and Contradiction in Social Analysis.* Berkeley: University of California Press.

Gilham, Steven A. 1981. "State, Law and Modern Economic Exchange." Pp. 129–152 in *Networks, Exchange and Coercion*, edited by D. Willer and B. Ander. New York: Elsevier/Greenwood.

Goldthorpe, John H. 1980. *Social Mobility and Class Structure in Modern Britain.* New York: Oxford University Press.

Granovetter, Mark. 1973. "The Strength of Weak Ties." *American Journal of Sociology* 78:1360–1380.

1974. *Getting a Job.* Cambridge, MA: Harvard University Press.

1982. "The Strength of Weak Ties: A Network Theory Revisited." Pp. 105–130 in *Social Structure and Network Analysis*, edited by Nan Lin and Peter V. Marsden. Beverly Hills, CA: Sage.

1985. "Economic Action and Social Structure: The Problem of Embeddedness." *American Journal of Sociology* 91:481–510.

1986. "Labor Mobility, Internal Markets, and Job Matching: A Comparison of the Sociological and Economic Approaches." *Research in Social Stratification and Mobility* 5:3–39.

1995. *Getting a Job* (rev. ed.). Chicago: University of Chicago Press.

Greeley, Andrew. 1997a. "Coleman Revisited: Religious Structures as a Source of Social Capital." *American Behavioral Scientist* 40(5, March–April): 587–594.

1997b. "The Other Civic America: Religion and Social Capital." *The American Prospect* 32 (May–June):68–73.

1997c. "The Strange Reappearance of Civic America: Religion and Volunteering," Department of Sociology, University of Chicago.

Green, Gary P., Leann M. Tigges, and Irene Browne. 1995. "Social Resources, Job Search, and Poverty in Atlanta." *Research in Community Sociology* 5:161–182.

Grief, Avner. 1989. "Reputation and Coalitions in Medieval Trade: Evidence of the Haghribi Traders." *Journal of Economic History* 49 (December):857–882.

Gurak, Laura J. 1999. "The Promise and the Peril of Social Action in Cyberspace: Ethos, Delivery, and the Protests Over Marketplace and the Clipper Chip." Pp. 243–263 in *Communities in Cyberspace*, edited by M. A. Smith and P. Kollock. London: Routledge.

Guy-Sheftall, Beverly. 1995. *Women's Studies: A Retrospective.* New York: Ford Foundation.

Hall, Alan and Barry Wellman. 1985. "Social Networks and Social Support." Pp. 23–42 in *Social Support and Health*, edited by S. Cohen and S. L. Syme. Orlando, FL: Academic Press.

Han, Minmo. 1987. *History of Chinese Sociology.* Tianjin: Tianjin Renmin Press.

Hannan, Michael T. 1992. "Rationality and Robustness in Multilevel Systems." Pp. 120–136 in *Rational Choice Theory: Advocacy and Critique*, edited by J. S. Coleman and T. J. Fararo. Newbury Park, CA: Sage.

Hardin, Russell. 1998. "Conceptions of Social Capital." Presented at the International Conference on Social Networks and Social Capital, October 30–November 1, Duke University.

Hechter, Michael. 1983. "A Theory of Group Solidarity." Pp. 16–57 in *The Microfoundations of Macrosociology*, edited by M. Hechter. Philadelphia: Temple University Press.

Heying, Charles H. 1997. "Civil Elites and Corporate Delocalization." *American Behavioral Scientist* (March–April) 408(5):657–668.

Homans, George C. 1950. *The Human Group*. New York: Harcourt, Brace.

    1958. "Human Behavior as Exchange." *American Journal of Sociology* 63(6, May):597–606.

    1961. *Social Behavior: Its Elementary Forms*. New York: Harcourt, Brace & World.

House, James, Debra Umberson, and K. R. Landis. 1988. "Structures and Processes of Social Support." *Annual Review of Sociology* 14:293–318.

Howe, Florence. 1977. *Seven Years Later: Women's Studies Programs in 1976*. Washington, DC: National Advisory Council on Women's Educational Programs.

Howe, Florence and Carol Ahlum. 1973. "Women's Studies and Social Change." Pp. 393–423 in *Academic Women on the Move*, edited by A. S. Rossi and A. Calderwood. New York: Russell Sage Foundation.

Hsung, Ray-May and Hwang, Yih-Jib. 1992. "Social Resources and Petit Bourgeois." *Chinese Sociological Quarterly* 16:107–138.

Hsung, Ray-May and Ching-Shan Sun. 1988. *Social Resources and Social Mobility: Manufacturing Employees*. Taiwan: National Science Council.

Irving, Larry. July 1995, 1998, 1999. *Falling Through the Net: Defining the Digital Divide*: I, II, III. Washington, DC: U.S. Department of Commerce.

Jacobs, Jerry. 1989. *Revolving Doors: Sex Segregation and Women's Careers*. Stanford, CA: Stanford University Press.

Jarvis, Craig. 1999. "Engineer Admits Securities Fraud." *News & Observers*, June 22, pp. 1–2.

Jenkins, Richard. 1992. *Pierre Bourdieu*. Long: Loutledge.

Jeter, Jon. 1999. "Internet Romance Ends with Death." *The Washington Post*, March 6, p. A2.

Johnson, Harry G. 1960. "The Political Economy of Opulence." *Canadian Journal of Economics and Political Science* 26:552–564.

Jones, Steven G., ed. 1997a. *Virtual Culture*. London: Sage.

Jones, Steven G. 1997b. "The Internet and Its Social Landscape." In *Virtual Culture*, edited by S. G. Jones. London: Sage.

Kadushin, Charles. 1983. "Mental Health and the Interpersonal Environment: A Re-Examination of Some Effects of Social Structure on Mental Health." *American Sociological Review* 48:188–198.

Kalleberg, Arne L. 1988. "Comparative Perspectives on Work Structures and Inequality." *Annual Review of Sociology* 14:203–225.

Kalleberg, Arne L. and James R. Lincoln. 1988. "The Structure of Earnings Inequality in the United States and Japan." *American Journal of Sociology* 94(Supplement):S121–S153.

Kelley, Jonathan. 1990. "The Failure of a Paradigm: Log-Linear Models of Social Mobility." Pp. 319–346, 349–357 in *John H. Goldthorpe: Consensus and Controversy*, edited by J. Clark, C. Modgil, and S. Modgil. London: Falmer Press.

Kelly, Kevin. 1998. *New Rules for the New Economy*. New York: Penguin.

Kelman, H. C. 1961. "Processes of Opinion Change." *Public Opinion Quarterly* 25:57–78.

Kenworthy, Lane. 1997. "Civil Engagement, Social Capital, and Economic Corporation." *American Behavioral Scientist* (March–April) 40(5):645–656.

Kessler-Harris, Alice. 1982. *Out to Work: A History of Wage-Earning Women in the United States*. New York: Oxford University Press.

Kilbourne, Barbara Stanek, Paula England, George Farkas, Kurt Beron, and Dorothea Weir. 1994. "Returns to Skill, Compensating Differentials, and Gender Bias: Effects of Occupational Characteristics on the Wages of White Women and Men." *American Journal of Sociology* 100(3, November): 689–719.

Klein, B. and K. Leffler. 1981. "The Role of Market Forces in Assuring Contractual Performance." *Journal of Political Economy* 81:615–641.

Kollock, Peter. 1999. "The Economics of Online Cooperation: Gifts and Goods in Cyberspace." Pp. 220–239 in *Communities in Cyberspace*, edited by Marc A. Smith and Peter Kollock. London: Routledge.

Kornai, Janos. 1992. *The Socialist System: The Political Economy of Communism*. Princeton, NJ: Princeton University Press.

Kreps, David and Robert Wilson. 1982. "Reputation and Imperfect Information." *Journal of Economic Theory* 27:253–279.

Krymkowski, Daniel H. 1991. "The Process of Status Attainment Among Men in Poland, the U.S., and West Germany." *American Sociological Review* 56:46–59.

Lai, Gina Wan-Foon, Nan Lin, and Shu-Yin Leung. 1998. "Network Resources, Contact Resources, and Status Attainment." *Social Networks* 20(2, April): 159–178.

Laumann, Edward O. 1966. *Prestige and Association in an Urban Community*. Indianapolis: Bobbs-Merrill.

Lazarsfeld, Paul F. and Robert K. Merton. 1954. "Friendship as Social Process: A Substantive and Methodological Analysis." Pp. 298–348 in *The Varied Sociology of Paul F. Lazarsfeld*, edited by P. L. Kendall. New York: Columbia University Press.

Ledeneva, Alena. 1998. *Russia's Economy of Favours: Blat, Networking, and Informal Exchange*. New York: Cambridge University Press.

Levi-Strauss, Claude. 1949. *Les Structures Elementaires de la Parente*. Paris: Presses Universitaires de France.

——— 1989. *The Elementary Structure of Kinship*. Boston: Beacon Press.

Li, Hongzhi. 1993 and 1994 (2nd ed.). *Zhong-Guo Fa-Lun Gong (Chinese Cultivation of the Wheel of the Law)*. Beijing: Military Literature Press.

——— 1996. *Fa-Lun Da-Fa Yi Jie (Explicating the Principles of the Wheel of the Law)*. Changchun: Changchun Press.

Lin, Nan. 1973. *The Study of Human Communication*. Indianapolis: Bobbs-Merrill.

1982. "Social Resources and Instrumental Action." Pp. 131–145 in *Social Structure and Network Analysis*, edited by P. V. Marsden and N. Lin. Beverly Hills, CA: Sage.

1986. "Conceptualizing Social Support." Pp. 17–30 in *Social Support, Life Events, and Depression*, edited by N. Lin, A. Dean, and W. Ensel. Orlando, FL: Academic Press.

1989. "Chinese Family Structure and Chinese Society." *Bulletin of the Institute of Ethnology* 65:382–399.

1990. "Social Resources and Social Mobility: A Structural Theory of Status Attainment." Pp. 247–271 in *Social Mobility and Social Structure*, edited by R. L. Breiger. New York: Cambridge University Press.

1992a. "Social Resources Theory." Pp. 1936–1942 in *Encyclopedia of Sociology*, Volume 4, edited by E. F. Borgatta and M. L. Borgatta. New York: Macmillan.

1992b. *The Struggle for Tiananmen: Anatomy of the 1989 Mass Movement*. Westport, CT: Praeger.

1994a. "Action, Social Resources, and the Emergence of Social Structure: A Rational Choice Theory." *Advances in Group Processes* 11:67–85.

1994b. "Institutional Capital and Work Attainment." Unpublished manuscript, Durham, NC.

1995a. "Les Resources Sociales: Une Theorie Du Capital Social." *Revue Française de Sociologie* XXXVI(4, October–December):685–704.

1995b. "Persistence and Erosion of Institutional Resources and Institutional Capital: Social Stratification and Mobility in Taiwan." Presented at the International Conference on Social Change in Contemporary Taiwan, June, Academia Sinica, Taipei, Taiwan.

1999a. "Building a Network Theory of Social Capital." *Connections* 22(1): 28–51.

1999b. "Social Networks and Status Attainment." *Annual Review of Sociology* 25:467–487.

Forthcoming. "Guanxi: A Conceptual Analysis." In *The Chinese Triangle of Mainland, Taiwan, and Hong Kong: Comparative Institutional Analysis*, edited by A. So, N. Lin, and D. Poston. Westport, CT: Greenwood.

Lin, Nan and Yanjie Bian. 1991. "Getting Ahead in Urban China." *American Journal of Sociology* 97(3, November):657–688.

Lin, Nan, Paul Dayton, and Peter Greenwald. 1978. "Analyzing the Instrumental Use of Relations in the Context of Social Structure." *Sociological Methods and Research* 7:149–166.

Lin, Nan, Alfred Dean, and Walter Ensel. 1986. *Social Support, Life Events, and Depression*. Orlando, FL: Academic Press.

Lin, Nan and Mary Dumin. 1986. "Access to Occupations Through Social Ties." *Social Networks* 8:365–385.

Lin, Nan and Walter M. Ensel. 1989. "Life Stress and Health: Stressors and Resources." *American Sociological Review* 54:382–399.

Lin, Nan, Walter M. Ensel, and John C. Vaughn. 1981. "Social Resources and Strength of Ties: Structural Factors in Occupational Status Attainment." *American Sociological Review* 46(4, August):393–405.

Lin, Nan and Gina Lai. 1995. "Urban Stress in China." *Social Science and Medicine* 41(8):1131–1145.

Lin, Nan and M. Kristen Peek. 1999. "Social Networks and Mental Health." Pp. 241–258 in *The Sociology of Mental Health and Illness*, edited by A. Horwitze and T. L. Scheid. New York: Cambridge University Press.

Lin, Nan, R. S. Simeone, W. M. Ensel, and W. Kuo. 1979. "Social Support, Stressful Life Events, and Illness: A Model and an Empirical Test." *Journal of Health and Social Behavior* 20:108–119.

Lin, N., Vaughn, John C., and Ensel, Walter M. 1981. "Social Resources and Occupational Status Attainment." *Social Forces* 59(4):1163–1181.

Lin, Nan and Xiaolan Ye. 1997. "Revisiting Social Support: Integration of Its Dimensions." Presented at the International Conference on Life Events/ Stress, Social Support and Mental Health: Cross-Cultural Perspectives, June 17–19, Taipei, Taiwan.

Lin, Nan, Xiaolan Ye, and Walter M. Ensel. 1999. "Social Support and Mental Health: A Structural Approach." *Journal of Health and Social Behavior* 40:344–359.

Lindenberg, Siegwart. 1992. "The Method of Decreasing Abstraction." Pp. 3–20 in *Rational Choice Theory: Advocacy and Critique*, edited by J. S. Coleman and T. J. Fararo. Newbury Park, CA: Sage.

Loury, G. 1977. "A Dynamic Theory of Racial Income Differences." Pp. 153–186 in *Women, Minorities, and Employment Discrimination*, edited by P. A. Wallace and A. Le Mund. Lexington, MA: Lexington Books.

　1987. "Why Should We Care About Group Inequality?" *Social Philosophy and Policy* 5:249–271.

Luhmann, Niklas. 1979. *Trust and Power*. Chichester, UK: Wiley.

　1988. "Familiarity, Confidence, Trust: Problems and Alternatives." Pp. 94–107 in *Trust: Making and Breaking Cooperative Relations*, edited by D. Gambetta. New York: Basil Blackwell.

MacKinnon, Richard C. 1997. "Punishing the Persona: Correctional Strategies for the Virtual Offender." Pp. 206–235 in *Virtue Culture*, edited by S. G. Jones. London: Sage.

Malinowski, Bronslaw. 1922. *Argonauts of the Western Pacific*. London: Routledge & Kegan Paul.

Mao, Zedong. 1940. "On New Democracy." Pp. 106–156 in *Selected Works of Mao Tse-Tung*, Vol. III. London: Lawrence Wishant, 1954.

　1942. "Talks at the Yenan Forum on Literature and Art." Pp. 250–286 in *Selected Readings from the Works of Mao Zedong*. Peking: Foreign Language Press, 1971.

　1949. "On the People's Democratic Dictatorship." Pp. 371–388 in *Selected Works of Mao Zedong*. Peking: Foreign Language Press, 1971.

Marini, Margaret Mooney. 1992. "The Role of Models of Purposive Action in Sociology." Pp. 21–48 in *Rational Choice Theory: Advocacy and Critique*, edited by J. S. Coleman and T. J. Fararo. Newbury Park, CA: Sage.

Marsden, Peter V. and Karen E. Campbell. 1984. "Measuring Tie Strength." *Social Forces* 63 (December):482–501.

Marsden, Peter V. and Jeanne S. Hurlbert. 1988. "Social Resources and Mobility Outcomes: A Replication and Extension." *Social Forces* 66(4):1038–1059.

Marx, Karl. 1933 (1849). *Wage-Labour and Capital*. New York: International Publishers.

1935 (1865). *Value, Price and Profit*. New York: International Publishers.

Marx, Karl (David McLellan, ed.). 1995 (1867, 1885, 1894). *Capital: A New Abridgement*. Oxford: Oxford University Press.

McLaughlin, Magaret L., Kerry K. Osborne, and Nicole B. Ellison. 1997. "Virtual Community in a Telepresence Environment." Pp. 146–168 in *Virtual Culture*, edited by S. G. Jones. London: Sage.

Mele, Christopher. 1999. "Cyberspace and Disadvantaged Communities: The Internet as a Tool for Collective Action." Pp. 290–310 in *Communities in Cyberspace*, edited by M. A. Smith and P. Kollock. London: Routledge.

Merrit, Karen. 1984. "Women's Studies: A Discipline Takes Shape." Pp. 253–262 in *Women and Education: Equity or Equality*, edited by E. Fennema and M. J. Ayer. Berkeley, CA: McCutchan.

Merton, Robert K. 1940. "Bureaucratic Structure and Personality." *Social Forces* 18:560–568.

1995. "Opportunity Structure: The Emergence, Diffusion, and Differentiation of a Sociological Concept, 1930s–1950s." Pp. 3–78 in *Advances in Criminological Theory: The Legacy of Anomie Theory*, edited by F. Adler and W. S. Laufer. New Brunswick, NJ: Transaction Books.

Metcalfe, Bob. 1999. "The Internet in 1999: This Will Prove to Be the Year of the Bills, Bills, and Bills." *Infoworld*, January 18, p. 90.

Meyer, John W. and Brian Rowan. 1977. "Institutionalized Organizations: Formal Structure as Myth and Ceremony." *American Journal of Sociology* 83:340–363.

Meyer, John W. and W. Richard Scott. 1992. *Organizational Environments: Ritual and Rationality*. Newbury Park, CA: Sage.

Miller, Michael J. 1999. "The Net Changes Everything." *PC Magazine* (February 9):4.

Minkoff, Debra C. 1997. "Producing Social Capital: National Social Movements and Civil Society." *American Behavioral Scientist* 40(5, March–April):606–619.

Misztal, Barbara A. 1996. *Trust in Modern Societies: The Search for the Bases of Social Order*. Cambridge: Polity Press.

Mitra, Ananda. 1997. "Virtual Commonality: Looking for India on the Internet." Pp. 55–79 in *Virtue Culture*, edited by S. G. Jones. London: Sage.

Mobilization Society of Wuhan. 1939. *K'ang-Ta Ti Chiao-Yu Fang-Fa (Pedagogical Methods of K'ang-Da)*. Wuhan: Mobilization Society of Wuhan.

Moerbeek, Hester, Wout Ultee, and Henk Flap. 1995. "That's What Friends Are For: Ascribed and Achieved Social Capital in the Occupational Career." Presented at the The European Social Network Conference, London.

Morrow, James. 1999. "Watching Web Speech." *U.S. News & World Report*, February 15, p. 32.

Newton, Kenneth. 1997. "Social Capital and Democracy." *American Behavioral Scientist* 40(5, March–April):575–586.

North, Douglass C. 1990. *Institutions, Institutional Change and Economic Performance*. Cambridge: Cambridge University Press.

Parsons, Talcott. 1963. "On the Concept of Influence." *Public Opinion Quarterly* 27:37–62.

Paxton, Pamela. 1999. "Is Social Capital Declining in the United States? A Multiple Indicator Assessment." *American Journal of Sociology* 105(1, July):88–127.

Pepper, Suzanne. 1996. *Radicalism and Education Reform in 20th-Century China*. New York: Cambridge University Press.

Pizzorno, Alessandro. 1991. "On the Individualistic Theory of Social Order." Pp. 209–231 in *Social Theory for a Changing Society*, edited by P. Bourdieu and J. S. Coleman. Boulder, CO: Westview Press.

Podolny, Joel M. and James N. Baron. 1997. "Social Networks and Mobility." *American Sociological Review* 62 (October):673–693.

Portes, Alejandro. 1998. "Social Capital: Its Origins and Applications in Modern Sociology." *Annual Review of Sociology* 22:1–24.

Portes, Alejandro and Julia Sensenbrenner. 1993. "Embeddedness and Immigration: Notes on the Social Determinants of Economic Action." *American Journal of Sociology* 98(6, May):1320–1350.

Poster, Mark. 1998. "Virtual Ethnicity: Tribal Identity in an Age of Global Communications." Pp. 184–211 in *Cybersociety 2.0: Revisiting Computer-Mediated Communication and Community*, edited by S. G. Jones. Thousand Oaks, CA: Sage.

Powell, Walter W. and Paul J. DiMaggio, eds. 1991. *The New Institutionalism in Organizational Analysis*. Chicago: University of Chicago Press.

Putnam, Robert D. 1993. "The Prosperous Community: Social Capital and Public Life." *The American Prospect* 13 (Spring):35–42.

  1995a. "Bowling Alone: American's Declining Social Capital." *Journal of Democracy* 6(1, January):65–78.

  1995b. "Tuning In, Tuning Out: The Strange Disappearance of Social Capital in America." *P.S.: Political Science and Politics* 28(4, December): 1–20.

Qiu Shi. 1999. "Insisting on Atheism and Criticizing Falun Gong." Editorial, *Seeking the Truth*, 15, August 1, pp. 2–4.

Qu, Shipei. 1985. *Higher Education in the Liberated Areas in the Period of the War of Resistance Against Japan*. Beijing: Beijing University Press.

Radcliffe-Brown, A. R. 1952. *Structure and Function in Primitive Society*. New York: Free Press.

Reid, Elizabeth. 1999. "Hierarchy and Power: Social Control in Cyberspace." Pp. 107–133 in *Communities in Cyberspace*, edited by M. A. Smith and P. Kollock. London: Routledge.

Requena, Felix. 1991. "Social Resources and Occupational Status Attainment in Spain: A Cross-National Comparison with the United States and the

Netherlands." *International Journal of Comparative Sociology* XXXII(3–4):233–242.

Reskin, Barbara. 1988. "Bringing the Men Back In: Sex Differentiation and the Devaluation of Women's Work." *Gender and Society* 2:58–81.

——— 1993. "Sex Segregation in the Workplace." *Annual Review of Sociology* 19:241–270.

Reskin, Barbara and Patricia Roos. 1990. *Job Queues, Gender Queues: Explaining Women's Inroads Into Male Occupations*. Philadelphia: Temple University Press.

Ruan, Danching. 1998. "The Content of the General Social Survey Discussion Networks: An Exploration of General Social Survey Discussion Name Generator in a Chinese Context." *Social Networks* 20(3, July):247–264.

Rus, Andrej. 1995. "Access and Mobilization – Dual Character of Social Capital: Managerial Networks and Privatization in Eastern Europe." Unpublished manuscript, Columbia University.

Sassen, Saskia and Kwame Anthony Appiah. 1998. *Globalization and Its Discontents*. New York: New Press.

Scheff, Thomas J. 1992. "Rationality and Emotion: Homage to Norbert Elias." Pp. 101–119 in *Rational Choice Theory: Advocacy and Critique*, edited by J. S. Coleman and T. J. Fararo. Newbury Park, CA: Sage.

Schmitz, Joseph. 1997. "Structural Relations, Electronic Media, and Social Change: The Public Electronic Network and the Homeless." Pp. 80–101 in *Virtue Culture*, edited by S. G. Jones. London: Sage.

Schram, Stuart R. 1963. *The Political Thought of Mao Tse-Tung*. New York: Praeger.

Schudson, Michael. 1996. "What If Civic Life Didn't Die?" *The American Prospect* 25 (March–April):17–20.

Schultz, Theodore W. 1961. "Investment in Human Capital." *The American Economic Review* LI(1, March):1–17.

Scott, W. Richard and John W. Meyer. 1994. *Institutional Environments and Organizations: Structural Complexity and Individualism*. Beverley Hills, CA: Sage.

Sewell, William H., Jr. 1992. "A Theory of Structure: Duality, Agency, and Transformation." *American Journal of Sociology* 98(1, July):1–29.

Sewell, William H., Jr. and Robert M. Hauser. 1975. *Education, Occupation and Earnings: Achievement in the Early Career*. New York: Academic Press.

Seybolt, Perter J. 1973. *Revolutionary Education in China*. White Plains, NY: International Arts and Sciences Press.

Shanghai Jiaoyu Chubanshe (Shanghai Educational Press). 1983. *Hunan Diyi Shifan Xiaoshi 1903–49 (History of Hunan #1 Normal School 1903–49)*. Shanghai: Shanghai Jiaoyu Chubanshe.

Shapiro, Carl and Hal R. Varian. 1999. *Information Rules: A Strategic Guide to the Network Economy*. Boston: Harvard Business School Press.

Simmel, Georg (trans. and ed. Kurt H. Wolff). 1950. *The Sociology of Georg Simmel*. Glencoe, IL: Free Press.

(ed. Donald N. Levine). 1971. *Georg Simmel on Individuality and Social Forms.* Chicago: University of Chicago Press.

1978. *The Philosophy of Money.* London: Routledge.

Skocpol, Theda. 1996. "Unravelling from Above." *The American Prospect* 25 (March–April):20–25.

Smith, Adam. 1937. *The Wealth of Nations.* New York: Modern Library.

Smith, Marc A. 1999. "The Economies of Online Cooperation: Gifts and Public Goods in Cyberspace." Pp. 220–242 in *Communities in Cyberspace*, edited by M. A. Smith and P. Kollock. London: Routledge.

Smith, Marc A. and Peter Kollock, eds. 1999. *Communities in Cyberspace.* London: Routledge.

Smith, Michael R. 1990. "What Is New in 'New Structuralist' Analyses of Earnings?" *American Sociological Review* 55 (December):827–841.

Sprengers, Maarten, Fritz Tazelaar, and Hendrik Derk Flap. 1988. "Social Resources, Situational Constraints, and Reemployment." *Netherlands Journal of Sociology* 24:98–116.

Stanton-Salazar, Ricardo D. 1997. "A Social Capital Framework for Understanding the Socialization of Racial Minority Children and Youths." *Harvard Educational Review* 67(1, Spring):1–40.

Stanton-Salazar, Ricard D. and Sanford M. Dornbusch. 1995. "Social Capital and the Reproduction of Inequality: Information Networks Among Mexican-Origin High School Students." *Sociology of Education* 68 (April):116–135.

Stimpson, Catharine R. 1986. *Women's Studies in the United States.* New York: Ford Foundation.

Tam, Tony. 1997. "Sex Segregation and Occupational Gender Inequality in the United States: Devaluation or Specialized Training?" *American Journal of Sociology* 102(6, May):1652–1692.

Tardos, Robert. 1996. "Some Remarks on the Interpretation and Possible Uses of the 'Social Capital' Concept with Special Regard to the Hungarian Case." *Bulletin de Methodologie Sociologique* 53 (December):52–62.

Taylor & Jerome. 1999. "Karma." *PC Computing*, June, p. 87.

Thomas, Karen. 1999. "Hate Groups Snare Youths with Web Games." *USA Today*, July 8, p. D1.

Tobias, Sheila. 1970. "Female Studies – an Immodest Proposal," Ithaca, NY: Cornell University.

Tomaskovic-Devey, Donald. 1993. *Gender and Race Inequality at Work: The Sources and Consequences of Job Segregation.* Ithaca, NY: ILR Press.

Treiman, Donald. 1970. "Industrialization and Social Stratification," Pp. 207–234 in *Social Stratification: Research and Theory for the 1970s*, edited by E. O. Laumann. Indianapolis: Bobbs-Merrill.

Treiman, Donald and Kermit Terrell. 1975. "Women, Work, and Wages – Trends in the Female Occupational Structure Since 1940." Pp. 157–200 in *Social Indicator Models*, edited by K. C. Land and S. Spilerman. New York: Russell Sage Foundation.

Uncapher, Willard. 1999. "Electronic Homesteading on the Rural Frontier: Big Sky Telegraph and Its Community." Pp. 264–289 in *Communities in Cyberspace*, edited by M. A. Smith and P. Kollock. London: Routledge.

Verba, Sidney, Schlozman, Kay Lehman, and Henry E. Brady. 1995. *Voice and Equality: Civil Voluntarism in American Politics*. Cambridge, MA: Harvard University Press.

——— 1997. "The Big Tilt: Participatory Inequality in America." *The American Prospect* 32:74–80.

Volker, Beate and Henk Flap. 1999. "Getting Ahead in the GDR: Social Capital and Status Attainment Under Communism." *Acta Sociologica* 41(1, April): 17–34.

von Thunen, H. (trans. B. F. Hoselitz). 1875. *Der Isolierte Staat*. Chicago: Comparative Education Center, University of Chicago.

Wacquant, L. D. 1989. "Toward a Reflexive Sociology: A Workshop with Pierre Bourdieu." *Sociological Theory* 7:26–63.

Watson, Nessim. 1997. "Why We Argue About Virtual Community: A Case Study of the Phish.Net Fan Community." Pp. 102–132 in *Virtual Culture*, edited by S. G. Jones. London: Sage.

Weber, Max. 1946. *Max Weber: Essays in Sociology* (trans. H. H. Gerth and C. Wright Mills). New York: Oxford University Press.

——— 1947. *The Theory of Social and Economic Organizations*. New York: Oxford University Press.

Weber, Max. (ed. G. Roth and C. Wittich). 1968. *Economy and Society*. Berkeley: University of California Press.

Wegener, Bernd. 1991. "Job Mobility and Social Ties: Social Resources, Prior Job and Status Attainment." *American Sociological Review* 56 (February):1–12.

Wellman, Barry. 1981. "Applying Network Analysis to the Study of Social Support." Pp. 171–200 in *Social Networks and Social Support*, edited by B. H. Gottlieb. Beverly Hills: Sage.

Wellman, Barry, ed. 1998. *Networks in the Global Village*. Boulder, CO: Westview Press.

Wellman, Barry and Milena Gulia. 1999. "Virtual Communities as Communities: Net Surfers Don't Ride Alone." Pp. 167–194 in *Communities in Cyberspace*, edited by M. A. Smith and P. Kollock. London: Routledge.

Willer, David. 1985. "Property and Social Exchange." Pp. 123–142 in *Advances in Group Processes*, edited by E. J. Lawler. Greenwich, CT: JAI Press.

Williamson, Oliver E. 1985. *Markets and Hierarchies: Analysis and Antitrust Implications*. New York: Free Press.

——— 1993. "Calculativeness, Trust, and Economic Organization." *Journal of Law and Economics* 36(1–2, April):453–486.

——— 1985. *The Economic Institutions of Capitalism*. New York: Free Press.

Wilson, Beth. 1999. "Vital Signs." *PC Computing*, March, p. 14.

Wood, Richard L. 1997. "Social Capital and Political Culture." *American Behavioral Scientist* (March–April) 40(5):595–605.

Wright, Erik Olin. 1979. *Class Structure and Income Determination.* New York: Academic Press.

Yamagishi, Toshio, Mary R. Gillmore, and Karen S. Cook. 1988. "Network Connections and the Distribution of Power in Exchange Networks." *American Journal of Sociology* 93(4, January):833–851.

Zhou, Xueguang. 1999. "Reputation as a Social Institution: A Macrosociological Approach." Unpublished manuscript, Duke University.

Zickmund, Susan. 1997. "Approaching the Radical Other: The Discursive Culture of Cyberspace." Pp. 185–205 in *Virtue Culture*, edited by S. G. Jones. London: Sage.

Zucker, Lynne G. 1988. "Where Do Instituional Patterns Come From? Organizations as Actors in Social Systems." Pp. 23–49 in *Institutional Patterns and Organizations: Culture and Environment*, edited by L. G. Zucker. Cambridge, MA: Ballinger.

Zuckerman, Mortimer B. 1999. "The Time of Our Lives." *U.S. News & World Report* (May 17):72.

Index